20/04
~mes & nobles
$19.95.

Santa Fe Community
College Library
6401 Richards Ave.
Santa Fe, NM 87508

DATE DUE

	NOV 0 8 2005		

D0620116

Walt Whitman's "Song of Myself"

Walt Whitman's "Song of Myself"

A Mosaic of Interpretations by Edwin Haviland Miller

University of Iowa Press Iowa City

University of Iowa Press, Iowa City 52242

Copyright © 1989 by the University of Iowa

All rights reserved

Printed in the United States of America

First paperback printing, 1991

Design by Richard Hendel

Typesetting by G&S Typesetters, Austin, Texas

Printing and binding by Malloy Lithographing,
Ann Arbor, Michigan

No part of this book may be reproduced or utilized in any
form or by any means, electronic or mechanical, including
photocopying and recording, without permission in writing
from the publisher.

Library of Congress Cataloging-in-Publication Data
Miller, Edwin Haviland.
  [Song of myself]
  Walt Whitman's "song of myself": a mosaic of
interpretations/by Edwin Haviland Miller.
    p. cm.
  Bibliography: p.
  Includes index.
  ISBN 0-87745-227-X, ISBN 0-87745-345-4 (pbk.)
  1. Whitman, Walt, 1819–1892. Song of myself.
I. Title.
PS3222.S63M55   1989   88-38069
811′.3—dc19   CIP

Dedicated to almost 300 critics

of "Song of Myself" who in the past

130 years have contributed to the

creation of A MOSAIC

OF INTERPRETATIONS

Contents

Preface

I undertook the preparation of what I call "A Mosaic of Interpretations" for two reasons. For more than twenty-five years in print and in the classroom I have wrestled with "Song of Myself" as much perhaps for my own enlightenment as my readers' or students'. I have also had for some time deep reservations as to the adequacy of any single approach, regardless of its breadth or depth, in reflecting the resonances and meanings of one of the most difficult and exciting poems in our literature.

Second, I think readers and students need assistance, a guide as it were, in coping with a commentary that I estimate now runs to thousands of pages.

Four Whitman scholars read and commented on the manuscript in early stages, and I have profited from their guidance in a number of ways. I am glad to acknowledge publicly my indebtedness to Harold Aspiz, Ed Folsom, Arthur Golden, and Jerome Loving. They are not responsible, I quickly add, for errors in judgment, omissions, or the final organization of the "Mosaic." I also want to record my appreciation of the assistance of librarians at the New York University Library and the New York Public Library and of the aid of Ivan Marki and Kenneth Price. Finally, I want to recognize the usefulness and stimulation of two prior studies: Gay Wilson Allen's *Walt Whitman Handbook* (1946) and James E. Miller Jr.'s *Whitman's "Song of Myself"—Origin, Growth, Meaning* (1964).

As for my debt to my wife, Rosalind, I still after forty-two years have not found the appropriate words.

Introduction

In July 1855, about the time Americans were again celebrating their independence, an oversized book with the strange title *Leaves of Grass* was published in Brooklyn. The embossed, gayly decorated letters of the title seem almost to dance across the green cover. Neither on the cover nor on the title page is the author identified, an omission not unusual in an era when many books appeared anonymously. What is unusual is the frontispiece, an engraving based on a daguerreotype, of an unidentified workingman with a straw hat perched foppishly on his forehead, an exposed undershirt, said to have been red, and, paradoxically, the eyes of a seemingly detached dreamer / observer. The copyright in the name of Walter Whitman appears on the verso of the title page.

The author is not named until about the middle of the first poem, on page twenty-nine, to be exact, in one of the most grandiose and immodest lines in literature—"Walt Whitman, an American, one of the roughs, a kosmos."

Early readers, of whom there were but a few, could not recognize the significance of the line. At age thirty-six a man previously known publicly as Walter Whitman during a career that included employment in printing shops, on newspapers as reporter and editor in Brooklyn, briefly in schools on Long Island, baptized himself Walt Whitman and soon was to establish a first-name relationship with his audience.

The book of twelve poems without titles was a more personal creation than anyone could have imagined. Even its production in almost every detail was closely supervised by the author: he set part of the type himself and designed the cover. The color and the title introduce one of the symbols of his poetry, grass, and the dancing letters evoke the kosmic (to use his spelling) choreography and the universal "procreant urge," which in turn will be part of a democratic choreography created by a perceptive observer—and lover—of the heterogeneous, classless American society.

In Section Seven he commands, "Undrape," but earlier in Section Two he presents himself "undisguised and naked," and promptly proceeds to undrape himself as he itemizes with loving care and imaginative verbiage bodily parts usually draped anatomically and always verbally in a freewheeling republic seemingly without genitals—"neuter" is Whitman's word for the collective castration or fear. Not only does the poet shed his clothes but he also seeks with unconcealed seductiveness a personal and erotic bond with each reader. His book, while physically a collection of twelve poems, is in a sense a person about to engage in a kind of dialogue with you the reader. "Gentle Readers" had been courted since the invention of the printing press, but usually within the parameters of genteel society and a well-established tradition. Whitman deliberately and delightedly wraps his arms about his naked body, his voice as seductive as his self-embrace, to attract attention, of course to shock, but also to establish his voice, his poetry, and his credo.

His goal is to be loved by the democratic society of which he is a self-appointed spokesman, the first democratic bard. But "Song of Myself" has never spoken to a mass audience. Its originality, the absence of rime and conventional meter, the quirkiness of the lines, and the sometimes obscure subject matter, erotic at times and sometimes puzzling, limits access to an elite readership. An early commentator, in the 1880s, quite rightly declares that Whitman "has always been truly caviare to the multitude."[1]

Despite what some critics were to say, Whitman was an astute self-critic, his brag resting on insight. In an anonymous review of his book in 1855 (Traubel, Bucke, and Harned, 19),[2] the first of his promotional releases, Whitman observes, in one of Nathaniel Hawthorne's favored images, that the twelve poems are "curiously veiled. Theirs is no writer to be gone through in a day or a month. Rather it is his pleasure to elude you and provoke you for deliberate purposes of his own." At the end of his life in a conversation with Horace Traubel (6:33) he professes to pity the person "who grapples with *Leaves of Grass*. It is so hard a tussle." On another occasion (6:408) he comments that his poems must be read "again and again. . . . before they enter into the reader, are grasped—filter their way to the undersoil." No one perhaps has stated more cogently the problems of his poetry, the source of his inspiration, or the depth of appeal—"to the undersoil."

Amy Lowell (503, 505), who should have known better, believes that Whitman "fell into his own peculiar form through ignorance, and not, as is commonly supposed, through a high sense of fitness. . . . Whitman never had the slightest idea of what cadence is, and I think it does not take much reading to force the conviction that he had very little rhythmical sense. . . . He was seeking something, but he never knew quite what, and he never found it."

Edmund Gosse (1900, 97–98), an English critic, explains the problem of the Whitman critic this way: Because Whitman "is literature in the condition of protoplasm," the critic "is immediately confronted with his own image stamped upon that viscid and tenuous surface. He finds, not what Whitman has to give, but what he himself has brought."

A wonderful English woman, Anne Gilchrist (297), one of the first of her sex to extol the American original in print, understood at once how to approach his verse. When she came upon what she called "enumerations," and others later referred to as telephone directories and worse, she "murmured not a little at first." Soon she realized that "not only is their purpose a justification, but that the musical ear and vividness of perception of the poet have enabled him to perform this task also with strength and grace, and that they are harmonious as well as necessary parts of the great whole." Hers is a positive, humble approach to the complex and elusive "great whole" that we still seek to understand more than 130 years after its appearance.

From the beginning Whitman had no doubts as to the importance of his great-est poem. Despite all the rearrangements of his other poems and his endless re-visions over the next thirty-five years, "Song of Myself" always appears early in each edition of *Leaves of Grass*, as the centerpiece: everything, in short, leads to and away from it. At its first appearance the poem of 1336 lines has neither line numbers nor divisions. Eventually the poem is divided into fifty-two sections, and although Whitman made a few deletions and inserted a few clarifying lines, he never essentially changed order or substance.

Yet despite his seeming self-confidence (colossal egoism, some have said) and his unlimited faith in a democratic society where all are equal, Whitman engaged in a lifelong manipulation of the public and posterity through an unrelenting publicity campaign to shape his public image in newspapers and magazines as well as through close supervision and direction of his most intimate friends in the articles and books that they wrote about him. He left nothing to chance. When Richard Maurice Bucke, a Canadian neurologist, a mystic, and one of the poet's literary executors, began to prepare a critical biography, he guided its preparation as an unacknowledged collaborator and arranged for its publication, and subsequently decreed that it was not to be altered.

Bucke (1883, 159) discusses at some length the content or meanings of "Song of Myself." It is, he writes,

> perhaps the most important poem that has so far been written at any time, in any language. Its magnitude, its depth and fulness of meaning, make it difficult, indeed impossible, to comment satisfactorily upon. In the first place, it is a celebration or glorification of Walt Whitman, of his body, and of his mind and soul, with all their functions and attributes—and then, by a subtle but inevitable implication, it becomes equally a song of exultation, as sung by any and every individual, man or woman, upon the beauty and per-fection of his or her body and spirits, the material part being treated as equally divine with the immaterial part, and the immaterial part as equally real and godlike with the material. Beyond this it has a third sense, in which it is the chant of cosmical man. . . . —of the whole race considered as one immense and immortal being. From a fourth point of view it is a most sub-lime hymn of glorification of external Nature. The way these different senses lie in some passages one behind the other, and are in others inextricably blended together, defies comment. But, above all, the chief difficulty in criti-cising this, as all other poems in *Leaves of Grass*, is that the ideas expressed are of scarcely any value or importance compared with the passion, the never-flagging emotion, which is in every line, almost in every word, and which cannot be set forth or even touched by commentary.

If this is not precisely the official reading of the poem, it is an approved reading.

Few of the early commentators, however, accept "Song of Myself" as Whitman's greatest achievement. Usually they single out "Out of the Cradle Endlessly Rock-ing," "When Lilacs Last in the Dooryard Bloom'd," or "Crossing Brooklyn Ferry."

It was not until the 1950s, after the celebration of the centennial of "Song of Myself" and the appearance of Gay Wilson Allen's biography *The Solitary Singer,* that it was accepted widely as Whitman's and the nation's greatest poem.

Serious examination of the content and structure of "Song of Myself" began about 1938 in the era of the so-called New Criticism, which was not attracted to Whitman, to his optimistic credo, or to a poem of such length as "Song of Myself." Carl Strauch is the first critic to find in a poem usually characterized as formless a logical and defensible structure, although, like many of his successors, he passes over aspects of the poem that do not support his interpretation of its meaning. Few later interpreters have accepted his structural outline in every detail—they too have had to shape the poem according to their own constructions of its meanings—but Strauch's example has led over the years to more than twenty similar analyses, as we shall see.

Whitman was often neglected in the post-war Eliotic era of disillusionment and an almost fashionable despair: Eliot, Pound, and Stevens had little of much significance to say about the poet, in contrast with D. H. Lawrence's free-floating, exuberant conferral of classical status upon Whitman and others. In a critical gem worthy of its subject Randall Jarrell points out with unfailing taste and generosity the incredible verbal felicities and delicacies of a poet whose "barbaric yawp" has by some been taken too literally—it is neither barbaric nor a yawp but, as Emerson was the first to recognize, an eccentric fusion of "wit & wisdom." Writing in the era of André Malraux's *Museum Without Walls,* with its sometimes excessive emphasis on details of paintings and sculptures at the expense of the whole, Jarrell delights in the jewels of the poem but pays little attention to the large tapestry.

Kenneth Burke was to prove one of the most perceptive readers of the poem and to make all admirers of Whitman regret that his essay of 1955 did not evolve into an extended analysis in depth. In the same year Richard Chase took up Emerson's point and Constance Rourke's delightful elaboration (but simplification) in *American Humor—A Study of the National Character,* to establish Whitman's legitimacy not only in the American comic tradition but in the English as well.

Richard P. Adams's undeservedly neglected essay in the *Tulane Studies in English* in 1955 is one of the best studies of the poem and proof that the principles of New Criticism can be applied creatively to Whitman's poetry. James E. Miller, Jr., coins the term "inverted mystical experience" in an attempt to merge the mystical tradition as defined by Evelyn Underhill and the sensuousness and explicit eroticism of Whitman's poem. Even when one disagrees with Miller's conclusions, one respects his acumen and the meticulous readings.

In this period Malcolm Cowley and Roy Harvey Pearce argue with cogency for the superiority of the early versions of the poems in the first three editions between 1855 and 1860 over the revisions and alterations Whitman made during his lifetime, as with age he occasionally muted excesses and even deleted a few controversial lines. Whitman had his nerve, as some critics have said, perhaps too often, but after the Civil War he deliberately modified his public image while denying that he was doing so.

During the 1960s James E. Miller modified some of his earlier views, and R. W. B. Lewis paid more attention to "Song of Myself" than he had in his influential *The American Adam,* with many illuminating insights. Tony Tanner proved himself a worthy successor of such English interpreters as Basil De Selincourt and David Daiches. In *Walt Whitman's Poetry: A Psychological Journey,* with debts to Jean Catel, Burke, Lawrence, and others, I examined the poem from a psychological focus in one of the longest analyses up to that time. It influenced the readings of such later commentators as Ivan Marki, Stephen A. Black, and David Cavitch.

In the 1970s the most significant interpreters were probably John Berryman,[3] who follows more or less in the tradition of Jarrell although he sometimes makes Whitman over in his own image; Diane Wood Middlebrook, who unfolds "a chronicle tracing the growth of the poet's mind"; Albert Gelpi, who advances a complex analysis of the psyche of the poet; Robert K. Martin, who places Whitman in a "homosexual tradition"; and Harold Bloom, probably despite his cumbersome terminology the most influential of recent interpreters.

In the present decade Whitman criticism has been enriched by the insights of, among others, Harold Aspiz, Lewis Hyde, Ernest Lee Tuveson, Paul Zweig, and, most recently, M. Wynn Thomas.

"Song of Myself"—The Search for Genre

More than 130 years after its appearance readers still search for a genre or a rubric. Mutlu Blasing (134), in 1987, asks: "how is 'Song of Myself' to be classified? Is the poem a lyric or an epic; is its 'I' the observed or an observer; and does the poem unify a fragmented objective experience, or does it fragment a unified subjective state?" One would think that at this late date these questions would no longer have to be asked or answered, but the poem has stubbornly, like Whitman himself, resisted classification.

Despite the jaunty parody of the *Aeneid* in the opening line—"I celebrate myself"—the poem does not unfold itself as parody or as epic of the Homeric or Miltonic order. The scope is large—the democratic American society in a vast landscape, North, South, East, and West—but epic conventions like deity are blithely ignored or mocked. The traditional epic has its cast of characters, and heroes as well as villains have names. In Whitman's depiction of his America, hundreds of people appear briefly but have no names, and no one establishes identity through individualized speech. The hero is the I, or Walt Whitman, and the voice is the poet's.

Unlike many later commentators who find it necessary to redefine the epic in order to incorporate "Song of Myself," one of Whitman's contemporaries, Jones

Very, that idiosyncratic classicist and poet who fell into the void of madness early in life, places no obstacles in the path of inevitable change (Pearce 1961, 69–70):

> To complain of this [progressive] tendancy [sic] of the human mind and its influence on literature, to sigh that we cannot have another Homeric poem is like weeping for the feeble days of childhood; and shows an insensibility to the ever-increasing beauty and grandeur developed by the Spirit in its endless progress; a forgetfulness of those powers of the soul, which result from this very progress; which enable it, while enjoying the present, to add to that joy by the remembrance of the past, and to grasp at a higher form the anticipations of the future.[4]

In effect confirming Very's judgment, Pearce (1961, 73, 83) recognizes "for the success of the poem that it be in no way externally or generically structured"; and eventually arrives at this formulation: "This is a new heroic poetry—not an epic, but an American equivalent of an epic. In this proto-epic, the hero releases the full creative force of the self, defines the *realia* of his world and takes from them his name, his office, and his phenomenal, existential qualities. . . . The new heroic poem, the specifically American epic, is one of ordering, not of order; of creation, not confirmation; of revealing, not memorializing."

Lawrence Buell (1973, 326) believes that only in "Song of Myself" is "anything like the feeling of epic scope really attained." In his judgment *Leaves of Grass* "stands as both the culmination and the epitaph of literary Transcendentalism." The observation may be extended to include "Song of Myself," which, although a new beginning in American poetry, is at the same time an epitaph to Victorian faith in self-reliance and inevitable progress.

For V. K. Chari (127) "Song of Myself," because of its "unity in theme, tone, and image," is "an epic of the self set in the framework of heroic and cosmic concepts, comparable in its expansive quality to *Paradise Lost*, or, better yet, the heroic Song of Krishna in the *Bhagavad-Gita.*"

Free of thesis and with greater critical acumen, David Daiches (1955a, 110) observes that Whitman "saw himself epically; his most trivial experience was thus potentially heroic, and his least observation could be presented as cosmic. He does not write epics, but he cultivates an epic pose in order to write lyrics." Gay Wilson Allen (1955a, 164) concurs in Daiches's judgment: "The final effect of 'Song of Myself' is . . . lyrical, and as a lyric it should be judged."

But many commentators want Whitman to be something presumably greater than and different from a lyricist. Malcolm Cowley (xi), for instance, declares with emphasis and, some would say, with hyperbole: "'Song of Myself' should be judged, I think, as one of the great inspired (and sometimes insane) prophetic works that have appeared at intervals in the western world, like [Christopher Smart's] *Jubilate Agno* (which is written in a biblical style sometimes suggesting Whitman's), like [Rimbaud's] *Illuminations*, like [Nietzsche's] *Thus Spake Zarathustra.*" While Cowley universalizes Whitman, G. Thomas Couser (85) argues that the poet "imitates the pattern of composition of the Quaker journal; a conversion narrative is supplemented periodically by installments probing the significance of subsequent experience in the light of a new vision."

Because "Song of Myself," like *Moby-Dick,* resists classification, some critics have offered multiple perspectives from which we can view the poem. To Leslie A. Fiedler (14, 16 – 17) *Leaves of Grass* is Whitman's "odd autobiographical Epic, his mythicized Portrait of the Artist as a Middle-Aged Hero." "Song of Myself," he writes,

> intended to define the ethos of a nation, is also a love-poem: simultaneously a love-song, a love-affair (the poet's only successful one), and a love-child (the only real offspring of his passion. . . .). As the hero of his poem is called "I," so the loved one is called "you"; and their vague pronominal romance is the thematic center of "Song of Myself." It is an odd subject for the Great American Poem: the celebration (half-heroic, half-ironic) of the mating between an "I" whose reality is constantly questioned and the even more elusive "you."

Paul Zweig (18, 135, 249, 251, 255 – 56), a poet as well as a critic of the loving order, states that the poem "is probably the finest enactment in all literature of the adventure of self-making, akin to such great quest poems as *The Epic of Gilgamesh*[5] and *The Divine Comedy.*" But it is also "a pastoral poem" with a difference because "its happy place is not a green meadow beside a brook, but the onrushing world of ordinary experience." It is also, Zweig writes, "an opera . . . , in which all the voices are one." At another point, "the poem is not about anything, . . . It is simply happening; it is about itself," a statement that owes something to current critical cant. Finally, Zweig's associative process bubbling, "The world exists for [Whitman] as food, and he devours it with his song." Fiedler and Zweig are in their enthusiasm given to tossing out provocative suggestions without attempting the more difficult task of elaboration and substantiation.

Richard Chase (1955a, 58, 72, 97, 67) describes "Song of Myself" as "the profound and lovely comic drama of the self," combining "Dionysian gaiety and an impulse toward verbal artificiality with the tone and cultural presuppositions of American humor—a striking feat of hybridization—certainly, yet no more so than that which produced *Moby-Dick.*" This "comedy of human thought" unfolds Whitman's "drama of identity."

Constance Rourke (143) may have been the first to point out that Whitman's "monologue or rhapsody" is "not far from the so-called stream of consciousness" in depicting "moods, shades of feeling, fragments of thought." Writing about the same time, the astute Danish critic Frederik Schyberg (100) maintains that the "stream of imagery, of associations, . . . particularly in 'Song of Myself,' many times has the appearance of being unconscious, of the subconscious acting on its own. As often happens in dreams, the poet, without realizing it, betrays himself in this imagery." Schyberg notes the anticipation of "surrealism and James Joyce, whose 'stream-of-consciousness' flows in an absolute parallel with Whitman's, though in a really less poetically inspired manner."

Daiches (1959, 48) elaborates on Whitman's influence on the twentieth-century sensibility: "the mosaic of ideas in Eliot, the stream of consciousness in the modern novel, and all those extraordinarily subtle devices through which the modern novelist and poet have tried to explore ways in which an individual sensibility can be modulated into an inclusive consciousness, are in the tradition of Whitman. How to escape the prison of the self and cultivate simultaneously self-consciousness and sympathy, using the sense of self-identity as a means of projecting oneself into the identity of others—that, I think, is Whitman's most valuable legacy to modern literature."[6]

E. H. Miller (1968, 39) suggests that the poem is a meditation after the fashion of Montaigne, who "uses the analogy of a seesaw to characterize the flux of the contradictory personality and to describe at the same time his essays." Ivan Marki (115) singles out "an often elliptic 'interior monologue' by a man profoundly alone. ["Song of Myself"] is, in fact, a meditation induced by what may be called an inner landscape and thus akin to the secular 'meditation on the creatures' that M. H. Abrams has identified as the distinctive feature of the 'descriptive-meditative poem' or 'greater Romantic lyric.'"

John Berryman (233) creates a new genre when he writes: "I take the work in fact to be one of Welcome, self-*wrestling*, inquiry, and wonder—conditional, open, and astonished (not exulting as over an accomplished victory, but gradually revealing, puzzling, discovering.)"

A summary of the views of "Song of Myself" presented here is as complex and inconclusive as the guesses of the "I" of the poem in answer to the child's question, "What is the grass?" For "Song of Myself" is epic (proto-epic, autobiographical epic, or epical in scope), heroic poem, lyric, prophetic or mystical (inverted or no) vision, a conversion narrative, a love poem, a comic drama, a drama of identity, an American pastoral, an opera, a self-making (simultaneously of person and poem), a reverie or meditation. And perhaps there is no end. Surely it is, among other things, a "grass-poem," since, as Tony Tanner (78) suggests, "the poem to some extent organizes itself" around the grass.[7]

"Song of Myself"—The Search for Structure

Whitman published "Song of Myself" without formal divisions until the appearance of the fourth edition of *Leaves of Grass* in 1867, when he created fifty-two sections—chants, poems, songs, or clusters, depending upon the taste of the critic—which may, as some have proposed, evoke the annual cycle. Clearly a poem of such length requires divisions, and if they are absent, critics will create them for purposes of understanding and discussion.

Those critics who deliberately avoid imposing order upon the poem out of respect for what they conceive to be Whitman's intentions are inevitably compelled to resort to such loose and indefinite formulations as musical analogies, which necessarily will rise at intervals in crescendos and culminate in climaxes. Clearly the poem has some kind of structure, conscious and unconscious, but "Song of Myself" poses formidable difficulties, as the lack of consensus among readers testifies. Those given to ingenious paradoxes of the Gilbert and Sullivan order can gleefully claim that nonform is form, as absence is said to be presence in this era of verbal and textual conundrums.

At the same time, some of those who propose structures—Lewis, Roy Pearce, and Marki, for example—are aware that their diagrams limit the resonance of the poetry and its meanings, and, more important, that linear constructions are basically at odds with the cyclical and rhythmic nature of "the procreant urge" and the sexuality at the center of the poem and at the center of creativity itself.

In an ingenious proposal derived from Whitman's democratic idealizations, Lewis (1965, 11) writes: "In a real sense, the poem was intended to have as many structures as there were readers; and the reason was that Whitman aimed not simply to create a poet and then a god, but to assist at the creation of the poetic and godlike in every reader."

Even the greatest of the poet's early American admirers, John Burroughs (1896, 121), does not perceive a clearly established structure. Rather it is, he declares, "a series of utterances, ejaculations, apostrophes, enumerations, associations, pictures, parables, incidents, suggestions, with little or no structural or logical connection, but all emanating from a personality whose presence dominates the page, and whose eye is ever upon us. Without this vivid and intimate sense of the man back of all, of a sane and powerful spirit sustaining ours, the piece would be wild and inchoate."[8]

William Sloane Kennedy (1896, 102), a young contemporary admirer of the poet, proposes a three-part structure so loose that it perhaps deserves little consideration except that it is apparently one of the first attempts to rein in Whitman's free-flowing poem. "Broadly speaking, the first part of this poem—#1 to that part of #33 beginning, 'I understand the large hearts of heroes' [818]—celebrates nature and the body ('physiology'); the second portion—#33 to that portion of #41 beginning, 'Magnifying and applying come I' [1020]—sets forth the democratic principle (comradeship, compassion, etc.); the last portion—#41 to the end—deals chiefly with religion (death, the stars, and immortality)."

Strauch (599) is the first analyst to advance a tenable structural order, but in effect by denying the eroticism of the poem. The five divisions reflect quite logically his primary emphasis upon the almost mystical emergence of the Self. (For the sake of clarity and consistency, I have standardized the formats of the proposed structures. Roman numerals are used for the divisions; Arabic numbers for the sections of the poem. The analyses are presented in order of appearance.)

I, 1–18: "the Self; mystical interpenetration of the Self with all life and experience";

II, 19–25: "definition of the Self; identification with the degraded, and transfiguration of it; final merit of Self withheld; silence; end of first half";

III, 26–38: "life flowing in upon the Self; then evolutionary interpenetration
  of life";

IV, 39–41: "the Superman";

V, 42–52: "larger questions of life—religion, faith, God, death; immortality
  and happiness mystically affirmed."

In *The American Way of Poetry* Henry W. Wells (36–37) asserts that Whitman
"groups his lyrics in such a way that his poem is virtually an effusion in five acts
and fifty-two scenes."

I, 1–7: Act 1, "Metaphysical, and . . . distinctly philosophical and subjective,"
  speculations upon the soul;

II, 8–16: Act 2, "predominantly objective, reportorial, and descriptive";

III, 17–30: Act 3, same as I;

IV, 31–36: Act 4, same as II, except "more varied, dramatic, and accumulative
  in effect";

V, 37–52: Act 5, same as I.

Whitman's "speculations," Wells (39) asserts, "treat the gravest spiritual problems which faced the American transcendentalists—the relation of the Self to
society, of soul to body, of the elemental to the sophisticated—together with
questions on science and faith, happiness, evolution, truth, immortality, religion,
and God. The chief conclusion is that God should be spelled with a small letter
and Self with a capital."

James E. Miller, Jr. (1957, 7), proposes the following "dramatic representation
of an inverted mystical experience," which is based on Evelyn Underhill's study:[9]

I, 1–5: "Entry into the mystical state";

II, 6–16: "Awakening of self";

III, 17–32: "Purification of self";

IV, 33–37: "Illumination and the dark night of the soul";

V, 38–43: "Union (faith and love)";

VI, 44–49: "Union (perception)";

VII, 50–52: "Emergence from the mystical state."

The five-fold structure of Richard P. Adams (129–30) rests on two principles:
"the growth of knowledge through the assimilation and integration of diverse
experience, and the growth of personality through the pattern of death and
rebirth."

I, 1–7: death and rebirth: "in the fusion of the ego—the 'I' . . . with the soul
  in #5, and certainly in the direct references to death and immortality in
  #6 and #7";

II, 8–16: assimilation and integration "of diverse experiences";

III, 17–30: death and rebirth: "The touch passage [#28–29] is the most
  intense climax of the poem";

IV, 31–36: assimilation and integration again, but now "the speaker is

overwhelmed by his empathic relation to the multitude of struggling and
suffering animals and persons . . . until he bethinks himself of his similar
relation to Christ";

V, 37–52: "a delivery of the poet-prophet's life-giving—or immortality-giving
message."

Adams acknowledges that because of "a very complex tissue of relations . . . it
seems almost impossible to mark off any boundaries corresponding to real divisions between one part and another."

John Berryman (233, 237, 241) draws upon the affinities between music and
"Song of Myself" when he posits four movements and at the same time, as one
would perhaps expect, concentrates upon the "I" or poet.

I, 1–5: "Double invitation from 'I,' or the human body, to the human soul and
from 'I,' or the poet, to the reader";

II, 6–19: "concerned after this prelude of the grass and death, with 'I's'
identification *outward*";

III, 20–38: the theme is "Being, 'What is a man anyhow?' [20:390]," to which
there are "two series of answers . . . of the *Self*" and "*not* of the Self";

IV, 39–52: "addressed to his 'Eleves'—disciples—'lovers of me.'" Whitman
gradually withdraws.

If the I assumes some of Berryman's own turbulences, it confirms Gosse's obser-
vations that readers will find their own images in Whitman's self-portrait.

Malcolm Cowley (xvii–xx) discovers in "Song of Myself" an "irreversible order,
like the beginning, middle, and end of any good narrative." In nine "sequences"
he delineates his version of the "prophetic" Whitman and at the same time gives
long overdue attention to "the procreant urge."

I, 1–4: "the poet or hero introduced to his audience . . . He is also in love
with his deeper self or soul, but explains that it is not to be confused with
mere personality";

II, 5: "the ecstasy . . . the rapt union of the poet and his soul, . . . described—
figuratively, on the present occasion—in terms of sexual union";

III, 6–19: the grass, "symbolizing the miracle of common things and the
divinity . . . of ordinary persons";

IV, 20–25: "the poet in person . . . he venerates himself as august and
immortal, but so . . . is everyone else";

V, 26–29: "ecstasy through the senses . . . With the sense of touch, [the poet]
finds himself rising to the ecstasy of sexual union";

VI, 30–38: "the power of identification . . . with every object and with every
person living or dead, heroic or criminal";

VII, 39–41: "the superman";

VIII, 42–50: "the sermon. He is about to offer a statement of the doctrines
implied by the narrative";

IX, 51–52: "the poet's farewell."

Roy Harvey Pearce (1961, 74) proposes an intellectual reading of the poem or "argument" that "moves in gross outline something like this" in "four phases":

I, 1–5: "The initial insight into the creative nature ('the procreant urge') of the self and the initiating of creative power which follows spontaneously upon that insight";

II, 6–16: "Recognition of the relation of the self to its world and a seeking after the metamorphoses which follow spontaneously upon that recognition";

III, 17–25: "The roles of the self in and through its world . . . Now the poet is not simply a force, but a force defined in terms of the world; now he is fully a person and can name himself";

IV, 26–52: "The poet (as person) fully at home in his newly defined world, . . . he can openly and lovingly address it, as he at once creates and controls it and as he is created and controlled by it. He is thus a religion, God-like in himself."

R. W. B. Lewis's reading (1965, 12–15) takes into account the didactic or religious theme, the emergence of a democratic poet, and the archetypal descent of the "I."

I, 1–2: invocation, "transition from the artificial to the natural";

II, 3–5: recollection of the union of body and soul, "mystical in kind, sexual in idiom";

III, 6–17: as a result of the union with democratic society, "the man becomes a *poet*. . . . The democratic aesthetic is most palpably at work here";

IV, 18–24: "Claims for himself the gradually achieved role of poet . . . of every mode of equality";

V, 25–32: prepares for "second great adventure, the long journey . . . toward *godhead*," in preparation for which "he undergoes a second ecstatic experience . . . of an almost overpoweringly sensuous kind." Health and sanity are endangered in the "touch" scene;

VI, 33–38: poet revives and now experiences "the familiar, archetypal descent into Jungian darkness or hell and resurrection";

VII, 39–51: proclaims "his divine inheritance . . . exhorting every man to his supreme and unique effort . . . for the divine potential of all men";

VIII, 52: he departs, his mission fulfilled.

Howard J. Waskow (163–89) delineates the poet's struggle to free himself from didacticism, to which he invariably retreats, to achieve his poetic vision. The poem is a kind of agon as Waskow perceives it, in the course of which the sexuality and poetry itself receive limited attention, although his study as a whole is marked by many insights.

I, 1–4: "a portrait of a man torn between celebration of his ideal self, the self harmonious with readers and all the world and acknowledgment of his 'actual self' [which] must contend with . . . everyday difficulties";

II, 5–7: "the first stage in his approach to the vision";

III, 8–15: "'Undrape' . . . leads into the second stage of Whitman's approach toward his poetic vision." He shows "tenacious acquisitiveness" as he "witnesses";

IV, 16–25: "the impatience of the hero's poetic imagination with the limitations imposed by didacticism" interferes with the realization of his vision;

V, 26–32: the I listens, becomes involved in "the mad whirl of imagination," and retreats briefly into didacticism;

VI, 33–37: imaginative journey or flight, now really "'in contact' with the atmosphere and with all other beings";

VII, 38–52: "The self is born anew . . . a secular Christ." The hero is "setting out on the 'perpetual journey' of development, the never-ending discovery of himself and everything that is."

The thesis of E. Fred Carlisle (177–78) is that the poem "moves essentially from concentration on the monological self to a discovery of the dialogical self— the man who shares his being and experience with the external world and others." This "drama of identity" takes place in six "stages."

I, 1–5: "the 'idle, unitary self' announces himself and asserts that he contains a multitude of characteristics";

II, 6–17: "after his sudden expansion of consciousness, he begins to recognize the world beyond him and to establish relations with it. . . . he sees the world as little more than a reflection of himself";

III, 18–32: "He realizes the uniqueness and reality of the world, and he opens himself completely to it";

IV, 33–38: "he risks his whole person, [and] the poet's identity is threatened and almost destroyed";

V, 39–50: "he emerges intact with his discoveries both earned and confirmed";

VI, 51–52: "the drama of identity ends as the self is absorbed into the world—leaving his reader with his experiences of encounter and his vision of wholeness."

According to Todd M. Lieber (76, 78, 84, 88, 94, 98), "Song of Myself" is "essentially a poem about selfhood as understood through the examination and dramatic presentation of one particular self."

I, 1–6: largely a prologue in which "we find the central paradox of the poem and the central tension of Whitman's thought: how the self can be at once both individual and cosmic and how the poem can be the 'thoughts of all men in all ages' and at the same time be uniquely personal";

II, 7–16: "as each thing is observed, . . . it becomes figuratively a part of the self. . . . the movement is inward";

III, 17–32: "now Whitman turns his attention . . . to a more reflective discussion of the meaning and significance of the poem and an examination of the fundamental qualities of cosmic selfhood";

> IV, 33–43: "the self-image of the poet becomes completely unlimited, . . . facing the full implications of his cosmic nature by including the harsh unpleasant aspects of experience";
>
> V, 44–52: "the final paradox of cosmic selfhood is that the hero's identity can never be complete, despite the fact that it is 'perfect' at any given moment."

Diane Wood Middlebrook (27–28, 35, 49, 72–73) focuses on the growth of the imagination and approaches Whitman through Coleridge and Wallace Stevens, as perhaps mediated by Bloom. She argues that the poem "is structured according to the fluctuations of that imagination as it operates in areas of reality which more and more challenge its pleasure-giving capacity for insight and incorporation."

> I, 1–5: Preface, "'I' is the consciousness of the poet. 'Myself' is an ideal abstracted from the poet's ego. At #5 they are made one; 'Myself' subsumes 'I' and becomes the speaker of the poem";
>
> II, 6–19: First phase, "virtually a casebook of demonstrations of Coleridge's idea about the imagination";
>
> III, 20–30: Second phase begins "to test that assumption. The Real Me takes up a subject for poetry which demands the most honest 'acceptation': his own sexuality";
>
> IV, 31–38: Third phase: "Acknowledging his error, the Real Me recovers his creative energy, only to have it diminished again . . . by another seizure of powerful feeling";
>
> V, 39–47: Fourth phase: Whitman presents the Real Me as the "hero of the epic of democracy . . . capable of maintaining a viable morality by mediating the pressure of instinct from within and the demands of social existence from without";
>
> VI, 48–52: Closure.

Albert Gelpi (169–209) in an illuminating, sometimes difficult discussion of the poem fuses the search for identity and the mystical and psychological aspects of the poem.

> I, 1–7: "transformative tendencies of self," including in #5 "a conversion-experience, simultaneously sexual and religious, simultaneously personal and cosmic";
>
> II, 8–17: procession of catalogues "substantiating and enlarging" upon the first part, in what Gelpi terms "the auto-apotheosis of the bacchic poet-prophet fleshing his personal identity in his natural and democratic environment";
>
> III, 18–24: more reflective speculations as to "the moral attitude and character of the poet-prophet; climaxes in a celebration of the 'mystic'";
>
> IV, 25–32: Because of his "psychic vulnerability" Whitman yields to the senses—first to sounds, then to touch, the danger being overcome by #30;

V, 33–38: "generating vision" of great catalogues, and by #38 he has recovered
and "replenished" himself;

VI, 39–52: a universal lover, a "phallic overman," then "the archetype of
Deity," and finally "Guru, Wise Man, and High Priest to all priesthoods"—of
"Cosmic Man," who "is rooted in organic nature and in man's sexuality."

Ivan Marki (152–85) in a nine-part structure traces the protagonist's journey
after the transformation in #5 to self-awareness and "social identity." Marki ig-
nores Whitman's sections and creates his own divisions to establish his thesis.

I, 1:1–5:81: "Introductory lines";

II, 5:82–8:145: "the protagonist's crisis and transformation . . . the very
heart-beat of life";

III, 8:146–16:352: Phase 1, the I as passive observer of the "nightmarish
urban landscape" and then of the pastoral landscape;

IV, 17:353–19:380: Phase 2, an attempt to clarify what he is doing; "oral and
musical" imagery predominates as he becomes preoccupied with failure;

V, 19:381–24:546: Phase 3, "What am I?", the answer being, I am the poet of
the body *and* the soul;

VI, 24:547–32:706: Phase 4, "intellectual uncertainty" following "sensuous
self-realization";

VII, 32:707–38:963: Phase 5, elaboration of the protagonist's announcement,
"I am afoot with my vision," its substance being "the flight of the fluid and
swallowing soul"; a "growing obsession with morbidity";

VIII, 38:964–50:1308: Phase 6, "The 'I' has acquired the social identity
commensurate with the visionary mode of his being"; overcomes "his
ultimate crisis by . . . making his personal myth of salvation coincide with
all mankind's pre-eminent myth of salvation";

IX, 51:1309–52:1336: Phase 7, "ever the one who has plenty of help to offer
but will never acknowledge that he might use some himself, offers his
audience a last reassurance: don't worry, 'I'll stop somewhere waiting
for you.'"

Harold Bloom (1976, 248–62) has attempted to make over the American literary landscape by means of an idiosyncratic, often brilliant fusion of Freudianism,
Emersonianism, and rhetorical embellishments in which he takes immense
delight.

I, 1–6: "overtly a celebration, . . . a return of the repressed, an ecstatic union
of soul and self, of primary and antithetical, or, more simply, they celebrate
the American Sublime of influx, of Emersonian self-recognition and
consequent self-reliance";

II, 7–27: "Whitman . . . makes of a linked sex-and-death a noble synechdoche
for all of existence. . . . A universalizing flood tide of reversals into-the-
opposite reaches a great climax in #24, which is an antithetical completion
of the self without rival in American poetry";

xxvi   INTRODUCTION

III, 28–30: masturbation becomes "a metonymic reduction of the self, where touch substitutes for the whole being";

IV, 31–38: "the most awesome repression in our literature, the greatest instance yet of the American Sublime";

V, 39–49: "an attempt at a sublimating consolidation of the self, . . . as inside reciprocally addressing the natural world as a supposedly answering outside";

VI, 50–52: "a miraculous transumption of all that has gone before. It is the reader, and not the poet, who is challenged directly to make his belatedness into an earliness."

Harold Aspiz (1980, 174–76) in an interpretation grounded in a close analysis of nineteenth-century interest in the occult, health, and fads delineates "the clairvoyant persona's extended sleep-walking experience one summer's day from early morning to 'the last scud of day.'"

I, 1–6: the persona, "possibly cataleptic," becomes "possessed by his 'soul' or associate spirit" in #5, and then "makes his first halting efforts to interpret nature's 'uniform hieroglyphic'";

II, 7–15: the I now "sees more clearly . . . even though his associate spirit (or inner self) has not yet achieved complete rapport with the associate spirits of those whom he observes";

III, 16–32: proceeding to a higher plane, the persona "becomes the spokesman for the 'many long dumb voices' and . . . acts as the mystic galvanometer of the divine spirit";

IV, 33–38: in plumbing "the depths of misery with his mediumistic senses, the persona has deranged the electrical balance so essential to his mediumistic communication with the spirit world";

V, 39–52: as a "flowing savage," he is "a clairvoyant healer of bodies, minds, and souls . . . , a teacher of the highest wisdom, and a spiritual being who can meet the gods on equal terms."

M. L. Rosenthal and Sally Gall (30) attempt no breakthrough in interpretation but bring to the poem the kind of delight and refinement Jarrell introduced many years earlier.

I, 1–7: "varied centers of emotional reference: key notations of sensibility";

II, 8–17: "varied projections of identity: objects of love";

III, 18–25: "negative extensions of II: the defeated, the forbidden passion for elemental realities";

IV, 26–29: "the sensitized responder; 'touch' poems at the heart of the sequence";

V, 30–36: "credo-poems converted into particular moments fixed in historical memory";

VI, 37–43: "the prophetic, divine, *crucified* self";

VII, 44–52: "mystical and cosmic extensions of the self; the open road of reaching into the unknown, including death; recapitulations."

In proposing the resemblance of "Song of Myself" to a "five-act comic drama," Ronald Wallace (73–75) draws on the discussions of Wells, Chase, and Rourke as well as on the comic theory of Northrop Frye. His thesis is that the poem incorporates "a persona that combines a character from early American humor with a character from Old Greek comedy in a plot that reflects patterns of exposure and integration, in a spirit of fun, nonsense, satire, self-parody, exaggeration, deflation, celebration, and surprise."

I, 1–5: Act 1 "introduces the comic hero as both egotist of an exposure comedy and lover of a romance comedy. His comic concerns with the grass, the self, the body, and the soul both elevate and deflate him, as does the dramatic conflict between ego and *eiron,* poet and paramour";

II, 6–33: Act 2 replaces "the conventional unfestive and destructive society with a new world that satisfactorily solves the puzzle of being";

III, 34–37: Act 3 "exposes the hero to a ritual death in which reality, society, and history conspire to separate the poet from his creations, the lover from his love";

IV, 38–49: Act 4, the hero overcomes "the blocks to his happiness, emerging as an absurdly buoyant god";

V, 50–52: Act 5, "having created a world that reaches from the grass to heaven and back again to the grass, the speaker waits confidently for the reader-lover, who is purged of pretense and negativity, to catch up and join him in a harmonious union."

As Calvin Bedient (29) reads the poem, "Organic dynamism and diversity are made possible through a mutual modification between the part and the whole. This dialectic provides the plan for 'Song of Myself.' The plan is incremental, with now 'identity' and now 'sympathy' returning with redoubled force, thanks to the loving tussle between them." He then treats the fifty-two sections "as flip pictures" of the poet's comic affirmation:

I, 1–6: "Whitman first taking a bow for no more or less reason than that he exists";

II, 7–16: appoints himself "mate and companion";

III, 17–23: "taking an even deeper bow, now as the bountiful artist";

IV, 24–29: now "doting on his body, which surprisingly shades and amorously slips into the body of the world";

V, 30–37: displaying an "'infinite and omnigenous' capacity for sympathy";

VI, 38–45: "posing as a jaunty, best-yet prophet jetting 'the stuff of finer republics'";

VII, 46–52: "finally, in a beautifully extended and mounting valediction, running on before his readers ('I see God') but warmly calling back to them to join him." [10]

Doubtless partitive structures will continue to appear, but there can be few substantial rearrangements so long as critics continue to emphasize the significance and resonances of the following sections: 1, 5, 6, 24–25, 28–29, 33–38, 39, 50–52. Yet it is only Whitmanesque to believe that in the future a reader will uncover, no doubt by happy accident, patterns embedded in the rich details of the mosaic that at last produce the harmonious consensus that has eluded generations of reader-lovers.

The mosaic of interpretations presented here consists of excerpts from the commentary of almost 300 readers who have brought various skills and insights to the poem during the past 130 years. Collectively these readers have written thousands of pages, adding up no doubt to hundreds of thousands of words, to explicate a poem consisting of 1336 lines at its first appearance in 1855.

These interpreters have approached "Song of Myself" from a wide variety of perspectives—mystical, religious, social-political, social-literary, aesthetic, linguistic, quests for identity, psychological-psychoanalytic, autobiographical—or by means of various combinations.

The 300 readers provide an elaborate and sensitive commentary on the poem, establishing its breadth and depths, its variety, as well as confirming its enduring mysteries that elude criticism. Even narrow approaches to the poem provide rewards by demonstrating that what appears to be trivia on superficial examination merges into larger configurations, into the endless flow of the poet's choreography. The seeming irrelevancies of much of the material in the catalogues take on greater significance if, like Mrs. Gilchrist, we stop condescending to a poet who is incredibly subtle and deeply reflective. Whitman's seeming nonselectivity is not nonselective: the whole is the sum of the parts.

What is clear, it seems to me, is that no single approach to "Song of Myself," no matter how acute and seemingly complete, can encompass the whole mosaic. Biases and methodologies get in the way and finally lose out to Walt Whitman. The commentary has, perhaps, exhausted many of the traditional critical approaches and is moving rapidly to a full exploitation of other, including postmodern, approaches. The poem has been tested by all kinds of methodologies, without achieving a breakthrough to a widely acclaimed consensual reading. Even in the most perceptive and sensitive interpretations, too many resonances are silenced, multifaceted affects are constricted by intellectualizations (mind taking precedence over feelings), and significant parts of the poem are sometimes arbitrarily dismissed if they do not confirm the reader's theories. Too many approaches have, not surprisingly, proved reductive, and the poem is still greater than the sum of its readings.

The commentary, however, establishes, if demonstration is needed, that according to his interpreters Whitman, an American of humble origins and limited education, walks in the company of the great and the elite. Despite his sometimes barbed and outrageously unfair attacks upon his predecessors and his desire to be an "original," his readers have placed him among mystics and prophets such as

Jesus, Buddha, Oriental and Indian mystics, and Blake; among the greatest writers and poets such as Homer, Vergil, Dante, Shakespeare, Goethe, Wordsworth, and Coleridge; among artists such as Michelangelo, Raphael, Breughel, Eakins, and Jackson Pollock; and among composers such as Hector Berlioz, Franz Schubert, Gustav Mahler, Charles Ives, and Richard Wagner.

The Plan of the Mosaic of Interpretations

The interpretations as arranged here provide a running commentary on the poem almost line by line, from section to section, somewhat in the fashion of a variorum. I have tried to allow the critics so far as possible to speak for themselves, but of necessity I have abridged comments, at times perhaps, but unintentionally, fractured arguments. It is, however, possible through reference to the index to follow more or less an individual critic's interpretation, that is, if he presents an extended discussion of the entire poem.

I have sought to be as objective as my biases will permit. However, I have not hesitated to make editorial decisions and evaluations: I have, for example, not quoted derivative criticism that adds nothing to our appreciation or foolish comments that should never have been published. Some absurd constructions too wonderfully funny not to be quoted brighten the endnotes, which may be one reason to read them, if one wishes to discover such dubiously useful information as why Whitman can be termed a "symbolic turkey." I see no reason why an editor should be denied his admittedly fallible judgments, and if in doubt, readers can, and should, consult the author whose views are only summarized here. In fairness to all critics I have listed their articles in the Bibliography.

Since textual matters are dealt with in detail in the three-volume *Leaves of Grass: A Textual Variorum of the Printed Poems,* in the New York University Press edition of Whitman, they are omitted here except in those few instances in which additions to the poems are either important to the argument of a critic or useful to our understanding.

The text of the 1855 edition is used because in my judgment the first version is closest to the inspiration and excited, almost panting, germination of the poem from 1850 to 1855, when Whitman's life and art were suddenly and dramatically transformed. The text is a facsimile of the first printing of the poem to which have been added line and section numbers. The following errors in the poem have been corrected: 2:14, Echoes (not Echos), 7:128, as (not a), 15:320, adobe (not abode) and canvas (not canvass), 17:361, the tasteless (not the the tasteless), 17:362, the federal (not th federal), 21:431, development (not developement), 31:664, chef d'oeuvre (not chef-d'ouvre), 33:771, firs (not furs), 33:859, indispensable (not indispensible), 40:1010, an armed (not am armed), 42:1080, omnivorous (not omniverous), 46:1227, life. (not life), 52:1334, fetch me (not fetch me me), 52:1336, you. (not you).

In quoting critics I have made the following alterations to eliminate confusion.

(1) The fifty-two divisions of the poem have been variously called song, chant, poem, paragraph, or, most commonly, section; I have used the last and in turn simplified to #1, etc. (2) Errors by critics in references to lines or sections and typographical errors have been silently corrected, without the use of brackets, and quotations from later texts of the poem have been transferred to the 1855 version or explained in a note, when necessary.

The following abbreviations appear in the text and notes and, with one exception, refer to the twenty-two-volume edition of *The Collected Writings of Walt Whitman* published by the New York University Press since 1961.

Corr.   *The Correspondence,* ed. Edwin Haviland Miller.
CRE   *Leaves of Grass: Comprehensive Reader's Edition,* eds. Harold W. Blodgett and Sculley Bradley.
DBN   *Daybooks and Notebooks,* ed. William White.
NUPM   *Notebooks and Unpublished Prose Manuscripts,* ed. Edward F. Grier.
PW   *Prose Works 1892,* ed. Floyd Stovall.
UPP   *The Uncollected Prose and Poetry,* ed. Emory Holloway. Garden City: Doubleday, Page & Company, 1921.

I CELEBRATE myself, [1]
And what I assume you shall assume,
For every atom belonging to me as good belongs to you.

I loafe and invite my soul,
I lean and loafe at my ease .... observing a spear of summer grass. 5

Houses and rooms are full of perfumes....the shelves are crowded with perfumes, [2]
I breathe the fragrance myself, and know it and like it,
The distillation would intoxicate me also, but I shall not let it.

The atmosphere is not a perfume....it has no taste of the distillation .... it is
odorless,
It is for my mouth forever .... I am in love with it, 10
I will go to the bank by the wood and become undisguised and naked,
I am mad for it to be in contact with me.

The smoke of my own breath,
Echoes, ripples, and buzzed whispers .... loveroot, silkthread, crotch and vine,
My respiration and inspiration .... the beating of my heart .... the passing of blood
and air through my lungs, 15
The sniff of green leaves and dry leaves, and of the shore and darkcolored sea-
rocks, and of hay in the barn,
The sound of the belched words of my voice .... words loosed to the eddies of
the wind,
A few light kisses .... a few embraces .... a reaching around of arms,
The play of shine and shade on the trees as the supple boughs wag,
The delight alone or in the rush of the streets, or along the fields and hillsides, 20
The feeling of health .... the full-noon trill .... the song of me rising from bed
and meeting the sun.

Have you reckoned a thousand acres much ? Have you reckoned the earth much ?
Have you practiced so long to learn to read ?
Have you felt so proud to get at the meaning of poems ?

25   Stop this day and night with me and you shall possess the origin of all poems,
You shall possess the good of the earth and sun .... there are millions of suns left,
You shall no longer take things at second or third hand .... nor look through the
       eyes of the dead .... nor feed on the spectres in books,
You shall not look through my eyes either, nor take things from me,
You shall listen to all sides and filter them from yourself.

30 [3]   I have heard what the talkers were talking .... the talk of the beginning and the end,
But I do not talk of the beginning or the end.

There was never any more inception than there is now,
Nor any more youth or age than there is now ;
And will never be any more perfection than there is now,
35   Nor any more heaven or hell than there is now.

Urge and urge and urge,
Always the procreant urge of the world.

Out of the dimness opposite equals advance .... Always substance and increase,
Always a knit of identity .... always distinction .... always a breed of life.

40   To elaborate is no avail .... Learned and unlearned feel that it is so.

Sure as the most certain sure .... plumb in the uprights, well entretied, braced in
       the beams,
Stout as a horse, affectionate, haughty, electrical,
I and this mystery here we stand.

Clear and sweet is my soul .... and clear and sweet is all that is not my soul.

45   Lack one lacks both .... and the unseen is proved by the seen,
Till that becomes unseen and receives proof in its turn.

Showing the best and dividing it from the worst, age vexes age,
Knowing the perfect fitness and equanimity of things, while they discuss I am silent,
       and go bathe and admire myself.

Welcome is every organ and attribute of me, and of any man hearty and clean,
50   Not an inch nor a particle of an inch is vile, and none shall be less familiar than the rest.

I am satisfied .... I see, dance, laugh, sing ;

As God comes a loving bedfellow and sleeps at my side all night and close on tho
    peep of the day,
And leaves for me baskets covered with white towels bulging the house with their
    plenty,
Shall I postpone my acceptation and realization and scream at my eyes,
That they turn from gazing after and down the road,   55
And forthwith cipher and show me to a cent,
Exactly the contents of one, and exactly the contents of two, and which is ahead?

Trippers and askers surround me,   [4]
People I meet . . . . . the effect upon me of my early life . . . . of the ward and city I
    live in . . . . of the nation,
The latest news . . . . discoveries, inventions, societies . . . . authors old and new,   60
My dinner, dress, associates, looks, business, compliments, dues,
The real or fancied indifference of some man or woman I love,
The sickness of one of my folks — or of myself . . . . or ill-doing . . . . or loss or lack
    of money . . . . or depressions or exaltations,
They come to me days and nights and go from me again,
But they are not the Me myself.   65

Apart from the pulling and hauling stands what I am,
Stands amused, complacent, compassionating, idle, unitary,
Looks down, is erect, bends an arm on an impalpable certain rest,
Looks with its sidecurved head curious what will come next,
Both in and out of the game, and watching and wondering at it.   70

Backward I see in my own days where I sweated through fog with linguists and
    contenders,
I have no mockings or arguments . . . . I witness and wait.

I believe in you my soul . . . . the other I am must not abase itself to you,   [5]
And you must not be abased to the other.

Loafe with me on the grass . . . . loose the stop from your throat,   75
Not words, not music or rhyme I want . . . . not custom or lecture, not even the best,
Only the lull I like, the hum of your valved voice.

I mind how we lay in June, such a transparent summer morning;
You settled your head athwart my hips and gently turned over upon me,
And parted the shirt from my bosom-bone, and plunged your tongue to my barestript
    heart,   80
And reached till you felt my beard, and reached till you held my feet.

Swiftly arose and spread around me the peace and joy and knowledge that pass all
    the art and argument of the earth;
And I know that the hand of God is the elderhand of my own,

And I know that the spirit of God is the eldest brother of my own,
And that all the men ever born are also my brothers . . . . and the women my sisters
85   and lovers,
And that a kelson of the creation is love ;
And limitless are leaves stiff or drooping in the fields,
And brown ants in the little wells beneath them,
And mossy scabs of the wormfence, and heaped stones, and elder and mullen and
          pokeweed.

90 [6]   A child said, What is the grass ? fetching it to me with full hands ;
How could I answer the child ? . . . . I do not know what it is any more than he.

I guess it must be the flag of my disposition, out of hopeful green stuff woven.

Or I guess it is the handkerchief of the Lord,
A scented gift and remembrancer designedly dropped,
Bearing the owner's name someway in the corners, that we may see and remark,
95   and say Whose ?

Or I guess the grass is itself a child . . . . the produced babe of the vegetation.

Or I guess it is a uniform hieroglyphic,
And it means, Sprouting alike in broad zones and narrow zones,
Growing among black folks as among white,
Kanuck, Tuckahoe, Congressman, Cuff, I give them the same, I receive them the
100   same.

And now it seems to me the beautiful uncut hair of graves.

Tenderly will I use you curling grass,
It may be you transpire from the breasts of young men,
It may be if I had known them I would have loved them ;
It may be you are from old people and from women, and from offspring taken soon
105   out of their mothers' laps,
And here you are the mothers' laps.

This grass is very dark to be from the white heads of old mothers,
Darker than the colorless beards of old men,
Dark to come from under the faint red roofs of mouths.

110   O I perceive after all so many uttering tongues !
And I perceive they do not come from the roofs of mouths for nothing.

I wish I could translate the hints about the dead young men and women,
And the hints about old men and mothers, and the offspring taken soon out of their
          laps.

What do you think has become of the young and old men ?
And what do you think has become of the women and children ?   115

They are alive and well somewhere ;
The smallest sprout shows there is really no death,
And if ever there was it led forward life, and does not wait at the end to arrest it,
And ceased the moment life appeared.

All goes onward and outward . . . . and nothing collapses,   120
And to die is different from what any one supposed, and luckier.

Has any one supposed it lucky to be born ?   [7]
I hasten to inform him or her it is just as lucky to die, and I know it.

I pass death with the dying, and birth with the new-washed babe . . . . and am not
    contained between my hat and boots,
And peruse manifold objects, no two alike, and every one good,   125
The earth good, and the stars good, and their adjuncts all good.

I am not an earth nor an adjunct of an earth,
I am the mate and companion of people, all just as immortal and fathomless as
    myself;
They do not know how immortal, but I know.

Every kind for itself and its own . . . . for me mine male and female,   130
For me all that have been boys and that love women,
For me the man that is proud and feels how it stings to be slighted,
For me the sweetheart and the old maid . . . . for me mothers and the mothers of
    mothers,
For me lips that have smiled, eyes that have shed tears,
For me children and the begetters of children.   135

Who need be afraid of the merge ?
Undrape . . . . you are not guilty to me, nor stale nor discarded,
I see through the broadcloth and gingham whether or no,
And am around, tenacious, acquisitive, tireless . . . . and can never be shaken away.

The little one sleeps in its cradle,   [8] 140
I lift the gauze and look a long time, and silently brush away flies with my hand.

The youngster and the redfaced girl turn aside up the bushy hill,
I peeringly view them from the top.

The suicide sprawls on the bloody floor of the bedroom,
It is so . . . . I witnessed the corpse . . . . there the pistol had fallen.   145

The blab of the pave .... the tires of carts and sluff of bootsoles and talk of the
    promenaders,
The heavy omnibus, the driver with his interrogating thumb, the clank of the shod
    horses on the granite floor,
The carnival of sleighs, the clinking and shouted jokes and pelts of snowballs ;
The hurrahs for popular favorites .... the fury of roused mobs,
150   The flap of the curtained litter — the sick man inside, borne to the hospital,
The meeting of enemies, the sudden oath, the blows and fall,
The excited crowd — the policeman with his star quickly working his passage to the
    centre of the crowd ;
The impassive stones that receive and return so many echoes,
The souls moving along .... are they invisible while the least atom of the stones is
    visible ?
155   What groans of overfed or half-starved who fall on the flags sunstruck or in fits,
What exclamations of women taken suddenly, who hurry home and give birth to
    babes,
What living and buried speech is always vibrating here .... what howls restrained
    by decorum,
Arrests of criminals, slights, adulterous offers made, acceptances, rejections with
    convex lips,
I mind them or the resonance of them .... I come again and again.

160 [9]   The big doors of the country-barn stand open and ready,
The dried grass of the harvest-time loads the slow-drawn wagon,
The clear light plays on the brown gray and green intertinged,
The armfuls are packed to the sagging mow :
I am there .... I help .... I came stretched atop of the load,
165   I felt its soft jolts .... one leg reclined on the other,
I jump from the crossbeams, and seize the clover and timothy,
And roll head over heels, and tangle my hair full of wisps.

[10]   Alone far in the wilds and mountains I hunt,
Wandering amazed at my own lightness and glee,
170   In the late afternoon choosing a safe spot to pass the night,
Kindling a fire and broiling the freshkilled game,
Soundly falling asleep on the gathered leaves, my dog and gun by my side.

The Yankee clipper is under her three skysails .... she cuts the sparkle and scud,
My eyes settle the land .... I bend at her prow or shout joyously from the deck.

175   The boatmen and clamdiggers arose early and stopped for me,
I tucked my trowser-ends in my boots and went and had a good time,
You should have been with us that day round the chowder-kettle.

I saw the marriage of the trapper in the open air in the far-west .... the bride was
    a red girl,

Her father and his friends sat near by crosslegged and dumbly smoking .... they
      had moccasins to their feet and large thick blankets hanging from their
      shoulders ;
On a bank lounged the trapper .... he was dressed mostly in skins .... his luxuriant
      beard and curls protected his neck,   180
One hand rested on his rifle .... the other hand held firmly the wrist of the red girl,
She had long eyelashes .... her head was bare ...,. her coarse straight locks
      descended upon her voluptuous limbs and reached to her feet.

The runaway slave came to my house and stopped outside,
I heard his motions crackling the twigs of the woodpile,
Through the swung half-door of the kitchen I saw him limpsey and weak,   185
And went where he sat on a log, and led him in and assured him,
And brought water and filled a tub for his sweated body and bruised feet,
And gave him a room that entered from my own, and gave him some coarse clean
      clothes,
And remember perfectly well his revolving eyes and his awkwardness,
And remember putting plasters on the galls of his neck and ankles ;   190
He staid with me a week before he was recuperated and passed north,
I had him sit next me at table .... my firelock leaned in the corner.

Twenty-eight young men bathe by the shore,   [11]
Twenty-eight young men, and all so friendly,
Twenty-eight years of womanly life, and all so lonesome.   195

She owns the fine house by the rise of the bank,
She hides handsome and richly drest aft the blinds of the window.

Which of the young men does she like the best ?
Ah the homeliest of them is beautiful to her.

Where are you off to, lady ? for I see you,   200
You splash in the water there, yet stay stock still in your room.

Dancing and laughing along the beach came the twenty-ninth bather,
The rest did not see her, but she saw them and loved them.

The beards of the young men glistened with wet, it ran from their long hair,
Little streams passed all over their bodies.   205

An unseen hand also passed over their bodies,
It descended tremblingly from their temples and ribs.

The young men float on their backs, their white bellies swell to the sun .... they do
      not ask who seizes fast to them,

They do not know who puffs and declines with pendant and bending arch,
210   They do not think whom they souse with spray.

[12]   The butcher-boy puts off his killing-clothes, or sharpens his knife at the stall in the market,
I loiter enjoying his repartee and his shuffle and breakdown.

Blacksmiths with grimed and hairy chests environ the anvil,
Each has his main-sledge .... they are all out .... there is a great heat in the fire.

215   From the cinder-strewed threshold I follow their movements,
The lithe sheer of their waists plays even with their massive arms,
Overhand the hammers roll — overhand so slow — overhand so sure,
They do not hasten, each man hits in his place.

[13]   The negro holds firmly the reins of his four horses .... the block swags underneath on its tied-over chain,
The negro that drives the huge dray of the stoneyard .... steady and tall he stands
220   poised on one leg on the stringpiece,
His blue shirt exposes his ample neck and breast and loosens over his hipband,
His glance is calm and commanding .... he tosses the slouch of his hat away from his forehead,
The sun falls on his crispy hair and moustache .... falls on the black of his polish'd and perfect limbs.

I behold the picturesque giant and love him .... and I do not stop there,
225   I go with the team also.

In me the caresser of life wherever moving .... backward as well as forward slue-ing,
To niches aside and junior bending.

Oxen that rattle the yoke or halt in the shade, what is that you express in your eyes?
It seems to me more than all the print I have read in my life.

230   My tread scares the wood-drake and wood-duck on my distant and daylong ramble,
They rise together, they slowly circle around.
.... I believe in those winged purposes,
And acknowledge the red yellow and white playing within me,
And consider the green and violet and the tufted crown intentional;
235   And do not call the tortoise unworthy because she is not something else,
And the mockingbird in the swamp never studied the gamut, yet trills pretty well to me,
And the look of the bay mare shames silliness out of me.

[14]   The wild gander leads his flock through the cool night,

Ya-honk ! he says, and sounds it down to me like an invitation ;
The pert may suppose it meaningless, but I listen closer,   240
I find its purpose and place up there toward the November sky.

The sharphoofed moose of the north, the cat on the housesill, the chickadee, the
    prairie-dog,
The litter of the grunting sow as they tug at her teats,
The brood of the turkeyhen, and she with her halfspread wings,
I see in them and myself the same old law.   245

The press of my foot to the earth springs a hundred affections,
They scorn the best I can do to relate them.

I am enamoured of growing outdoors,
Of men that live among cattle or taste of the ocean or woods,
Of the builders and steerers of ships, of the wielders of axes and mauls, of the drivers
    of horses,   250
I can eat and sleep with them week in and week out.

What is commonest and cheapest and nearest and easiest is Me,
Me going in for my chances, spending for vast returns,
Adorning myself to bestow myself on the first that will take me,
Not asking the sky to come down to my goodwill,   255
Scattering it freely forever.

The pure contralto sings in the organloft,   [15]
The carpenter dresses his plank .... the tongue of his foreplane whistles its wild
    ascending lisp,
The married and unmarried children ride home to their thanksgiving dinner,
The pilot seizes the king-pin, he heaves down with a strong arm,   260
The mate stands braced in the whaleboat, lance and harpoon are ready,
The duck-shooter walks by silent and cautious stretches,
The deacons are ordained with crossed hands at the altar,
The spinning-girl retreats and advances to the hum of the big wheel,
The farmer stops by the bars of a Sunday and looks at the oats and rye,   265
The lunatic is carried at last to the asylum a confirmed case,
He will never sleep any more as he did in the cot in his mother's bedroom ;
The jour printer with gray head and gaunt jaws works at his case,
He turns his quid of tobacco, his eyes get blurred with the manuscript ;
The malformed limbs are tied to the anatomist's table,   270
What is removed drops horribly in a pail ;
The quadroon girl is sold at the stand .... the drunkard nods by the barroom stove,
The machinist rolls up his sleeves .... the policeman travels his beat .... the gate-
    keeper marks who pass,

The young fellow drives the express-wagon .... I love him though I do not know him;

275 The half-breed straps on his light boots to compete in the race,

The western turkey-shooting draws old and young .... some lean on their rifles, some sit on logs,

Out from the crowd steps the marksman and takes his position and levels his piece ;

The groups of newly-come immigrants cover the wharf or levee,

The woollypates hoe in the sugarfield, the overseer views them from his saddle ;

The bugle calls in the ballroom, the gentlemen run for their partners, the dancers

280   bow to each other ;

The youth lies awake in the cedar-roofed garret and harks to the musical rain,

The Wolverine sets traps on the creek that helps fill the Huron,

The reformer ascends the platform, he spouts with his mouth and nose,

The company returns from its excursion, the darkey brings up the rear and bears the well-riddled target,

The squaw wrapt in her yellow-hemmed cloth is offering moccasins and beadbags for

285   sale,

The connoisseur peers along the exhibition-gallery with halfshut eyes bent sideways,

The deckhands make fast the steamboat, the plank is thrown for the shoregoing passengers,

The young sister holds out the skein, the elder sister winds it off in a ball and stops now and then for the knots,

The one-year wife is recovering and happy, a week ago she bore her first child,

The cleanhaired Yankee girl works with her sewing-machine or in the factory or

290   mill,

The nine months' gone is in the parturition chamber, her faintness and pains are advancing ;

The pavingman leans on his twohanded rammer — the reporter's lead flies swiftly over the notebook — the signpainter is lettering with red and gold,

The canal-boy trots on the towpath — the bookkeeper counts at his desk — the shoemaker waxes his thread,

The conductor beats time for the band and all the performers follow him,

295 The child is baptised — the convert is making the first professions,

The regatta is spread on the bay .... how the white sails sparkle !

The drover watches his drove, he sings out to them that would stray,

The pedlar sweats with his pack on his back — the purchaser higgles about the odd cent,

The camera and plate are prepared, the lady must sit for her daguerreotype,

300 The bride unrumples her white dress, the minutehand of the clock moves slowly,

The opium eater reclines with rigid head and just-opened lips,

The prostitute draggles her shawl, her bonnet bobs on her tipsy and pimpled neck,

The crowd laugh at her blackguard oaths, the men jeer and wink to each other,

(Miserable !   I do not laugh at your oaths nor jeer you,)

305 The President holds a cabinet council, he is surrounded by the great secretaries,

On the piazza walk five friendly matrons with twined arms;
The crew of the fish-smack pack repeated layers of halibut in the hold,
The Missourian crosses the plains toting his wares and his cattle,
The fare-collector goes through the train — he gives notice by the jingling of loose
    change,
The floormen are laying the floor — the tinners are tinning the roof — the masons
    are calling for mortar,   310
In single file each shouldering his hod pass onward the laborers;
Seasons pursuing each other the indescribable crowd is gathered .... it is the
    Fourth of July .... what salutes of cannon and small arms!
Seasons pursuing each other the plougher ploughs and the mower mows and the
    wintergrain falls in the ground;
Off on the lakes the pikefisher watches and waits by the hole in the frozen surface,
The stumps stand thick round the clearing, the squatter strikes deep with his axe,   315
The flatboatmen make fast toward dusk near the cottonwood or pekantrees,
The coon-seekers go now through the regions of the Red river, or through those
    drained by the Tennessee, or through those of the Arkansas,
The torches shine in the dark that hangs on the Chattahoochee or Altamahaw;
Patriarchs sit at supper with sons and grandsons and great grandsons around them,
In walls of adobe, in canvas tents, rest hunters and trappers after their day's sport.   320
The city sleeps and the country sleeps,
The living sleep for their time .... the dead sleep for their time,
The old husband sleeps by his wife and the young husband sleeps by his wife;
And these one and all tend inward to me, and I tend outward to them,
And such as it is to be of these more or less I am.   325

I am of old and young, of the foolish as much as the wise,   [16]
Regardless of others, ever regardful of others,
Maternal as well as paternal, a child as well as a man,
Stuffed with the stuff that is coarse, and stuffed with the stuff that is fine,
One of the great nation, the nation of many nations — the smallest the same and the
    largest the same,   330
A southerner soon as a northener, a planter nonchalant and hospitable,
A Yankee bound my own way .... ready for trade .... my joints the limberest
    joints on earth and the sternest joints on earth,
A Kentuckian walking the vale of the Elkhorn in my deerskin leggings,
A boatman over the lakes or bays or along coasts .... a Hoosier, a Badger, a
    Buckeye,
A Louisianian or Georgian, a poke-easy from sandhills and pines,   335
At home on Canadian snowshoes or up in the bush, or with fishermen off New-
    foundland,
At home in the fleet of iceboats, sailing with the rest and tacking,
At home on the hills of Vermont or in the woods of Maine or the Texan ranch,
Comrade of Californians .... comrade of free northwesterners, loving their big
    proportions,

340   Comrade of raftsmen and coalmen — comrade of all who shake hands and welcome
              to drink and meat ;
         A learner with the simplest, a teacher of the thoughtfulest,
         A novice beginning experient of myriads of seasons,
         Of every hue and trade and rank, of every caste and religion,
         Not merely of the New World but of Africa Europe or Asia .... a wandering
              savage,
345   A farmer, mechanic, or artist .... a gentleman, sailor, lover or quaker,
         A prisoner, fancy-man, rowdy, lawyer, physician or priest.

         I resist anything better than my own diversity,
         And breathe the air and leave plenty after me,
         And am not stuck up, and am in my place.

350   The moth and the fisheggs are in their place,
         The suns I see and the suns I cannot see are in their place,
         The palpable is in its place and the impalpable is in its place.

[17]   These are the thoughts of all men in all ages and lands, they are not original with
              me,
         If they are not yours as much as mine they are nothing or next to nothing,
355   If they do not enclose everything they are next to nothing,
         If they are not the riddle and the untying of the riddle they are nothing,
         If they are not just as close as they are distant they are nothing.

         This is the grass that grows wherever the land is and the water is,
         This is the common air that bathes the globe.

360   This is the breath of laws and songs and behaviour,
         This is the tasteless water of souls .... this is the true sustenance,
         It is for the illiterate .... it is for the judges of the supreme court .... it is for the
              federal capitol and the state capitols,
         It is for the admirable communes of literary men and composers and singers and
              lecturers and engineers and savans,
         It is for the endless races of working people and farmers and seamen.

[18]   This is the trill of a thousand clear cornets and scream of the octave flute and strike
365   of triangles.

         I play not a march for victors only .... I play great marches for conquered and
              slain persons.

         Have you heard that it was good to gain the day ?
         I also say it is good to fall .... battles are lost in the same spirit in which they are
              won.

I sound triumphal drums for the dead .... I fling through my embouchures the
    loudest and gayest music to them,
Vivas to those who have failed, and to those whose war-vessels sank in the sea,
    and those themselves who sank in the sea,   370
And to all generals that lost engagements, and all overcome heroes, and the number-
    less unknown heroes equal to the greatest heroes known.

This is the meal pleasantly set .... this is the meat and drink for natural hunger,   [19]
It is for the wicked just the same as the righteous ...., I make appointments with all,
I will not have a single person slighted or left away,
The keptwoman and sponger and thief are hereby invited .... the heavy-lipped slave
    is invited ..... the venerealee is invited,   375
There shall be no difference between them and the rest.

This is the press of a bashful hand .... this is the float and odor of hair,
This is the touch of my lips to yours .... this is the murmur of yearning,
This is the far-off depth and height reflecting my own face,
This is the thoughtful merge of myself and the outlet again.   380

Do you guess I have some intricate purpose?
Well I have .... for the April rain has, and the mica on the side of a rock has.

Do you take it I would astonish?
Does the daylight astonish? or the early redstart twittering through the woods?
Do I astonish more than they?   385

This hour I tell things in confidence,
I might not tell everybody but I will tell you.

Who goes there! hankering, gross, mystical, nude?   [20]
How is it I extract strength from the beef I eat?

What is a man anyhow? What am I? and what are you?   390
All I mark as my own you shall offset it with your own,
Else it were time lost listening to me.

I do not snivel that snivel the world over,
That months are vacuums and the ground but wallow and filth,
That life is a suck and a sell, and nothing remains at the end but threadbare crape
    and tears.   395

Whimpering and truckling fold with powders for invalids .... conformity goes to
    the fourth-removed,
I cock my hat as I please indoors or out.

Shall I pray? Shall I venerate and be ceremonious?

I have pried through the strata and analyzed to a hair,
And counselled with doctors and calculated close and found no sweeter fat than
400   sticks to my own bones.

In all people I see myself, none more and not one a barleycorn less,
And the good or bad I say of myself I say of them.

And I know I am solid and sound,
To me the converging objects of the universe perpetually flow,
405 All are written to me, and I must get what the writing means.

And I know I am deathless,
I know this orbit of mine cannot be swept by a carpenter's compass,
I know I shall not pass like a child's carlacue cut with a burnt stick at night.

I know I am august,
410 I do not trouble my spirit to vindicate itself or be understood,
I see that the elementary laws never apologize,
I reckon I behave no prouder than the level I plant my house by after all.

I exist as I am, that is enough,
If no other in the world be aware I sit content,
415 And if each and all be aware I sit content.

One world is aware, and by far the largest to me, and that is myself,
And whether I come to my own today or in ten thousand or ten million years,
I can cheerfully take it now, or with equal cheerfulness I can wait.

My foothold is tenoned and mortised in granite,
420 I laugh at what you call dissolution,
And I know the amplitude of time.

[21] I am the poet of the body,
And I am the poet of the soul.

The pleasures of heaven are with me, and the pains of hell are with me,
The first I graft and increase upon myself .... the latter I translate into a new
425   tongue.

I am the poet of the woman the same as the man,
And I say it is as great to be a woman as to be a man,
And I say there is nothing greater than the mother of men.

I chant a new chant of dilation or pride,
430 We have had ducking and deprecating about enough,
I show that size is only development.

Have you outstript the rest ?   Are you the President ?
It is a trifle .... they will more than arrive there every one, and still pass on.

I am he that walks with the tender and growing night ;
I call to the earth and sea half-held by the night.   435

Press close barebosomed night !   Press close magnetic nourishing night !
Night of south winds !   Night of the large few stars !
Still nodding night !   Mad naked summer night !

Smile O voluptuous coolbreathed earth !
Earth of the slumbering and liquid trees !   440
Earth of departed sunset !   Earth of the mountains misty-topt !
Earth of the vitreous pour of the full moon just tinged with blue !
Earth of shine and dark mottling the tide of the river !
Earth of the limpid gray of clouds brighter and clearer for my sake !
Far-swooping elbowed earth !   Rich apple-blossomed earth !   445
Smile, for your lover comes !

Prodigal ! you have given me love ! .... therefore I to you give love !
O unspeakable passionate love !

Thruster holding me tight and that I hold tight !
We hurt each other as the bridegroom and the bride hurt each other.   450

You sea !   I resign myself to you also .... I guess what you mean,   [22]
I behold from the beach your crooked inviting fingers,
I believe you refuse to go back without feeling of me ;
We must have a turn together .... I undress .... hurry me out of sight of the land,
Cushion me soft .... rock me in billowy drowse,   455
Dash me with amorous wet .... I can repay you.

Sea of stretched ground-swells !
Sea breathing broad and convulsive breaths !
Sea of the brine of life !   Sea of unshovelled and always-ready graves !
Howler and scooper of storms !   Capricious and dainty sea !   460
I am integral with you .... I too am of one phase and of all phases.

Partaker of influx and efflux .... extoler of hate and conciliation,
Extoler of amies and those that sleep in each others' arms.

I am he attesting sympathy ;
Shall I make my list of things in the house and skip the house that supports them ?   465

I am the poet of commonsense and of the demonstrable and of immortality ;
And am not the poet of goodness only .... I do not decline to be the poet of wick-
    edness also.

Washes and razors for foofoos .... for me freckles and a bristling beard.

What blurt is it about virtue and about vice ?
470   Evil propels me, and reform of evil propels me .... I stand indifferent,
My gait is no faultfinder's or rejecter's gait,
I moisten the roots of all that has grown.

Did you fear some scrofula out of the unflagging pregnancy ?
Did you guess the celestial laws are yet to be worked over and rectified ?

I step up to say that what we do is right and what we affirm is right .... and some
475   is only the ore of right,
Witnesses of us .... one side a balance and the antipodal side a balance,
Soft doctrine as steady help as stable doctrine,
Thoughts and deeds of the present our rouse and early start.

This minute that comes to me over the past decillions,
480   There is no better than it and now.

What behaved well in the past or behaves well today is not such a wonder,
The wonder is always and always how there can be a mean man or an infidel.

[23]   Endless unfolding of words of ages !
And mine a word of the modern .... a word en masse.

485   A word of the faith that never balks,
One time as good as another time .... here or henceforward it is all the same to
            me.

A word of reality .... materialism first and last imbueing.

Hurrah for positive science !   Long live exact demonstration !
Fetch stonecrop and mix it with cedar and branches of lilac ;
This is the lexicographer or chemist .... this made a grammar of the old
490   cartouches,
These mariners put the ship through dangerous unknown seas,
This is the geologist, and this works with the scalpel, and this is a mathematician.

Gentlemen I receive you, and attach and clasp hands with you,
The facts are useful and real .... they are not my dwelling .... I enter by them to
            an area of the dwelling.

495   I am less the reminder of property or qualities, and more the reminder of life,
And go on the square for my own sake and for others' sakes,

And make short account of neuters and geldings, and favor men and women fully
    equipped,
And beat the gong of revolt, and stop with fugitives and them that plot and conspire.

Walt Whitman, an American, one of the roughs, a kosmos,   [24]
Disorderly fleshy and sensual .... eating drinking and breeding,   500
No sentimentalist .... no stander above men and women or apart from them .... no
    more modest than immodest.

Unscrew the locks from the doors!
Unscrew the doors themselves from their jambs!

Whoever degrades another degrades me .... and whatever is done or said returns
    at last to me,
And whatever I do or say I also return.   505

Through me the afflatus surging and surging .... through me the current and index.

I speak the password primeval .... I give the sign of democracy;
By God! I will accept nothing which all cannot have their counterpart of on the
    same terms.

Through me many long dumb voices,
Voices of the interminable generations of slaves,   510
Voices of prostitutes and of deformed persons,
Voices of the diseased and despairing, and of thieves and dwarfs,
Voices of cycles of preparation and accretion,
And of the threads that connect the stars — and of wombs, and of the fatherstuff,
And of the rights of them the others are down upon,   515
Of the trivial and flat and foolish and despised,
Of fog in the air and beetles rolling balls of dung.

Through me forbidden voices,
Voices of sexes and lusts .... voices veiled, and I remove the veil,
Voices indecent by me clarified and transfigured.   520

I do not press my finger across my mouth,
I keep as delicate around the bowels as around the head and heart,
Copulation is no more rank to me than death is.

I believe in the flesh and the appetites,
Seeing hearing and feeling are miracles, and each part and tag of me is a miracle.   525

Divine am I inside and out, and I make holy whatever I touch or am touched from;
The scent of these arm-pits is aroma finer than prayer,
This head is more than churches or bibles or creeds.

If I worship any particular thing it shall be some of the spread of my body ;
530   Translucent mould of me it shall be you,
Shaded ledges and rests, firm masculine coulter, it shall be you,
Whatever goes to the tilth of me it shall be you,
You my rich blood, your milky stream pale strippings of my life ;
Breast that presses against other breasts it shall be you,
535   My brain it shall be your occult convolutions,
Root of washed sweet-flag, timorous pond-snipe, nest of guarded duplicate eggs, it
      shall be you,
Mixed tussled hay of head and beard and brawn it shall be you,
Trickling sap of maple, fibre of manly wheat, it shall be you ;
Sun so generous it shall be you,
540   Vapors lighting and shading my face it shall be you,
You sweaty brooks and dews it shall be you,
Winds whose soft-tickling genitals rub against me it shall be you,
Broad muscular fields, branches of liveoak, loving lounger in my winding paths, it
      shall be you,
Hands I have taken, face I have kissed, mortal I have ever touched, it shall be you.

545   I dote on myself .... there is that lot of me, and all so luscious,
Each moment and whatever happens thrills me with joy.

I cannot tell how my ankles bend .... nor whence the cause of my faintest wish,
Nor the cause of the friendship I emit .... nor the cause of the friendship I take
    again.

To walk up my stoop is unaccountable .... I pause to consider if it really be,
550   That I eat and drink is spectacle enough for the great authors and schools,
A morning-glory at my window satisfies me more than the metaphysics of books.

To behold the daybreak !
The little light fades the immense and diaphanous shadows,
The air tastes good to my palate.

555   Hefts of the moving world at innocent gambols, silently rising, freshly exuding,
Scooting obliquely high and low.

Something I cannot see puts upward libidinous prongs,
Seas of bright juice suffuse heaven.

The earth by the sky staid with .... the daily close of their junction,
560   The heaved challenge from the east that moment over my head,
The mocking taunt, See then whether you shall be master !

[25]   Dazzling and tremendous how quick the sunrise would kill me,
If I could not now and always send sunrise out of me.

We also ascend dazzling and tremendous as the sun,
We found our own my soul in the calm and cool of the daybreak.   565

My voice goes after what my eyes cannot reach,
With the twirl of my tongue I encompass worlds and volumes of worlds.

Speech is the twin of my vision .... it is unequal to measure itself.

It provokes me forever,
It says sarcastically, Walt, you understand enough .... why don't you let it out
        then ?   570

Come now I will not be tantalized .... you conceive too much of articulation.

Do you not know how the buds beneath are folded ?
Waiting in gloom protected by frost,
The dirt receding before my prophetical screams,
I underlying causes to balance them at last,   575
My knowledge my live parts .... it keeping tally with the meaning of things,
Happiness ..:.. which whoever hears me let him or her set out in search of this
        day.

My final merit I refuse you .... I refuse putting from me the best I am.

Encompass worlds but never try to encompass me,
I crowd your noisiest talk by looking toward you.   580

Writing and talk do not prove me,
I carry the plenum of proof and every thing else in my face,
With the hush of my lips I confound the topmost skeptic.

I think I will do nothing for a long time but listen,   [26]
And accrue what I hear into myself .... and let sounds contribute toward me. 585

I hear the bravuras of birds .... the bustle of growing wheat .... gossip of flames
        .... clack of sticks cooking my meals.

I hear the sound of the human voice .... a sound I love,
I hear all sounds as they are tuned to their uses .... sounds of the city and sounds
        out of the city .... sounds of the day and night;
Talkative young ones to those that like them .... the recitative of fish-pedlars and
        fruit-pedlars .... the loud laugh of workpeople at their meals,
The angry base of disjointed friendship .... the faint tones of the sick,   590
The judge with hands tight to the desk, his shaky lips pronouncing a death-sentence,
The heave'e'yo of stevedores unlading ships by the wharves .... the refrain of the
        anchor-lifters ;

The ring of alarm-bells .... the cry of fire .... the whirr of swift-streaking engines
    and hose-carts with premonitory tinkles and colored lights,
The steam-whistle .... the solid roll of the train of approaching cars;
595   The slow-march played at night at the head of the association,
They go to guard some corpse .... the flag-tops are draped with black muslin,

I hear the violincello or man's heart's complaint,
And hear the keyed cornet or else the echo of sunset.

I hear the chorus .... it is a grand-opera .... this indeed is music!

600   A tenor large and fresh as the creation fills me,
The orbic flex of his mouth is pouring and filling me full.

I hear the trained soprano .... she convulses me like the climax of my love-grip;
The orchestra whirls me wider than Uranus flies,
It wrenches unnamable ardors from my breast,
605   It throbs me to gulps of the farthest down horror,
It sails me .... I dab with bare feet .... they are licked by the indolent waves,
I am exposed .... cut by bitter and poisoned hail,
Steeped amid honeyed morphine .... my windpipe squeezed in the fakes of death,
Let up again to feel the puzzle of puzzles,
610   And that we call Being.

[27]   To be in any form, what is that?
If nothing lay more developed the quahaug and its callous shell were enough.

Mine is no callous shell,
I have instant conductors all over me whether I pass or stop,
615   They seize every object and lead it harmlessly through me.

I merely stir, press, feel with my fingers, and am happy,
To touch my person to some one else's is about as much as I can stand.

[28]   Is this then a touch? .... quivering me to a new identity,
Flames and ether making a rush for my veins,
620   Treacherous tip of me reaching and crowding to help them,
My flesh and blood playing out lightning, to strike what is hardly different from
    myself,
On all sides prurient provokers stiffening my limbs,
Straining the udder of my heart for its withheld drip,
Behaving licentious toward me, taking no denial,
625   Depriving me of my best as for a purpose,
Unbuttoning my clothes and holding me by the bare waist,
Deluding my confusion with the calm of the sunlight and pasture fields,

Immodestly sliding the fellow-senses away,
They bribed to swap off with touch, and go and graze at the edges of me,
No consideration, no regard for my draining strength or my anger,   630
Fetching the rest of the herd around to enjoy them awhile,
Then all uniting to stand on a headland and worry me.

The sentries desert every other part of me,
They have left me helpless to a red marauder,
They all come to the headland to witness and assist against me.   635

I am given up by traitors ;
I talk wildly .... I have lost my wits .... I and nobody else am the greatest
    traitor,
I went myself first to the headland .... my own hands carried me there.

You villain touch ! what are you doing ? .... my breath is tight in its throat ;
Unclench your floodgates ! you are too much for me.   640

Blind loving wrestling touch !   Sheathed hooded sharptoothed touch !   [29]
Did it make you ache so leaving me ?

Parting tracked by arriving .... perpetual payment of the perpetual loan,
Rich showering rain, and recompense richer afterward.

Sprouts take and accumulate .... stand by the curb prolific and vital,   645
Landscapes projected masculine full-sized and golden.

All truths wait in all things,   [30]
They neither hasten their own delivery nor resist it,
They do not need the obstetric forceps of the surgeon,
The insignificant is as big to me as any,   650
What is less or more than a touch ?

Logic and sermons never convince,
The damp of the night drives deeper into my soul.

Only what proves itself to every man and woman is so,
Only what nobody denies is so.   655

A minute and a drop of me settle my brain ;
I believe the soggy clods shall become lovers and lamps,
And a compend of compends is the meat of a man or woman,
And a summit and flower there is the feeling they have for each other,
And they are to branch boundlessly out of that lesson until it becomes omnific,   660
And until every one shall delight us, and we them.

[31]   I believe a leaf of grass is no less than the journeywork of the stars,
        And the pismire is equally perfect, and a grain of sand, and the egg of the wren,
        And the tree-toad is a chef d'oeuvre for the highest,
665   And the running blackberry would adorn the parlors of heaven,
        And the narrowest hinge in my hand puts to scorn all machinery,
        And the cow crunching with depressed head surpasses any statue,
        And a mouse is miracle enough to stagger sextillions of infidels,
        And I could come every afternoon of my life to look at the farmer's girl boiling her
            iron tea-kettle and baking shortcake.

        I find I incorporate gneiss and coal and long-threaded moss and fruits and grains and
670   esculent roots,
        And am stucco'd with quadrupeds and birds all over,
        And have distanced what is behind me for good reasons,
        And call any thing close again when I desire it.

        In vain the speeding or shyness,
675   In vain the plutonic rocks send their old heat against my approach,
        In vain the mastadon retreats beneath its own powdered bones,
        In vain objects stand leagues off and assume manifold shapes,
        In vain the ocean settling in hollows and the great monsters lying low,
        In vain the buzzard houses herself with the sky,
680   In vain the snake slides through the creepers and logs,
        In vain the elk takes to the inner passes of the woods,
        In vain the razorbilled auk sails far north to Labrador,
        I follow quickly .... I ascend to the nest in the fissure of the cliff.

[32]   I think I could turn and live awhile with the animals .... they are so placid and self-
            contained,
685   I stand and look at them sometimes half the day long.

        They do not sweat and whine about their condition,
        They do not lie awake in the dark and weep for their sins,
        They do not make me sick discussing their duty to God,
        Not one is dissatisfied .... not one is demented with the mania of owning things,
690   Not one kneels to another nor to his kind that lived thousands of years ago,
        Not one is respectable or industrious over the whole earth.

        So they show their relations to me and I accept them ;
        They bring me tokens of myself .... they evince them plainly in their possession.

        I do not know where they got those tokens,
695   I must have passed that way untold times ago and negligently dropt them,
        Myself moving forward then and now and forever,
        Gathering and showing more always and with velocity,

Infinite and omnigenous and the like of these among them ;
Not too exclusive toward the reachers of my remembrancers,
Picking out here one that shall be my amie,   700
Choosing to go with him on brotherly terms.

A gigantic beauty of a stallion, fresh and responsive to my caresses,
Head high in the forehead and wide between the ears,
Limbs glossy and supple, tail dusting the ground,
Eyes well apart and full of sparkling wickedness .... ears finely cut and flexibly
     moving.   705

His nostrils dilate .... my heels embrace him .... his well built limbs tremble with
     pleasure .... we speed around and return.

I but use you a moment and then I resign you stallion .... and do not need your
     paces, and outgallop them,
And myself as I stand or sit pass faster than you.

Swift wind ! Space ! My Soul ! Now I know it is true what I guessed at ;   [33]
What I guessed when I loafed on the grass,   710
What I guessed while I lay alone in my bed .... and again as I walked the beach
     under the paling stars of the morning.

My ties and ballasts leave me .... I travel .... I sail .... my elbows rest in the
     sea-gaps,
I skirt the sierras .... my palms cover continents,
I am afoot with my vision.

By the city's quadrangular houses .... in log-huts, or camping with lumbermen, ·   715
Along the ruts of the turnpike .... along the dry gulch and rivulet bed,
Hoeing my onion-patch, and rows of carrots and parsnips .... crossing savannas ...
     trailing in forests,
Prospecting .... gold-digging .... girdling the trees of a new purchase,
Scorched ankle-deep by the hot sand .... hauling my boat down the shallow river ;
Where the panther walks to and fro on a limb overhead .... where the buck turns
     furiously at the hunter,   720
Where the rattlesnake suns his flabby length on a rock .... where the otter is
     feeding on fish,
Where the alligator in his tough pimples sleeps by the bayou,
Where the black bear is searching for roots or honey .... where the beaver pats
     the mud with his paddle-tail ;
Over the growing sugar .... over the cottonplant .... over the rice in its low
     moist field ;
Over the sharp-peaked farmhouse with its scalloped scum and slender shoots from
     the gutters ;   725

Over the western persimmon .... over the longleaved corn and the delicate blue-
    flowered flax ;
Over the white and brown buckwheat, a hummer and a buzzer there with the rest,
Over the dusky green of the rye as it ripples and shades in the breeze ;
Scaling mountains .... pulling myself cautiously up .... holding on by low scrag-
    ged limbs,
730   Walking the path worn in the grass and beat through the leaves of the brush ;
Where the quail is whistling betwixt the woods and the wheatlot,
Where the bat flies in the July eve .... where the great goldbug drops through the
    dark ;
Where the flails keep time on the barn floor,
Where the brook puts out of the roots of the old tree and flows to the meadow,
Where cattle stand and shake away flies with the tremulous shuddering of their
735   hides,
Where the cheese-cloth hangs in the kitchen, and andirons straddle the hearth-slab,
    and cobwebs fall in festoons from the rafters ;
Where triphammers crash .... where the press is whirling its cylinders ;
Wherever the human heart beats with terrible throes out of its ribs ;
Where the pear-shaped balloon is floating aloft .... floating in it myself and look-
    ing composedly down ;
Where the life-car is drawn on the slipnoose .... where the heat hatches pale-
740   green eggs in the dented sand.
Where the she-whale swims with her calves and never forsakes them,
Where the steamship trails hindways its long pennant of smoke,
Where the ground-shark's fin cuts like a black chip out of the water,
Where the half-burned brig is riding on unknown currents,
745   Where shells grow to her slimy deck, and the dead are corrupting below ;
Where the striped and starred flag is borne at the head of the regiments ;
Approaching Manhattan, up by the long-stretching island,
Under Niagara, the cataract falling like a veil over my countenance ;
Upon a door-step .... upon the horse-block of hard wood outside,
750   Upon the race-course, or enjoying pic-nics or jigs or a good game of base-ball,
At he-festivals with blackguard jibes and ironical license and bull-dances and
    drinking and laughter,
At the cider-mill, tasting the sweet of the brown sqush .... sucking the juice
    through a straw,
At apple-pealings, wanting kisses for all the red fruit I find,
At musters and beach-parties and friendly bees and huskings and house-raisings ;
Where the mockingbird sounds his delicious gurgles, and cackles and screams and
755   weeps,
Where the hay-rick stands in the barnyard, and the dry-stalks are scattered, and the
    brood cow waits in the hovel,
Where the bull advances to do his masculine work, and the stud to the mare, and the
    cock is treading the hen,
Where the heifers browse, and the geese nip their food with short jerks ;

Where the sundown shadows lengthen over the limitless and lonesome prairie,
Where the herds of buffalo make a crawling spread of the square miles far and
    near ;   760
Where the hummingbird shimmers .... where the neck of the longlived swan is
    curving and winding ;
Where the laughing-gull scoots by the slappy shore and laughs her near-human
    laugh ;
Where beehives range on a gray bench in the garden half-hid by the high weeds ;
Where the band-necked partridges roost in a ring on the ground with their heads
    out ;
Where burial coaches enter the arched gates of a cemetery ;   765
Where winter wolves bark amid wastes of snow and icicled trees ;
Where the yellow-crowned heron comes to the edge of the marsh at night and feeds
    upon small crabs ;
Where the splash of swimmers and divers cools the warm noon ;
Where the katydid works her chromatic reed on the walnut-tree over the well ;
Through patches of citrons and cucumbers with silver-wired leaves,   770
Through the salt-lick or orange glade .... or under conical firs ;
Through the gymnasium .... through the curtained saloon .... through the office
    or public hall ;
Pleased with the native and pleased with the foreign .... pleased with the new
    and old,
Pleased with women, the homely as well as the handsome,
Pleased with the quakeress as she puts off her bonnet and talks melodiously,   775
Pleased with the primitive tunes of the choir of the whitewashed church,
Pleased with the earnest words of the sweating Methodist preacher, or any preacher
    .... looking seriously at the camp-meeting ;
Looking in at the shop-windows in Broadway the whole forenoon .... pressing the
    flesh of my nose to the thick plate-glass,
Wandering the same afternoon with my face turned up to the clouds ;
My right and left arms round the sides of two friends and I in the middle ;   780
Coming home with the bearded and dark-cheeked bush-boy .... riding behind him
    at the drape of the day ;
Far from the settlements studying the print of animals' feet, or the moccasin print ;
By the cot in the hospital reaching lemonade to a feverish patient,
By the coffined corpse when all is still, examining with a candle ;
Voyaging to every port to dicker and adventure ;   785
Hurrying with the modern crowd, as eager and fickle as any,
Hot toward one I hate, ready in my madness to knife him ;
Solitary at midnight in my back yard, my thoughts gone from me a long while,
Walking the old hills of Judea with the beautiful gentle god by my side ;
Speeding through space .... speeding through heaven and the stars,   790
Speeding amid the seven satellites and the broad ring and the diameter of eighty
    thousand miles,

Speeding with tailed meteors .... throwing fire-balls like the rest,
Carrying the crescent child that carries its own full mother in its belly :
Storming enjoying planning loving cautioning,
795   Backing and filling, appearing and disappearing,
I tread day and night such roads.

I visit the orchards of God and look at the spheric product,
And look at quintillions ripened, and look at quintillions green.

I fly the flight of the fluid and swallowing soul,
800   My course runs below the soundings of plummets.

I help myself to material and immaterial,
No guard can shut me off, no law can prevent me.

I anchor my ship for a little while only,
My messengers continually cruise away or bring their returns to me.

I go hunting polar furs and the seal .... leaping chasms with a pike-pointed staff
805   .... clinging to topples of brittle and blue.

I ascend to the foretruck .... I take my place late at night in the crow's nest ....
we sail through the arctic sea .... it is plenty light enough,
Through the clear atmosphere I stretch around on the wonderful beauty,
The enormous masses of ice pass me and I pass them .... the scenery is plain in
all directions,
The white-topped mountains point up in the distance .... I fling out my fancies
toward them ;
We are about approaching some great battlefield in which we are soon to be
810   engaged,
We pass the colossal outposts of the encampments .... we pass with still feet and
caution ;
Or we are entering by the suburbs some vast and ruined city .... the blocks and
fallen architecture more than all the living cities of the globe.

I am a free companion .... I bivouac by invading watchfires.

I turn the bridegroom out of bed and stay with the bride myself,
815   And tighten her all night to my thighs and lips.

My voice is the wife's voice, the screech by the rail of the stairs,
They fetch my man's body up dripping and drowned.

I understand the large hearts of heroes,
The courage of present times and all times ;

How the skipper saw the crowded and rudderless wreck of the steamship, and death   820
     chasing it up and down the storm,
How he knuckled tight and gave not back one inch, and was faithful of days and
     faithful of nights,
And chalked in large letters on a board, Be of good cheer, We will not desert you;
How he saved the drifting company at last,
How the lank loose-gowned women looked when boated from the side of their
     prepared graves,
How the silent old-faced infants, and the lifted sick, and the sharp-lipped unshaved
     men;   825
All this I swallow and it tastes good .... I like it well, and it becomes mine,
I am the man .... I suffered .... I was there.

The disdain and calmness of martyrs,
The mother condemned for a witch and burnt with dry wood, and her children
     gazing on;
The hounded slave that flags in the race and leans by the fence, blowing and
     covered with sweat,   830
The twinges that sting like needles his legs and neck,
The murderous buckshot and the bullets,
All these I feel or am.

I am the hounded slave .... I wince at the bite of the dogs,
Hell and despair are upon me .... crack and again crack the marksmen,   835
I clutch the rails of the fence .... my gore dribs thinned with the ooze of my skin,
I fall on the weeds and stones,
The riders spur their unwilling horses and haul close,
They taunt my dizzy ears .... they beat me violently over the head with their
     whip-stocks.

Agonies are one of my changes of garments;   840
I do not ask the wounded person how he feels .... I myself become the wounded
     person,
My hurt turns livid upon me as I lean on a cane and observe.

I am the mashed fireman with breastbone broken .... tumbling walls buried me in
     their debris,
Heat and smoke I inspired .... I heard the yelling shouts of my comrades,
I heard the distant click of their picks and shovels;   845
They have cleared the beams away .... they tenderly lift me forth.

I lie in the night air in my red shirt .... the pervading hush is for my sake,
Painless after all I lie, exhausted but not so unhappy,
White and beautiful are the faces around me .... the heads are bared of their fire-
     caps,
The kneeling crowd fades with the light of the torches.   850

Distant and dead resuscitate,
They show as the dial or move as the hands of me .... and I am the clock myself.

I am an old artillerist, and tell of some fort's bombardment .... and am there again.

Again the reveille of drummers .... again the attacking cannon and mortars and howitzers,
855   Again the attacked send their cannon responsive.

I take part .... I see and hear the whole,
The cries and curses and roar .... the plaudits for well aimed shots,
The ambulanza slowly passing and trailing its red drip,
Workmen searching after damages and to make indispensable repairs,
860   The fall of grenades through the rent roof .... the fan-shaped explosion,
The whizz of limbs heads stone wood and iron high in the air.

Again gurgles the mouth of my dying general .... he furiously waves with his hand,
He gasps through the clot .... Mind not me .... mind .... the entrenchments.

[34]   I tell not the fall of Alamo .... not one escaped to tell the fall of Alamo,
865   The hundred and fifty are dumb yet at Alamo.

Hear now the the tale of a jetblack sunrise,
Hear of the murder in cold blood of four hundred and twelve young men.

Retreating they had formed in a hollow square with their baggage for breastworks,
Nine hundred lives out of the surrounding enemy's nine times their number was the price they took in advance,
870   Their colonel was wounded and their ammunition gone,
They treated for an honorable capitulation, received writing and seal, gave up their arms, and marched back prisoners of war.

They were the glory of the race of rangers,
Matchless with a horse, a rifle, a song, a supper or a courtship,
Large, turbulent, brave, handsome, generous, proud and affectionate,
875   Bearded, sunburnt, dressed in the free costume of hunters,
Not a single one over thirty years of age.

The second Sunday morning they were brought out in squads and massacred .... it was beautiful early summer,
The work commenced about five o'clock and was over by eight.

None obeyed the command to kneel,
880   Some made a mad and helpless rush .... some stood stark and straight,
A few fell at once, shot in the temple or heart .... the living and dead lay together,

The maimed and mangled dug in the dirt . . . . the new-comers saw them there ;
Some half-killed attempted to crawl away,
These were dispatched with bayonets or battered with the blunts of muskets ;
A youth not seventeen years old seized his assassin till two more came to release
    him,   885
The three were all torn, and covered with the boy's blood.

At eleven o'clock began the burning of the bodies ;
And that is the tale of the murder of the four hundred and twelve young men,
And that was a jetblack sunrise.

Did you read in the seabooks of the oldfashioned frigate-fight ?   [35] 890
Did you learn who won by the light of the moon and stars ?

Our foe was no skulk in his ship, I tell you,
His was the English pluck, and there is no tougher or truer, and never was, and
    never will be ;
Along the lowered eve he came, horribly raking us.

We closed with him . . . . the yards entangled . . . . the cannon touched,   895
My captain lashed fast with his own hands.

We had received some eighteen-pound shots under the water,
On our lower-gun-deck two large pieces had burst at the first fire, killing all around
    and blowing up overhead.

Ten o'clock at night, and the full moon shining and the leaks on the gain, and five feet
    of water reported,
The master-at-arms loosing the prisoners confined in the after-hold to give them a
    chance for themselves.   900

The transit to and from the magazine was now stopped by the sentinels,
They saw so many strange faces they did not know whom to trust.

Our frigate was afire . . . . the other asked if we demanded quarters ? if our colors
    were struck and the fighting done ?

I laughed content when I heard the voice of my little captain,
We have not struck, he composedly cried, We have just begun our part of the
    fighting.   905

Only three guns were in use,
One was directed by the captain himself against the enemy's mainmast,
Two well-served with grape and canister silenced his musketry and cleared his decks.

The tops alone seconded the fire of this little battery, especially the maintop,
910   They all held out bravely during the whole of the action.

Not a moment's cease,
The leaks gained fast on the pumps .... the fire eat toward the powder-magazine,
One of the pumps was shot away .... it was generally thought we were sinking.

Serene stood the little captain,
915   He was not hurried .... his voice was neither high nor low,
His eyes gave more light to us than our battle-lanterns.

Toward twelve at night, there in the beams of the moon they surrendered to us.

[36]   Stretched and still lay the midnight,
Two great hulls motionless on the breast of the darkness,
Our vessel riddled and slowly sinking .... preparations to pass to the one we had
920   conquered,
The captain on the quarter deck coldly giving his orders through a countenance
       white as a sheet,
Near by the corpse of the child that served in the cabin,
The dead face of an old salt with long white hair and carefully curled whiskers,
The flames spite of all that could be done flickering aloft and below,
925   The husky voices of the two or three officers yet fit for duty,
Formless stacks of bodies and bodies by themselves .... dabs of flesh upon the
       masts and spars,
The cut of cordage and dangle of rigging .... the slight shock of the soothe of
       waves,
Black and impassive guns, and litter of powder-parcels, and the strong scent,
Delicate sniffs of the seabreeze .... smells of sedgy grass and fields by the shore ...
       death-messages given in charge to survivors,
930   The hiss of the surgeon's knife and the gnawing teeth of his saw,
The wheeze, the cluck, the swash of falling blood .... the short wild scream, the
       long dull tapering groan,
These so .... these irretrievable.

[37]   O Christ !   My fit is mastering me !
What the rebel said gaily adjusting his throat to the rope-noose,
What the savage at the stump, his eye-sockets empty, his mouth spirting whoops
935   and defiance,
What stills the traveler come to the vault at Mount Vernon,
What sobers the Brooklyn boy as he looks down the shores of the Wallabout and
       remembers the prison ships,
What burnt the gums of the redcoat at Saratoga when he surrendered his brigades,
These become mine and me every one, and they are but little,
940   I become as much more as I like.

I become any presence or truth of humanity here,
And see myself in prison shaped like another man,
And feel the dull unintermitted pain.

For me the keepers of convicts shoulder their carbines and keep watch,
It is I let out in the morning and barred at night.   945

Not a mutineer walks handcuffed to the jail, but I am handcuffed to him and walk
    by his side,
I am less the jolly one there, and more the silent one with sweat on my twitching
    lips.

Not a youngster is taken for larceny, but I go up too and am tried and sentenced.

Not a cholera patient lies at the last gasp, but I also lie at the last gasp,
My face is ash-colored, my sinews gnarl .... away from me people retreat.   950

Askers embody themselves in me, and I am embodied in them,
I project my hat and sit shamefaced and beg.

I rise extatic through all, and sweep with the true gravitation,
The whirling and whirling is elemental within me.

Somehow I have been stunned.   Stand back !   [38] 955
Give me a little time beyond my cuffed head and slumbers and dreams and gaping,
I discover myself on a verge of the usual mistake.

That I could forget the mockers and insults !
That I could forget the trickling tears and the blows of the bludgeons and hammers !
That I could look with a separate look on my own crucifixion and bloody crowning !   960

I remember .... I resume the overstaid fraction,
The grave of rock multiplies what has been confided to it .... or to any
    graves,
The corpses rise .... the gashes heal .... the fastenings roll away.

I troop forth replenished with supreme power, one of an average unending
    procession,
We walk the roads of Ohio and Massachusetts and Virginia and Wisconsin and
    New York and New Orleans and Texas and Montreal and San Francisco and
    Charleston and Savannah and Mexico,   965
Inland and by the seacoast and boundary lines .... and we pass the boundary lines.

Our swift ordinances are on their way over the whole earth,
The blossoms we wear in our hats are the growth of two thousand years.

Eleves I salute you,
I see the approach of your numberless gangs .... I see you understand yourselves
970   and me,
And know that they who have eyes are divine, and the blind and lame are equally
      divine,
And that my steps drag behind yours yet go before them,
And are aware how I am with you no more than I am with everybody.

[39]   The friendly and flowing savage .... Who is he?
975   Is he waiting for civilization or past it and mastering it?

Is he some southwesterner raised outdoors? Is he Canadian?
Is he from the Mississippi country? or from Iowa, Oregon or California? or from
      the mountains? or prairie life or bush-life? or from the sea?

Wherever he goes men and women accept and desire him,
They desire he should like them and touch them and speak to them and stay with
      them.

Behaviour lawless as snow-flakes .... words simple as grass .... uncombed head
980   and laughter and naivete;
Slowstepping feet and the common features, and the common modes and emanations,
They descend in new forms from the tips of his fingers,
They are wafted with the odor of his body or breath .... they fly out of the glance
      of his eyes.

[40]   Flaunt of the sunshine I need not your bask .... lie over,
985   You light surfaces only .... I force the surfaces and the depths also.

Earth! you seem to look for something at my hands,
Say old topknot! what do you want?

Man or woman! I might tell how I like you, but cannot,
And might tell what it is in me and what it is in you, but cannot,
990   And might tell the pinings I have .... the pulse of my nights and days.

Behold I do not give lectures or a little charity,
What I give I give out of myself.

You there, impotent, loose in the knees, open your scarfed chops till I blow grit
      within you,
Spread your palms and lift the flaps of your pockets,
995   I am not to be denied .... I compel .... I have stores plenty and to spare,
And any thing I have I bestow.

I do not ask who you are .... that is not important to me,
You can do nothing and be nothing but what I will infold you.

To a drudge of the cottonfields or emptier of privies I lean ...., on his right cheek
        I put the family kiss,
And in my soul I swear I never will deny him.   1000

On women fit for conception I start bigger and nimbler babes,
This day I am jetting the stuff of far more arrogant republics.

To any one dying .... thither I speed and twist the knob of the door,
Turn the bedclothes toward the foot of the bed,
Let the physician and the priest go home.   1005

I seize the descending man .... I raise him with resistless will.

O despairer, here is my neck,
By God! you shall not go down!   Hang your whole weight upon me.

I dilate you with tremendous breath .... I buoy you up;
Every room of the house do I fill with an armed force .... lovers of me, bafflers
        of graves: 1010
Sleep!   I and they keep guard all night;
Not doubt, not decease shall dare to lay finger upon you,
I have embraced you, and henceforth possess you to myself,
And when you rise in the morning you will find what I tell you is so.

I am he bringing help for the sick as they pant on their backs,   [41] 1015
And for strong upright men I bring yet more needed help.

I heard what was said of the universe,
Heard it and heard of several thousand years;
It is middling well as far as it goes .... but is that all?

Magnifying and applying come I,   1020
Outbidding at the start the old cautious hucksters,
The most they offer for mankind and eternity less than a spirt of my own seminal
        wet,
Taking myself the exact dimensions of Jehovah and laying them away,
Lithographing Kronos and Zeus his son, and Hercules his grandson,
Buying drafts of Osiris and Isis and Belus and Brahma and Adonai,   1025
In my portfolio placing Manito loose, and Allah on a leaf, and the crucifix engraved,
With Odin, and the hideous-faced Mexitli, and all idols and images,
Honestly taking them all for what they are worth, and not a cent more,
Admitting they were alive and did the work of their day,

1030
Admitting they bore mites as for unfledged birds who have now to rise and fly and
        sing for themselves,
Accepting the rough deific sketches to fill out better in myself .... bestowing them
        freely on each man and woman I see,
Discovering as much or more in a framer framing a house,
Putting higher claims for him there with his rolled-up sleeves, driving the mallet and
        chisel;
Not objecting to special revelations .... considering a curl of smoke or a hair on
        the back of my hand as curious as any revelation;

1035
Those ahold of fire-engines and hook-and-ladder ropes more to me than the gods of
        the antique wars,
Minding their voices peal through the crash of destruction,
Their brawny limbs passing safe over charred laths .... their white foreheads whole
        and unhurt out of the flames;
By the mechanic's wife with her babe at her nipple interceding for every person
        born;
Three scythes at harvest whizzing in a row from three lusty angels with shirts
        bagged out at their waists;

1040
The snag-toothed hostler with red hair redeeming sins past and to come,
Selling all he possesses and traveling on foot to fee lawyers for his brother and sit
        by him while he is tried for forgery:
What was strewn in the amplest strewing the square rod about me, and not filling
        the square rod then;
The bull and the bug never worshipped half enough,
Dung and dirt more admirable than was dreamed,

1045
The supernatural of no account .... myself waiting my time to be one of the
        supremes,
The day getting ready for me when I shall do as much good as the best, and be as
        prodigious,
Guessing when I am it will not tickle me much to receive puffs out of pulpit or
        print;
By my life-lumps! becoming already a creator!
Putting myself here and now to the ambushed womb of the shadows!

1050 [42]
.... A call in the midst of the crowd,
My own voice, orotund sweeping and final.

Come my children,
Come my boys and girls, and my women and household and intimates,
Now the performer launches his nerve .... he has passed his prelude on the reeds
        within.

1055
Easily written loosefingered chords!   I feel the thrum of their climax and close.

My head evolves on my neck,

Music rolls, but not from the organ .... folks are around me, but they are no
    household of mine.

Ever the hard and unsunk ground,
Ever the eaters and drinkers .... ever the upward and downward sun .... ever the
    air and the ceaseless tides,
Ever myself and my neighbors, refreshing and wicked and real,   1060
Ever the old inexplicable query .... ever that thorned thumb — that breath of itches
    and thirsts,
Ever the vexer's hoot! hoot! till we find where the sly one hides and bring him
    forth ;
Ever love .... ever the sobbing liquid of life,
Ever the bandage under the chin .... ever the tressels of death.

Here and there with dimes on the eyes walking,   1065
To feed the greed of the belly the brains liberally spooning,
Tickets buying or taking or selling, but in to the feast never once going ;
Many sweating and ploughing and thrashing, and then the chaff for payment re-
    ceiving,
A few idly owning, and they the wheat continually claiming.

This is the city .... and I am one of the citizens ;   1070
Whatever interests the rest interests me .... politics, churches, newspapers,
    schools,
Benevolent societies, improvements, banks, tariffs, steamships, factories, markets,
Stocks and stores and real estate and personal estate.

They who piddle and patter here in collars and tailed coats .... I am aware who
    they are .... and that they are not worms or fleas,
I acknowledge the duplicates of myself under all the scrape-lipped and pipe-legged
    concealments.   1075

The weakest and shallowest is deathless with me,
What I do and say the same waits for them,
Every thought that flounders in me the same flounders in them.

I know perfectly well my own egotism,
And know my omnivorous words, and cannot say any less,   1080
And would fetch you whoever you are flush with myself.

My words are words of a questioning, and to indicate reality ;
This printed and bound book .... but the printer and the printing-office boy ?
The marriage estate and settlement .... but the body and mind of the bridegroom ?
    also those of the bride ?
The panorama of the sea .... but the sea itself ?   1085

The well-taken photographs .... but your wife or friend close and solid in your
    arms ?

The fleet of ships of the line and all the modern improvements .... but the craft
    and pluck of the admiral ?

The dishes and fare and furniture .... but the host and hostess, and the look out of
    their eyes ?

The sky up there .... yet here or next door or across the way ?

1090   The saints and sages in history .... but you yourself?

Sermons and creeds and theology .... but the human brain, and what is called
    reason, and what is called love, and what is called life ?

[43]   I do not despise you priests;

My faith is the greatest of faiths and the least of faiths,

Enclosing all worship ancient and modern, and all between ancient and modern,

1095   Believing I shall come again upon the earth after five thousand years,

Waiting responses from oracles .... honoring the gods .... saluting the sun,

Making a fetish of the first rock or stump .... powowing with sticks in the circle of
    obis,

Helping the lama or brahmin as he trims the lamps of the idols,

Dancing yet through the streets in a phallic procession .... rapt and austere in the
    woods, a gymnosophist,

Drinking mead from the skull-cup .... to shasta and vedas admirant .... minding

1100   the koran,

Walking the teokallis, spotted with gore from the stone and knife — beating the
    serpent-skin drum ;

Accepting the gospels, accepting him that was crucified, knowing assuredly that he
    is divine,

To the mass kneeling — to the puritan's prayer rising — sitting patiently in a pew,

Ranting and frothing in my insane crisis — waiting dead-like till my spirit arouses me ;

1105   Looking forth on pavement and land, and outside of pavement and land,

Belonging to the winders of the circuit of circuits.

One of that centripetal and centrifugal gang,

I turn and talk like a man leaving charges before a journey.

Down-hearted doubters, dull and excluded,

1110   Frivolous sullen moping angry affected disheartened atheistical,

I know every one of you, and know the unspoken interrogatories,

By experience I know them.

How the flukes splash !

How they contort rapid as lightning, with spasms and spouts of blood !

1115   Be at peace bloody flukes of doubters and sullen mopers,

I take my place among you as much as among any ;

The past is the push of you and me and all precisely the same,
And the day and night are for you and me and all,
And what is yet untried and afterward is for you and me and all.

I do not know what is untried and afterward,   1120
But I know it is sure and alive and sufficient.

Each who passes is considered, and each who stops is considered, and not a single
    one can it fail.

It cannot fail the young man who died and was buried,
Nor the young woman who died and was put by his side,
Nor the little child that peeped in at the door and then drew back and was never
    seen again,   1125
Nor the old man who has lived without purpose, and feels it with bitterness worse
    than gall,
Nor him in the poorhouse tubercled by rum and the bad disorder,
Nor the numberless slaughtered and wrecked .... nor the brutish koboo, called the
    ordure of humanity,
Nor the sacs merely floating with open mouths for food to slip in, ,
Nor any thing in the earth, or down in the oldest graves of the earth,   1130
Nor any thing in the myriads of spheres, nor one of the myriads of myriads that in-
    habit them,
Nor the present, nor the least wisp that is known.

It is time to explain myself .... let us stand up.   [44]

What is known I strip away .... I launch all men and women forward with me into
    the unknown.

The clock indicates the moment .... but what does eternity indicate?   1135

Eternity lies in bottomless reservoirs .... its buckets are rising forever and ever,
They pour and they pour and they exhale away.

We have thus far exhausted trillions of winters and summers;
There are trillions ahead, and trillions ahead of them.

Births have brought us richness and variety,   1140
And other births will bring us richness and variety.

I do not call one greater and one smaller,
That which fills its period and place is equal to any.

Were mankind murderous or jealous upon you my brother or my sister?

1145   I am sorry for you .... they are not murderous or jealous upon me;
        All has been gentle with me ...... I keep no account with lamentation;
        What have I to do with lamentation?

        I am an acme of things accomplished, and I an encloser of things to be.

        My feet strike an apex of the apices of the stairs,
1150   On every step bunches of ages, and larger bunches between the steps,
        All below duly traveled — and still I mount and mount.

        Rise after rise bow the phantoms behind me,
        Afar down I see the huge first Nothing, the vapor from the nostrils of death,
        I know I was even there .... I waited unseen and always,
1155   And slept while God carried me through the lethargic mist,
        And took my time .... and took no hurt from the fœtid carbon.

        Long I was hugged close .... long and long.

        Immense have been the preparations for me,
        Faithful and friendly the arms that have helped me.

1160   Cycles ferried my cradle, rowing and rowing like cheerful boatmen;
        For room to me stars kept aside in their own rings,
        They sent influences to look after what was to hold me.

        Before I was born out of my mother generations guided me,
        My embryo has never been torpid .... nothing could overlay it;
        For it the nebula cohered to an orb .... the long slow strata piled to rest it on
1165   .... vast vegetables gave it sustenance,
        Monstrous sauroids transported it in their mouths and deposited it with care.

        All forces have been steadily employed to complete and delight me,
        Now I stand on this spot with my soul.

[45]   Span of youth!   Ever-pushed elasticity!   Manhood balanced and florid and full!

1170   My lovers suffocate me!
        Crowding my lips, and thick in the pores of my skin,
        Jostling me through streets and public halls .... coming naked to me at night,
        Crying by day Ahoy from the rocks of the river .... swinging and chirping over my
            head,
        Calling my name from flowerbeds or vines or tangled underbrush,
        Or while I swim in the bath .... or drink from the pump at the corner .... or the
            curtain is down at the opera .... or I glimpse at a woman's face in the
1175   railroad car;

Lighting on every moment of my life,
Bussing my body with soft and balsamic busses,
Noiselessly passing handfuls out of their hearts and giving them to be mine.

Old age superbly rising ! Ineffable grace of dying days !

Every condition promulges not only itself . . . , it promulges what grows after and out   1180
    of itself,
And the dark hush promulges as much as any.

I open my scuttle at night and see the far-sprinkled systems,
And all I see, multiplied as high as I can cipher, edge but the rim of the farther
    systems.

Wider and wider they spread, expanding and always expanding,
Outward and outward and forever outward.   1185

My sun has his sun, and round him obediently wheels,
He joins with his partners a group of superior circuit,
And greater sets follow, making specks of the greatest inside them.

There is no stoppage, and never can be stoppage ;
If I and you and the worlds and all beneath or upon their surfaces, and all the
    palpable life, were this moment reduced back to a pallid float, it would not
    avail in the long run,   1190
We should surely bring up again where we now stand,
And as surely go as much farther, and then farther and farther.

A few quadrillions of eras, a few octillions of cubic leagues, do not hazard the span,
    or make it impatient,
They are but parts . . . . any thing is but a part.

See ever so far . . . . there is limitless space outside of that,   1195
Count ever so much . . . . there is limitless time around that.

Our rendezvous is fitly appointed . . . . God will be there and wait till we come.

I know I have the best of time and space — and that I was never measured, and   [46]
    never will be measured.

I tramp a perpetual journey,
My signs are a rain-proof coat and good shoes and a staff cut from the woods ;   1200
No friend of mine takes his ease in my chair,
I have no chair, nor church nor philosophy ;
I lead no man to a dinner-table or library or exchange,

But each man and each woman of you I lead upon a knoll,
1205   My left hand hooks you round the waist,
My right hand points to landscapes of continents, and a plain public road.

Not I, not any one else can travel that road for you,
You must travel it for yourself.

It is not far .... it is within reach,
1210   Perhaps you have been on it since you were born, and did not know,
Perhaps it is every where on water and on land.

Shoulder your duds, and I will mine, and let us hasten forth ;
Wonderful cities and free nations we shall fetch as we go.

If you tire, give me both burdens, and rest the chuff of your hand on my hip,
1215   And in due time you shall repay the same service to me ;
For after we start we never lie by again.

This day before dawn I ascended a hill and looked at the crowded heaven,
And I said to my spirit, When we become the enfolders of those orbs and the plea-
      sure and knowledge of every thing in them, shall we be filled and satisfied then ?
And my spirit said No, we level that lift to pass and continue beyond.

1220   You are also asking me questions, and I hear you ;
I answer that I cannot answer .... you must find out for yourself.

Sit awhile wayfarer,
Here are biscuits to eat and here is milk to drink,
But as soon as you sleep and renew yourself in sweet clothes I will certainly kiss you
      with my goodbye kiss and open the gate for your egress hence.

1225   Long enough have you dreamed contemptible dreams,
Now I wash the gum from your eyes,
You must habit yourself to the dazzle of the light and of every moment of your
      life .

Long have you timidly waded, holding a plank by the shore,
Now I will you to be a bold swimmer,
To jump off in the midst of the sea, and rise again and nod to me and shout, and
1230   laughingly dash with your hair.

[47]   I am the teacher of athletes,
He that by me spreads a wider breast than my own proves the width of my own,
He most honors my style who learns under it to destroy the teacher.

The boy I love, the same becomes a man not through derived power but in his own
    right,
Wicked, rather than virtuous out of conformity or fear,   1235
Fond of his sweetheart, relishing well his steak,
Unrequited love or a slight cutting him worse than a wound cuts,
First rate to ride, to fight, to hit the bull's eye, to sail a skiff, to sing a song or play
    on the banjo,
Preferring scars and faces pitted with smallpox over all latherers and those that
    keep out of the sun.

I teach straying from me, yet who can stray from me ?   1240
I follow you whoever you are from the present hour ;
My words itch at your ears till you understand them.

I do not say these things for a dollar, or to fill up the time while I wait for a boat ;
It is you talking just as much as myself .... I act as the tongue of you,
It was tied in your mouth .... in mine it begins to be loosened.   1245

I swear I will never mention love or death inside a house,
And I swear I never will translate myself at all, only to him or her who privately
    stays with me in the open air.

If you would understand me go to the heights or water-shore,
The nearest gnat is an explanation and a drop or the motion of waves a key,
The maul the oar and the handsaw second my words.   1250

No shuttered room or school can commune with me,
But roughs and little children better than they.

The young mechanic is closest to me .... he knows me pretty well,
The woodman that takes his axe and jug with him shall take me with him all day,
The farmboy ploughing in the field feels good at the sound of my voice,   1255
In vessels that sail my words must sail .... I go with fishermen and seamen, and
    love them,
My face rubs to the hunter's face when he lies down alone in his blanket,
The driver thinking of me does not mind the jolt of his wagon,
The young mother and old mother shall comprehend me,
The girl and the wife rest the needle a moment and forget where they are,   1260
They and all would resume what I have told them.

I have said that the soul is not more than the body,   [48]
And I have said that the body is not more than the soul,
And nothing, not God, is greater to one than one's-self is,
And whoever walks a furlong without sympathy walks to his own funeral, dressed in
    his shroud,   1265

And I or you pocketless of a dime may purchase the pick of the earth,
And to glance with an eye or show a bean in its pod confounds the learning of all
     times,
And there is no trade or employment but the young man following it may become a
     hero,
And there is no object so soft but it makes a hub for the wheeled universe,
1270   And any man or woman shall stand cool and supercilious before a million universes.

And I call to mankind, Be not curious about God,
For I who am curious about each am not curious about God,
No array of terms can say how much I am at peace about God and about death.

I hear and behold God in every object, yet I understand God not in the least,
1275   Nor do I understand who there can be more wonderful than myself.

Why should I wish to see God better than this day ?
I see something of God each hour of the twenty-four, and each moment then,
In the faces of men and women I see God, and in my own face in the glass ;
I find letters from God dropped in the street, and every one is signed by God's name,
And I leave them where they are, for I know that others will punctually come for-
1280   ever and ever.

[49]   And as to you death, and you bitter hug of mortality .... it is idle to try to alarm
     me.

To his work without flinching the accoucheur comes,
I see the elderhand pressing receiving supporting,
I recline by the sills of the exquisite flexible doors .... and mark the outlet, and
     mark the relief and escape.

1285   And as to you corpse I think you are good manure, but that does not offend me,
I smell the white roses sweetscented and growing,
I reach to the leafy lips .... I reach to the polished breasts of melons.

And as to you life, I reckon you are the leavings of many deaths,
No doubt I have died myself ten thousand times before.

1290   I hear you whispering there O stars of heaven,
O suns .... O grass of graves .... O perpetual transfers and promotions .... if
     you do not say anything how can I say anything ?

Of the turbid pool that lies in the autumn forest,
Of the moon that descends the steeps of the soughing twilight,
Toss, sparkles of day and dusk .... toss on the black stems that decay in the muck,
1295   Toss to the moaning gibberish of the dry limbs.

I ascend from the moon .... I ascend from the night,
And perceive of the ghastly glitter the sunbeams reflected,
And debouch to the steady and central from the offspring great or small.

There is that in me .... I do not know what it is .... but I know it is in me.   [50]

Wrenched and sweaty .... calm and cool then my body becomes ;   1300
I sleep .... I sleep long.

I do not know it .... it is without name .... it is a word unsaid,
It is not in any dictionary or utterance or symbol.

Something it swings on more than the earth I swing on,
To it the creation is the friend whose embracing awakes me.   1305

Perhaps I might tell more .... Outlines ! I plead for my brothers and sisters.

Do you see O my brothers and sisters ?
It is not chaos or death .... it is form and union and plan .... it is eternal life ....
     it is happiness.

The past and present wilt .... I have filled them and emptied them,   [51]
And proceed to fill my next fold of the future.   1310

Listener up there !   Here you .... what have you to confide to me ?
Look in my face while I snuff the sidle of evening,
Talk honestly, for no one else hears you, and I stay only a minute longer.

Do I contradict myself ?
Very well then .... I contradict myself ;   1315
I am large .... I contain multitudes.

I concentrate toward them that are nigh .... I wait on the door-slab.

Who has done his day's work and will soonest be through with his supper ?
Who wishes to walk with me ?

Will you speak before I am gone ?   Will you prove already too late ?   1320

The spotted hawk swoops by and accuses me.... he complains of my gab and my   [52]
     loitering.

I too am not a bit tamed .... I too am untranslatable,
I sound my barbaric yawp over the roofs of the world.

The last scud of day holds back for me,

1325   It flings my likeness after the rest and true as any on the shadowed wilds,
         It coaxes me to the vapor and the dusk.

         I depart as air .... I shake my white locks at the runaway sun,
         I effuse my flesh in eddies and drift it in lacy jags.

         I bequeath myself to the dirt to grow from the grass I love,
1330   If you want me again look for me under your bootsoles.

         You will hardly know who I am or what I mean,
         But I shall be good health to you nevertheless,
         And filter and fibre your blood.

         Failing to fetch me at first keep encouraged,
1335   Missing me one place search another,
         I stop some where waiting for you .

The Mosaic of Interpretations

1:1–5

"I celebrate myself" resonates in American poetry as "Call me Ishmael" does in our fiction: the American sound system has never been quite the same since the appearance of these two works in that remarkable decade of the 1850s, which gave birth to *The Scarlet Letter* (1850), *Moby-Dick* (1851), *Walden* (1854), and *Leaves of Grass* (1855).

With a comic bow to Vergil and a gay farewell to Miltonic blank verse, Whitman confidently and wittily introduces the first great poem in American literature. He frees himself and modern poetry with a joyous, parodistic yawp from its subservience to forms and techniques appropriate to the expression of what he calls a feudalistic social order no longer viable in a democratic age. Vergil sings of arms and the man. Whitman, in the words of Albert Gelpi (170), "displays as symbolic talisman not the swordblade of Aeneas but 'a spear of summer grass.'"

"Whitman never claimed anything more significant about himself," Alfred Kazin (105) writes, than the opening words of his greatest poem. "His street pals in Brooklyn must have spoiled him, then become his type of sexual complement; many a Victorian eminence (Tennyson, Swinburne, Hopkins, George Eliot) was moved by Whitman's erotic lines but was abashed by his direct appeal to the reader."[1]

Whitman himself (Traubel, Bucke, and Harned, 30–31) in an anonymous review of his own book in the *American Phrenological Review* in 1855 anticipates the reception he in fact received: "It is indeed a strange voice! Critics and lovers and readers of poetry as hitherto written, may well be excused the chilly and unpleasant shudders which will assuredly run through them, to their very blood and bones, when they first read Whitman's poems. If this is poetry, where must its foregoers stand? . . . if the tan-faced man here advancing and claiming to speak for America and the nineteenth hundred of the Christian list of years, typifies indeed the natural and proper bard?"

"He sings himself with long-unequalled arrogance," James Thomson (29), author of "The City of Dreadful Night," is to note, but not pejoratively. "(Poetry is arrogance . . . chanted brave old Goethe in the *Divan*, but [Whitman] himself as average man, claiming nothing personally which shall not be conceded to every human being. . . .)" Contemporary and later critics of hostile persuasion were to censure the egotism. Harvey O'Higgins (704) is especially vehement in alleging that "I celebrate myself" is "the resolve of a Narcissan thinking only of his fiercely-loved physique. . . . It is the impulse that drove him to celebrate himself in his 'own flesh and form, undraped, regardless of modesty or law.'"

General Jan Christian Smuts (65) is more generous, although it is doubtful that egotism is ever wholly "*objective*," at least not to the extent of Smuts's italics, which even Whitman himself would not have resorted to. "He does not celebrate or glory," Smuts says, "in those qualities which differentiate him from his fellows, but in those which he possesses in common with them. What he celebrates in himself are just those qualities that make him one of the 'divine average' for whom he sings. . . . If he writes about himself—his thoughts, feelings, hopes, joys, aspirations—his object is to describe these states of mind as they exist more or less in all persons."

John Updike (33) takes another tack. "I celebrate myself," he observes, is "the superb subject of the poem, the exultant egotism which only an American could have voiced. By mid-nineteenth century the creed of American individualism was ascendant: the communal conscience of the Puritan villages was far behind, and the crushing personal burdens of industrialism were yet to be sharply felt. Our political institutions and our still vast unexploited territories permitted the enterprising individual an illusion of unlimited importance and sublime potential untasted since the Garden of Eden."

While Updike places Whitman in a political-social context in which he shares a collective "illusion," Harold Bloom (1976, 249), perceives a contradiction behind the three famous words: "Defensively, Whitman opens with a reaction-formation against his precursor Emerson, which rhetorically becomes not the digressiveness or 'permanent parabasis' of German Romantic irony, but the sharper, simpler irony of saying one thing while meaning another. Whitman says 'I celebrate' and he cunningly means: 'I contract and withdraw while asserting that I expand.'"

Mitchell Robert Breitwieser (134, 131) observes in somewhat clotted prose that in feigning conversation with the reader Whitman "calls attention to the unique, individual 'compactness' of the man who writes; calling attention to the writer's deadness for the reader, he emphasizes the transtemporal and transspatial mobility of the spoken 'I,' . . . but preserves perplexing 'I-ness.'" Whitman draws on "all the resources of language" in order to "so blur the boundaries between the alternating 'I's' and 'you's' that separate individuality will grow indistinct, 'atoms' that had been private property will fraternize, and, above the hum and buzz of this *concordia discordans,* the second 'I' will tally and rise. The conversation will be a 'common ground' for the 'perfect shape,' the poetic president."

Feeling his way as it were into the poem, the poet Robert Creeley (17–18) describes the relationship between the reader and the I without Breitwieser's intellectualizations, and delights in the "flexibility of diction" that sustains the human and erotic attraction of the poem. "It is," Creeley writes, "very open, familiar, at times very casual and yet able to be, on the instant, intensive, intimate, charged with complexly diverse emotion. This manner of address invites, as it were, the person reading to 'come unto' the activity and experience of the poems, to share with Whitman in a paradoxically unsentimental manner the actual texture and force of the emotions involved. When he speaks directly to the reader, there is an uncanny feeling of his literal presence, physically."

David Cavitch (1985, 46), however, comes to another conclusion. Whitman, he alleges, "subordinates" the reader immediately by putting up "a bridge that can be crossed emotionally in only one direction from him to us. . . . The fantasy of our assuming different roles together makes our range of feelings available to him while it prevents our empathizing with the poet except by sharing his enjoyment of fantasized roles and relationships."

Charmenz S. Lenhart (180) likens the early lines to the introduction in a symphony of "musical phrases that will be treated and repeated throughout the rest of the movement. The emphasis is upon the beginning of the musical line and not the close. So Whitman's lines depend upon a 'germ' idea immediately stated— and take their final effect from the treatment of that idea." Justin Kaplan (187) suggests that the first five lines function as an introit at the opening of a church service, "in spirit and structure a secular Mass."

The first picture in Whitman's tapestry—the I leaning on the earth "observing a spear of summer grass"—is as unconventional as the frontispiece of the poet dressed as a workingman. Yet we have the word of Bronson Alcott (286), one of the first to make a visit to the poet's home after the appearance of *Leaves of Grass,* that in life Whitman assumed the same posture: "When talking [he] will recline upon the couch at length, pillowing his head upon his bended arm, and informing you naively how lazy he is, and slow."

Whitman's pose leads Hawthorne's son Julian (261) to pontificate that the poet "abandons all personal dignity and reserve, and sprawls incontinently before us in his own proper person. It is no wonder that an experiment so desperate should attract attention: so do the gambols of a bull in a china-shop. In old times, a sort of sanctity and reverence was associated with idiots, insane persons and the victims of hysteria and epilepsy. . . . Analogous to this is the attitude of many of Whitman's admirers and disciples to-day. They cannot persuade themselves that a man who acts so grotesquely should be anything less than inspired."

Unlike Julian Hawthorne, whose snobbery he does not share, Edmund Gosse (1965, 29) writes: "'I loafe and invite my soul', he sings, and we must not shrink, if we wish to penetrate that soul, from the coarse and bracing perfume of its illustration. The one thing we must never do is to persuade ourselves that Whitman was 'after all', respectable. He was not; he rolled on the carpet of the world like a grown-up naked baby." Rosenthal and Gall (35) also delight in this "superbly casual posture of indolence . . . as of one of the elect in a pastoral paradise."

Kenneth Burke (90) arrives at a significant insight into these lines by means of a linguistic approach: "'lean and loafe' are here attitudinally identical. But further, lo! not only is 'loafe' tonally an ablaut form of 'leaf'—change the unvoiced 'f' to its voiced cognate, 'v,' and you have the close tonal proximity between 'loafe' and 'love.'" Leslie Fiedler (13) comes to a similar conclusion, too often neglected in the critical commentary: "Surely his deepest aim was to transcend the image, to make a kind of poetry which was the equivalent of action, a very act of love."

Seeking a parallel in literary tradition, Van Wyck Brooks (1915, 125) cites the similarity of Whitman's introductory lines and Montaigne's essays: "'I look within myself, I am only concerned with myself, I reflect on myself, I examine myself, I take pleasure in myself,' said Montaigne; and all France for the first time saw itself in a looking-glass and fell together in a common discipline."

According to Carl Strauch (600), three principal themes are introduced in this section: "the Self, the identification of Self with others, and 'Nature without check with original energy.'" Altering Strauch's view slightly, Daiches (1959, 32) proposes that Whitman presents a "picture of the relationship of his self, first to other selves, secondly to the external world of nature, and thirdly to other moments in time which he is experiencing now. There is both a spatial and a temporal relationship developed here."

Edward Dowden (44), one of the early Irish admirers, dwells on Whitman's celebration "of himself as a man and as an American." Whitman emphasizes what he "possesses in common" with his countrymen. "Manhood, then, and in particular American manhood, is the real subject of the poem." Henry Alonzo Myers (245) calls attention to Whitman's "unlimited, all-embracing personality," which he shares with others, as part of the poet's conception of a "spiritual democracy." Essentially in agreement with Dowden and Myers, Thomas J. Rountree (553) observes that Whitman, "knowing that the song must be a form of communication, boldly asserts that this will be 'democratic' communication." But as Rountree and others appear to forget, "Song of Myself" has proved inaccessible to a mass audience.

Howard J. Waskow (163) is one of the first interpreters to approach the poem primarily as "an act of the poetic imagination" or "singing." The central subject, then, is not the I as a complex and indirect self-portrait or a search for identity, the I in relation to others and nature, or a celebration of democracy. His study is, as his subtitle indicates, *Explorations in Form,* and the focus is on art and the portrait of an artist.

In an analysis of states of consciousness in the poem, Carmine Sarracino (5) emphasizes circular rather than linear movement, consciousness, in his words, "looping back on itself": "'I' is the first word of this poem of the Self. 'Celebrate' seems to draw consciousness back to its starting place: 'myself.' In the first line, then, we have the three components of ordinary waking-state awareness: experiencer (I), act of experiencing (celebrate) and object of experience (myself)."

The structural approach of M. Wynn Thomas (1987, 42, 41) rests on careful analysis of "myself" (line 1) and "you" (line 3). "Myself," he writes, "can then be understood as existing in what structuralists would call a 'vertical' or 'associative' relationship with the word 'mine,' which had in contemporary life effectively usurped its place at the center of people's conception and definition of themselves. The word 'mine' has a kind of absent presence in the first sentence." "You," Thomas maintains, assumes two different meanings: "It tells us that 'your atoms are every bit as good as my atoms,'" but at the same time Whitman is "making us an extraordinary offer, . . . to share every atom of himself with us. The two meanings, brought like a single pair of eyes to bear upon the opening phrase, give a stereoscopic prominence to its hitherto concealed meaning."[2]

In a letter that Whitman wrote for John Burroughs to recopy and sign, the poet (*NUPM,* 4:1515) avers that in his poetry "Cheerfulness overarches all, like a sky," which seems like a delightful description of the celebratory atmosphere of #1. However, as we have seen, Bloom alleges that Whitman is indulging in romantic irony. John Berryman (233) observes that the poem has "the form of a paean or exultation . . . unconditional, closed, reflexive." This is "misleading," he claims, because "we do not yet know what 'I' is," though we learn in the fourth line that it does not include the soul, "which is thus the first guest to be invited."

Stephen Black (1975, 93, and see 1969, 225) asserts that Whitman's "unconscious ambivalence toward himself is manifest in the ambiguity of the third line," which disguises the arrogance of the preceding lines. Thereupon Black points out Whitman's inconsistencies, or perhaps evasiveness. "If the atoms that belong 'as good' to others as to himself comprise his body, it is fair to ask who is the *me* to whom the atoms belong? The *me* must be separate from the body, but if the *me* is the soul, the soul must dominate the body. If Whitman intends a mystical assertion of faith, he must soon run afoul of his own conviction that body and soul are equally important. What begins as a celebration of the self becomes a troublesome question: who and what *am* I?"

Gelpi (171, 177) believes that the I from the beginning displays "a characteristic bisexuality. It is not just that . . . he must make room for 'the Female equally with the Male.' Political and social equality follows from psychological integration, and the sexual basis for Whitman's politics is there to begin with." According to Gelpi, Whitman seeks a fusion or knitting of man's and woman's psyche "into a personal identity."

In the 1881 edition of *Leaves of Grass* in which Whitman established the final text, he added to this section the following eight lines from "Starting from Paumanok":

> My tongue, every atom of my blood, form'd from this soil, this air,
> Born here of parents born here from parents the same, and their parents
>   the same,
> I, now thirty-seven years old in perfect health, begin,
> Hoping to cease not till death.
> Creeds and schools in abeyance,
> Retiring back a while sufficed at what they are, but never forgotten,
> I harbor for good or bad, I permit to speak at every hazard,
> Nature without check with original energy.   (*CRE*, 29)

Through this transfer the I acquires the parents, ancestry, and social context lacking in earlier versions. Despite the alteration, however, the I in effect remains a loner, the isolate in the lovely American landscape like Natty Bumppo and Ishmael, as well as their successors.

GRASS AS SYMBOL

Donna L. Henseler (30) proposes that Whitman himself is "a living grass-poem," and that "Song of Myself" "is a sprawling, magnificent grass-poem." Tony Tanner (78) observes that "the poem to some extent organizes itself" around such

"hints and echoes and accumulations of significances" as the grass provides. This
view essentially derives from those of Whitman himself, F. O. Matthiessen, and
Richard P. Adams.

The following passage in the biography written by Richard Maurice Bucke
(1883, 156) was approved and emended by the poet himself:

> Like the grass, while old as creation, [the book] is modern, fresh, universal,
> spontaneous, not following forms, taking its own form, perfectly free and un-
> constrained, common as the commonest things, yet its meaning inexhaust-
> ible by the greatest intellect, full of life itself, and capable of entering into
> and nourishing other lives, growing in the sunshine . . . , perfectly open and
> simple, yet having meanings underneath; always young, pure, delicate and
> beautiful to those who have hearts and eyes to feel and see, but coarse, in-
> significant and worthless to those who live more in the artificial . . . than in
> the natural.[3]

Matthiessen (547, 549) cites one of Whitman's jottings in a notebook during
the years in which he painfully gave birth to his masterpiece: "Bring all the art
and science of the world, and baffle and humble it with one spear of grass." In
Matthiessen's words, "he thus suggests how all the things that he is, equalitarian
democrat, sensualist, transcendental optimist, mystic, and pagan, are dissolving
into the elements, into light, air, cloud, and dirt, and the green life springing up
from it." R. P. Adams (131) states succinctly the pervasiveness and subtlety of
what has been called an image, symbol, organic metaphor. Grass, he writes,

> is more or less explicitly mentioned in Sections 1, 5, 6, 9, 17, 31, 33, 39, 49,
> and 52. Its meaning, as a symbol, is complex, multiple, and finally indetermi-
> nate, but some of its bearings and functions can be pointed out, if not fully
> explained. First and most obviously it represents the organic metaphor, but
> this meaning is not insisted upon. Second, it represents the book, the leaves
> of which are, in their organic representation of nature and the poetic rela-
> tion of the speaker to the natural world or universe, "leaves of grass." The
> book, that is, may be regarded as an embodiment of the organic whole
> of things.[4]

Recently George B. Hutchinson (72, 73, 76–77) has offered similar all-inclusive
claims for the grass as "the dominant symbol" of the poem. All dualisms, he
notes, "are joined in the grass, a riddle in itself . . . diversity merges with unity:
subject with object, good with evil, life with death . . . this symbol stands both for
the complementarity of life and death and for democracy." In fact, "the grass is
the emblem of cultural renewal." In part Hutchinson's is a restatement of a view
advanced in the poet's lifetime by Rudolf Schmidt (245), the perceptive Danish
critic. Whitman, Schmidt writes, "dwells upon [grass] everywhere with peculiar
fondness as nature's Democracy—it being, as it were, the first child of the vege-
table kingdom—the symbol of the new spiritual life which the poet very well
knows is to proceed from himself."

T. R. Rajasekharaiah (147) in *The Roots of Whitman's Grass* justifies the title in his book by suggesting a parallel with an Indian ceremony: "The priest then takes up two leaves of *cusa* grass and with another blade of the same grass, cuts off the length of a span, saying, 'Pure leaves! be sacred to VISHNÚ;' and throws them into a vessel of copper or another metal." Stephen J. Tapscott (65) draws upon *The Egyptian Book of the Dead* to explain the association of grass "with the self that is reborn or regenerated after the death of the individual body." In Egyptian writings, he observes, it is "consistently used . . . to signify the growth at the moment when the body becomes the sāhū, or spiritualized body."

The pun upon leaves of grass and the leaves of a book has often been noted. Robert Duncan (101), the poet, raises the discussion to another level: "The grass is the very language, embodying as it does the perennial human spirit and experience, in which the book we are reading is created; it is the green blades of words that we call Poetry because the pulse of that sea of grass enlivens them, common as grass, and having the mystery of the ultimately *real*, a living word, as Whitman most wanted his poetry to have." For Lewis Hyde (179) the grass "stands for the creative self, the singing self," and he notes that in 6:109–10 the grass speaks: "it is 'so many uttering tongues' emerging from 'the faint red roofs' of the mouths of the dead."

The phallic associations of "spears" of grass have often been noted as well as Whitman's equation of orgasm and the growth of grass: "Sprouts take and accumulate . . . / Landscapes projected masculine full-sized and golden" (29:645–46). William M. White (357) observes that Whitman accepts "the mystical bisexual mixture of his own personality, which is for him, like the blade of grass, a microcosm of the benevolent intricacy . . . of nature herself." William E. McMahon (41) writes with more wit than one usually finds in critical exegeses: "The deepest component to the formal coherence of 'Song of Myself' may well be the fact that the grass is not a bachelor. It has a spouse. The polarity of this male/female pair probably constitutes the strongest of all the symbolic bondings in the poem." Whether sound or no, it is a happy idea.

2:6–29

6–8

Bucke (1883, 161) offers a straightforward interpretation of the opening lines of this section which has had little effect upon subsequent interpretation: "'Houses and rooms' are the schools, religion, philosophies, literature; 'perfumes' are their modes of thought and feeling; the 'atmosphere' is the thought and feeling excited in a healthy and free individual by direct contact with Nature; to be 'naked' is to strip off the swathing, suffocating folds and mental trappings from civilization." Apparently approving of Bucke's construction in what was to be the official biography, Whitman added only the words "swathing, suffocating folds and."[5]

9–10

Later commentators have proposed more religious or mystical interpretations, sometimes perhaps almost too subtle. Hyde (173–74) suggests that Whitman invites us "to breathe the thinner 'atmosphere,' the original hieroglyphs, not the commentary of the scribes. As we inhale this atmosphere of primary objects, they exhale gnosis, a prolific, carnal science, not an intellectual knowledge. . . . As his body and its senses are the font of Whitman's religion, so the perception of natural objects is his sacrament." In J. Middleton Murry's judgment (131), "This is not, what it seems, a paean to the open air; it celebrates what Blake called 'the cleansing of the doors of perception,' and the entry into the new and ever-present world of things as they are. Whitman calls 'the atmosphere' what Spinoza calls the *species aeternitatis,* and more traditionally Christian mystics the all-sustaining love of God."

Rosenthal and Gall (37) dwell not on mystical avenues but on the sheer physical sensation of Whitman's lines. "This is a language of almost unbearable sensation," they write. "The state of arousal it presents is felt not as something shameful but as an absolute good. These lines are a touchstone for the most intensely alive moments of *Song of Myself,* found in #28 and #29." In loving phrases Diane Kepner (193) makes a similar point: "Every wind that blows, every breath he takes, every sound he hears, everything is reaching out to him, vinelike, to change his atomic make-up."

11–12

Here, according to Denis Donoghue (31, 33), Whitman employs for the first time in his poetry the word *contact,* which "reverberates through the poems and prose. . . . A life of such continuous intimacy, a life of contacts, is Whitman's ideal human image. It will blur the distinctions between man and God, thus setting up yet another equation, the largest in intention. . . . This divinity flows and sanctifies, by contact, everything it sees, hears, touches, tastes, or smells; it is Whitman's version of the laying on of hands."

13–17

Gelpi (175) points out that the contact "touches off" the first catalogue of the poem: "Images and perceptions rush in free association from the unconscious, and the poet sees and feels as would never be possible with intellectual control. William Blake would say that Whitman was not merely seeing with his eyes as physical organs gathering sensory data but seeing through his eyes into the mystery of being, . . . Jung might say that he is seeing with a double set of eyes, the full four-fold act of vision, like Blake's *Four Zoas.*"[6]

The air, according to Berryman (234), is "used as a prime symbol for equality and ubiquity—the earth's air and human air (symbol for life as well as singing, speech, the poem itself) coming together." Richard A. Law (92–93, 94) elaborates on what we may call the respiration motif: "among the life processes of an organism respiration is primary. It is the first source of nourishment, and it is basic to metabolism. . . . In the human being the critical center of exchange is the lungs, which by inspiration and expiration filter oxygen from the atmosphere into the blood and carbon dioxide from the blood into the atmosphere." In Law's opinion, "spiritual experience (L. *spiritus*, breath) can be represented in no better way than by figures or symbols of breathing and atmosphere."

Proposing a gigantic pictorial image not unlike those of modern artists such as Claes Oldenburg, Hyde (170–71) perceives the "self" in Whitman's song as "a sort of lung, inhaling and exhaling the world. Almost everything in the poem happens as a breathing, an incarnate give-and-take, which filters the world through the body. . . . The initial event of the poem, and of Whitman's aesthetic, is the gratuitous, commanding, strange and satisfying entry into the self of something that was previously separate and distinct. The corresponding gesture on Whitman's part is to give himself away [cites 14:254]. . . . These gestures—the inhalation and exhalation, the reception and bestowal—are the structuring elements of the poem, the passive and active phases of the self in the gifted state."[7]

Thomas (1983, 12) provides an ingenious structural analysis of this passage, which, as he says, lacks "a main verb." This discovery "involve[s] a realisation that these descriptive phrases are not simply a preparation for action, subject to and therefore subordinate to the directing presence of the verb. . . . as the reader adjusts so as finally to find meaning in the verbless 'sentence' so too does he simultaneously re-orientate himself in relation to himself and his world, and engage in a revaluation of life itself."

18–21

The increased gyrations of the lungs and the heartbeats, as well as the "belched" sound of words "loosed to the eddies of the wind," are part of the I's gradual sexual arousal in a pastoral setting near a pond. Luxuriating in his nakedness, the I is preoccupied with his genitals, which are described in romanticized, loving phrases. The scene culminates in "a reaching around of arms," a self-embrace that leads to orgasm.

"The rhythm is slowed down," David J. Johnson (52) suggests, "and the pauses between each experience—the kiss, the embrace, and the reach around of arms—indicates that the narrator is allowing himself time to thoroughly enjoy each one as a separate experience. The reader may join him."

The belching (E. H. Miller 1968, 89) parallels the orgasmic release in its pent-up rhythms, and Whitman's use of a vulgarism[8] reinforces the protagonist's liberation from social and sexual prohibitions. In addition, the expressive, but surprising, oral image anticipates the oral sexuality in #5, 11, and elsewhere. The tongue, then, relates to the words of the poet's song, to sexuality, and the fusion of art and orgasm in #3. Black (1975, 101–2) describes this "cathartic experience" as "basically regressive, resembling an infant's earliest experiences of being held, petted, kissed by his mother. The regressive impulse underlying Whitman's cathartic experiences parallels a conscious poetic theme: the attempt to return to his origins and find a new way to understand himself. . . . Once more he has found a way to imagine himself cradled by the universe, marked with the special sense of grace which defines infantile symbiosis."

Middlebrook (40) relates the scene to her Coleridgean thesis of the secondary imagination: "The gesture of undressing may be regarded as Whitman's characteristic rendering of what Coleridge describes as one mode of the secondary imagination, which 'dissolves, diffuses, dissipates, in order to re-create.' In this mode, the secondary imagination refuses pre-established forms in order to recover essences." Marki (105) believes the "poet's sexual climax is also the metaphor of his attainment of an ecstatic vision which fuses apparent discordances into universal harmony." He suggests that "an extroverted, 'centrifugal' impulse is reconciled by an opposing introverted, 'centripetal' impulse into a bipolar unity of rhetoric."

22–29
Gelpi (176) observes that the physical environment has been sexualized through the I's projection of his desire everywhere, a process that is to be repeated several times later. "The leap of associations pieces out its own unexpected and irregular pattern," Gelpi explains, "and the effect of the pattern is to make us sense with the poet all things seething with sexual vitality. In this divine passion the poet comes to 'possess the origin of all poems' and 'the meaning of poems,' which he instantly presses upon each of 'you' for realization." Couser (86) believes that the I "promises a vision [in #5] which will entirely supplant Franklinian values." Robert K. Martin (1979, 16) construes the invitation to spend "this day and night with me" as a playing out of the I's fantasy. Martin, almost alone in maintaining that the poem has a clear narrative line, proposes that "in fantasy at least, the request is granted, and the rest of the poem is an account of that day and night," of the poet and his lover.[9]

Mark Bauerlein (2), who like some other recent critics focuses on Whitman's "orality," argues that in line 27 (and later in 25:566–68) the poet "explicitly exalts speech, often at the expense of writing." Such passages, in his view, "indicate Whitman's trust in the unmediated power of speech. They also disclose his recognition that writing threatens this power. Because writing separates the author both from his own language and from his audience (who therefore 'take things at second or third hand'), writing precludes an immediate communal experience."

3:30–57

30–35
Thomas (1987, 55–56) construes this passage in which Whitman refutes those who pessimistically "talk of the beginning and the end" as an attack upon "acquisitive man . . . addicted in the name of spending time profitably," which is, Thomas argues, "false economy: true economy being always to live in the very nick of time, the present." Whitman is then a "'moral Alaric,' living (*pace* San-

tayana) with a *calculated* barbarism in the present." Berryman (234–35), on the other hand, states that in this section Whitman begins "the attack upon time that characterizes all great poets." Berryman believes that Whitman presents "a continuous present," which he may have derived from Hindoo poems, and quotes the 1855 preface: the poet "is to compete with the laws that pursue and follow time."

36–40

"'Urge and urge and urge,'" Robert Faner (190) writes, with its three accents and five syllables "conveys the slow, deep, eternal desires which make 'ending' impossible." Properly read, he declares, it and the following line, "disclose the fact that they can be molded into a perceptible contour." And, in the judgment of Tuveson (233), the two lines "perhaps are the most important in all Whitman."

To William Robert Dubois (53) the "urge" is "a metaphor for the 'life force,' the ground of the all which insures continuity of life." Joseph Warren Beach (388) perhaps makes Dubois's point more explicit: "Whitman's interpretation of sex is comprehensive and philosophical. He realizes that sex, taken broadly, is central to all human experience—the root of the affections and the foundation of government; that the radiating influence of this primary impulse is felt in art and morality. Moreover, his view of sex is metaphysical; sex is a physical symbol of the creative potency of the universe. His cult of sex is consciously religious, phallic."

Duncan (96, 97) hears in the resonances of "Urge and urge and urge" "a homosexuality in distress, not only in its cry for a mate—there are also the ardent raptures of its fulfillments—but in its generative loss . . . , in the longing for a woman not as a lover but as mother to his fathering desire":

"*Agonía, agonía, sueño, fermento y sueño . . . agonía, agonía,*" Lorca will reply, a poet who was himself obsessed with the longing of a woman to give birth, to have a child, and denied fulfillment.

So in Whitman, song is poured forth, love is poured forth, self is poured forth, as semen is jetted, in a life urgency at once triumphant and pathetic. His young friends, his comrades, as he grows older, will be no longer lovers but his boys or sons.

Tuveson (233) proposes that the sources of these lines may be the *Hermetica*, and that what Whitman "celebrates in 'Song of Myself' is bisexuality, for the individual ultimately is not complete without including in his being the principles of both sexes. Homosexuality is a corrective to the excessive maleness or femaleness of each individual, which the mores of Whitman's time produced, but to say he exalts homosexuality per se over all forms of love and sexuality is hardly accurate." Adrienne Rich (17), the poet, arrived at a similar conclusion years earlier: "It is worth noting that Whitman really does accept woman's lust as a good and natural part of her being, rather than as a devouring force or a self-destructive drive."

Aspiz[10] points out the significance of Whitman's early assumption in the poem of an anti-intellectual stance, reliance upon feeling rather than intellect, for confirmation of the "procreant urge": "To elaborate is no avail . . . . Learned and unlearned feel that it is so."

41–43

Here for the first time Whitman draws upon the vernacular of his and his father's trade as housebuilders—"plumb in the uprights, well entretied, braced in the beams"—which has its own kind of appropriateness in Whitman's poetic construction. Jarrell (116) in his usual fashion captures Whitman's wit: "Just for oddness, charactericalness, differentness, what more could you ask in a letter of recommendation? (Whitman sounds as if he were recommending a house—haunted, but what foundations!)"[11]

The horse, "affectionate, haughty, electrical," E. H. Miller (1968, 89) suggests, may be a stud, which will anticipate the arrival of the "loving bedfellow" and the appearance of the "gigantic beauty of a stallion" in 32:702 ff, which in turn may be a nineteenth-century Pegasus.[12]

44–50

Once again the I retreats from a society given to lengthy discussions of what he considers irrelevancies: "I am silent, and go bathe and admire myself."[13] Once more he caresses his body, verbally and visually, if not tactilely, Whitman mirroring the I's narcissism in his poetry. The caresses may indicate that the next scene is, as Black (1975, 102 n.) suggests, "an actual dream," or, more probably, another autoerotic fantasy.

David Reynolds (325) proposes that here Whitman places "his persona in the objective, clean realm of physiology, distant from the nasty arena of sensational sex," and thus removes "sex from the lurid indirections of the popular love plot." Many of Whitman's contemporaries would not have shared this conclusion.

51–57

The identity of the bedfellow becomes ambiguous through Whitman's alterations over the years:

> 1855: As God comes a loving bedfellow and sleeps at my side all night and close on the peep of day
> 1856: As the hugging and loving Bed-fellow sleeps at my side through the night, and withdraws at the peep of the day
> 1867: [added after "day"] with stealthy tread
> 1881: "Bed-fellow" is not capitalized.

The bedfellow, then, loses his divinity after the first edition, although the capitalized "Bed-fellow," which appeared until 1881, may have been Whitman's devious tactic to confer divinity through indirection.[14]

The fumbling changes are understandable since the orthodox, like Queen Victoria herself, would not have been amused. Jarrell (105) as a poet is filled with admiration and envy: "the Psalmist himself, his cup running over, would have looked at Whitman with dazzled eyes."

Eric W. Carlson explains the passage in its relation to and anticipation of #5: "symbolic God-inspired comradeship in terms of a mystical experience. . . . Here, then, is the theme of mystic affection of soul for body, of soul for soul, as a value that can only be accepted and realized, not measured or defined. As a bountiful gift of special value it is symbolized by the white-toweled baskets."

Hyde (164–65) reaches a somewhat similar, but less mystical, construction, the emphasis in conformity with the thesis of his essay, *The Gift—Imagination and the Erotic Life of Property*:

> it is God who shares the poet's bed and leaves the baskets of rising dough. In an early notebook, Whitman, thinking of various heroes (Homer, Columbus, Washington), writes that 'after none of them . . . does my stomach say enough and satisfied.—Except Christ; he alone brings the perfumed bread, ever vivifying to me, ever fresh and plenty, ever welcome and to spare' [*UPP*, 2:83]. Each of these breads, like that of the hunger fantasy, is a gift (from the god-lover, to the soul), and Whitman senses he would lose that gift were he to 'turn from gazing after' his lover and reckon its value or peek to see if the baskets hold whole wheat or rye.

Gelpi (178) observes that "the unspecified sex of the bedfellow leaves ambiguous here the homosexual feelings which surface time and again in Whitman's work." However, the "pregnant baskets" indicate sexual consummation and anticipate the union of body and soul in #5 as well as "the naked men's naked bellies" in #11. "The encounter," Gelpi concludes, "results in a sense of completion which is felt explicitly as androgynous."[15]

After noting that the lover—God in #3 and the Soul in #5—is male, Burke (85) adds parenthetically that "the passage may also be complicated by infantile memories of the mother." In other words, the seemingly insignificant visual image of baskets of rising dough leads to a psychological insight that Burke does not develop.[16]

The "baskets covered with white towels" may be, according to Marki (109), "an allusion to communion baskets" and thus an anticipation of #5 as a mystical sexual encounter. Aspiz (1980, 176) speculates that the I's "spiritual progress" may be measured by the appearance of the bread of life here as well as in 19:372 and 46:1223. Martin (1975, 89) interprets the "bulging basket" as the I's erection on "the coming of God at night . . . and permits him to accept the day in the knowledge of a forthcoming night."[17] To Thomas (1987, 64) the white towels mean that "the environment [is] progressively charged with libidinal energy, as the imagination is sensually aroused."

Allegorizing the episode, Esther Shephard (1953, 73) invokes the tale of Cupid and Psyche and notes that "the great god Love comes to her at night and departs in the early morning before dawn. . . . one wonders whether the original bedfellows were Love and the Soul, i.e., poetically, Walt Whitman."

4:58–72

58–65

"Here the real, personal Walt Whitman is introduced," Schyberg (116) alleges, "not the prophet, world-traveler and vagabond, the confident, grandiloquent 'I,' but the actual, existent young American . . . who often betrays himself in the poem in a characteristic fashion, and in a voice widely at variance with the voice of the confident, masculine braggadocio in which the poem is otherwise written." Schyberg may overstate somewhat his contrast between the I, "stout as a horse," and the second I, "strangely young and uncertain, strangely groping, strangely feminine in his emotions."

Henseler (32) believes that the "Trippers and askers" are the professional critics, "careful, clever, clean surgeons. . . . But their operations on 'Song of Myself' fail because the poem slips from under the knife and gets away, leaving only its shadow for them to carve and systematize." To Carlisle (179) the "Trippers and askers" are "inauthentic, desperate men," whom Whitman challenges here as in "Song of the Open Road." He resists not only these enemies but also external, emotionally shattering, "fitful" events such as (in a line added to the poem in 1867) "Battles, the horrors of fratricidal war, the fever of doubtful news." But, as Carlisle observes, "he can neither deny nor escape if he wishes to discover his genuine identity." Withdraw he must, for "they are not the Me myself."

66–72

Burroughs (1896, 96), who was one of Whitman's intimates for thirty years, describes the poet's "curious habit of standing apart, as it were, and looking upon himself and his career as of some other person. He was interested in his own cause, and took a hand in the discussion. From first to last he had the habit of regarding himself objectively." In the manuscript of "Pictures" (*NUPM,* 4:1299) Whitman himself writes: "Who is this, with rapid feet, curious, gay—going up and down Mannahatta, through the streets, along the shores, working his way through the crowds, observant and singing?"

Here we find, according to R. W. B. Lewis (1955, 47), "the new Adam. If we want a profile of him, we could start with the adjectives Whitman supplies: amused, complacent, compassionating, idle, unitary; especially unitary, and certainly very easily amused; too complacent, we frequently feel, but always compassionate."

The observer described in this section is in the judgment of mystical interpreters of the text the "kosmos self" free of egotism, "reflecting the divine self." Tuveson (207) states, "The true self, the 'unitary, compassionate' one, entered Whitman's experience in a loving form. . . . In all Gnostic systems, . . . the individual may have a double existence: one is that of a native and permanent inhabitant of this physical universe, subject to its laws and exigencies, like an animal; the other, in some manner, may rise above the limitations of existence. In optimistic gnosis, the new self is unlimited, divinized, world-embracing." Drawing upon parallels in the *Upanishads,* Chari (75) finds that Whitman's intuitive vision "had led him to believe that his role in the world was more or less that of a detached witness. With the attainment of fuller realization he became convinced that his real self was different from the fettered ego that acts, enjoys, or suffers, that the outward events are not he, that his self is not a doer but a mere spectator, sharing all experience, yet unattached to it, standing apart and watching the masquerade of life."

Gelpi (179) provides a Jungian explanation: "These words anticipate quite precisely the distinction Jung would make between ego and Self: the ego being the center of consciousness acting out the person of its public, social role; the Self being a more remote and mysterious identity, 'in and out of the game,' which includes all the potentialities and possibilities waiting latent in the unconscious to be brought into active play and realization as the Self."

Thomas (1987, 47), however, warns against a psychological explanation: "such a Self is better seen as a creative response to social pressure than as a neurotic or pathological symptom." Dennis K. Renner (1984, 122) draws upon social psychology to explain what he calls Whitman's "metaphor for anomic experience"— the I standing "Apart from the pulling and hauling." From this perspective "an identity is precarious, sustained . . . by 'conversation' with the social environment that bestows it. Disruptions of that conversation are 'anomic,' placing in doubt 'the fundamental order in terms of which the individual can "make sense" of his life and recognize his own identity.'"[18]

Maximilian Beck (21) offers a simpler explanation when he draws upon Thoreau's *Journal:* I "am sensible of a certain doubleness by which I can stand as remote from myself as from another. I am conscious of the presence and criticism of a part of me which, as it were, is not a part of me, but spectator, sharing no experience, but taking note of it, and that is no more I than it is you. When the play—it may be the tragedy of life—is over, the spectator goes his way."[19]

Jarrell (117) notes that within a few lines Whitman offers himself to everybody, but now stands "apart": "Tamburlaine is already beginning to sound like Hamlet: the employer feels uneasily, 'Why, I might as well hire myself?'" Apparently Jarrell forgets that the I acknowledges the dramatic shifts of "depressions or exaltations," which he claims are not "Me myself," but the poem confirms the emotional gyrations even as the I denies them. Roger Asselineau (1960, 68) observes that in a line such as "Backward I see in my own days where I sweated through fog with linguists and contenders," Whitman reveals that he "had not always possessed the faith and the certitude which now prompted his exultant optimism."[20]

5:73–89

"I witness and wait," the poet writes at the conclusion of #4, and then quietly begins the most famous chant in the poem and perhaps in American poetry: the fusion or marriage of the body and the soul. Marki (120) believes the pause should be longer, for what Cavitch (1985, 30) terms a "remembered experience," but Whitman seeks no dramatic effect: the poetic flow like "the procreant urge" itself never alters or falters and irresistibly flows on, as the lines recall "I loafe and invite my soul," as well as the arrival of the divine bedfellow, in an elaboration that evokes perhaps the prelude to Wagner's *Tristan und Isolde,* where sexuality and transcendence fuse in orgasmic excitement, release, and the radiant peace of consummation.

Murry (130) guesses that the experience described here is "the creative kernal of the whole of 'Song of Myself,'" or, if not, "the key to it." Since the key Murry finds here is not the one others always find, agreement as to interpretation has not emerged, and may never be effected, for a work like "Song of Myself" would appear to have, at Whitman's invitation, almost as many interpreters as readers.

According to Bucke's (1901, 227–28) account in his enormously popular work, *Cosmic Consciousness,* the experience occurred on a June morning in 1853 or 1854 "and took (though gently) absolute possession of him, at least for the time. Henceforth, he says, his life received its inspiration from the newcomer, the new self, whose tongue, as he expresses it, was plunged to his bare-stripped heart. His outward life, also, became subject to the dictation of the new self—*it held his feet.* Finally he tells in brief of the change wrought in his mind and heart by the birth within him of the new faculty. He says he was filled all at once with peace and joy and knowledge transcending all the art and argument of the earth."[21]

I have divided the lengthy discussion of this section into three parts—Mysticism, Sexuality, Art, with the alternative titles God, Man, Poet—and an epilogue consisting of interpretations of crucial lines.

MYSTICISM—GOD

Whitman's friend, William Sloane Kennedy (1926, 190), reduces the episode "simply" to "the duad of soul and body, as in the motto inscription, 'Come, Said my Soul.' It is a restatement once more of his cardinal Hegelian principle,—that for which he wrote his Leaves, mainly,—that the body is of equal rank and honor with the soul." In *The Varieties of Religious Experience,* William James (387) terms it "a classical expression of this sporadic type of mystical experience." Henry Bryan Binns (1905, 72–73), one of the early biographers, likens it to George Fox's account of his own mystical experience: "Now was I come up in spirit through the flaming sword into the Paradise of God. All things were new, and all the creation gave another smell unto me than before, beyond what words can utter."[22]

Leon Howard (1932, 81, 83) finds a similarity between #5 and Emerson's illumination in "Nature" in which in a magnificent image he becomes "a transparent eye-ball." Howard points out "one striking dissimilarity": "neither element of [Whitman's] enlarged, emotionally realized self was to abase itself before the other, while for [Emerson] the ultimate realization of man came from the complete obedience of the individual to the dictates of the over-soul."[23]

Although guesses as to sources, literary or religious, are interesting, and sometimes significant, they are suggestive rather than conclusive, particularly in the
case of illuminations or epiphanies. The episode may be, as Allen (1970, 129–30,
and 1955a, 159) suggests, "a myth" of Whitman's "creative imagination" or "an
esoteric description of some physical experience," but evidence, except for
Bucke's account, is lacking. Yet such moments are not uncommon in the nineteenth century, which had an active interest in occultism and extrasensory perceptions and longed for a "hero" to replace a tottering deity. Herman Melville
(*Letters*, 131) was not given to the usual mystical illuminations, but in one of
his passionately charged letters to Nathaniel Hawthorne, written at the time
Whitman was gradually finding his artistic self, Melville adds this postscript:

> N.B. This "all" feeling, though, there is some truth in. You must often have
> felt it, lying on the grass on a warm summer's day. Your legs seem to send out
> shoots into the earth. Your hair feels like leaves upon your head. This is the
> *all* feeling. But what plays the mischief with the truth is that men will insist
> upon the universal application of a temporary feeling or opinion.

In Melville's account the intrusion of the reality principle asserts the inevitable
transitoriness of such experiences and the equally inevitable feelings of deflation
afterwards.

Rajasekharaiah (284, 260) believes that #5 is "less the product of self-
dramatization than of 'lyricization' of the experiences of a yogi" recorded in
William Ward's *View of the History, Literature and Mythologies of the Hin-
doos* (London, 1817). According to Rajasekharaiah's fanciful account, Whitman
"read these pages of Ward 'in June, such a transparent summer morning' bathing
the streets around the Mercantile or the Astor Library; and perhaps he 'settled'
the book 'athwart' his 'hips and gently turned over' the pages, drew the pen from
his 'bosom' pocket, 'plunged' the nib on the 'bare' sheets, and made notes till [he
realized] 'that a kelson of the creation is love.'"

Geoffrey Dutton (66) describes this section as "one of the greatest mystical
visions in all poetry; and yet one hesitates to use the word 'mystical' about a vision that is also so precise and compassionate, and so perfectly, after the earlier
strutting and exaltation, introduces the theme of humility." Matthiessen (535)
also notes "a central problem in appreciation," which he proceeds to outline, until his own distaste or perhaps fear comes through: "Readers with a distaste for
loosely defined mysticism have plenty of grounds for objection in the way the
poet's belief in divine inspiration is clothed in imagery that obscures all distinctions between body and soul by portraying the soul as merely the sexual agent.
Moreover, in the passivity of the poet's body there is a quality vaguely pathological and homosexual. This is in keeping with the regressive, infantile fluidity,
imaginatively polyperverse, which breaks down all mature barriers."[24]

Although Clarence Gohdes (1954, 584) points out that eroticism is "not at all
unusual" in mystical experiences, he precedes this statement with the observation that the scene is "rather 'sexy,' and even ridiculous,"[25] and reveals the em-

barrassment shared by many commentators in dealing with the explicit oral sexuality depicted in the passage. Hermann Pongs (25), a German commentator, cautions readers "to remember from the beginning that with the word *you* the poet is addressing not a beloved, but his own soul," and notes a similar situation in one of Stefan George's poems in *Stern des Bundes* (26):

> On your breast where I can hear your heart beat,
> Let me lay my mouth to suck the festered
> Sores of former fevers, as a healing
> Stone upon a wound extracts the venom.

J. E. Miller (1962, 151, and 1957, 10) appears to have little difficulty reconciling his mystical construction of the poem and the "unmistakable" sexual imagery: "In another context the passage might well appear to be a physical drama of ecstatic sexual experience. But in its own context, it is a mystic interfusion of body and soul." Yet Miller seems in the process of reconciliation to de-eroticize the passage: "The imagery of the tongue and heart is ingenious: the spiritual tongue informs; the physical heart receives. Such imagery suggests that it is only through the intimate fusion of the physical and spiritual, the ennobling of the physical through the spiritual, that one can come to know transcendent reality."

With the support of yogi doctrine, O. K. Nambiar (42) offers a detailed explanation intended to account for the physicality of the episode, but one may wonder whether he does not render the passage "neuter," to borrow from Whitman, in a most unwhitmanesque fashion.

> Whitman's 'we' stands for the body and the soul. The sensations felt in and by the body are apparently what he has set forth in these lines. The sensation starts from a point or source situated 'athwart the hips', where he feels the beginning of an ascending movement. The line 'You settled your head athwart my hips and gently turned over upon me', describes an axial rotary movement. This is followed by a sensation of chill ascending along the body. As a consequence he feels a sense of physical exposure as if his shirt is being stript off his bosom. When the movement reaches the region of the heart he has another vivid tactual experience. Here he experiences the sensation, and what could possibly arise out of it, the vision of a tongue plunged deep into his heart—a very definite, unmistakable, physical pressure. From this point the sensation moves upward to the region of his throat. . . . This is followed by a descending movement reaching down to the lower extremity of the body, 'till you held my feet.'[26]

Lewis (1965, 12, and 1955, 52) characterizes the union as "mystical in kind, sexual in idiom—between the two dimensions of the poet's being: the limited, conditioned Whitman and the 'Me, myself,' his creative genius, what Emerson might have called the Over-Soul." Yet Lewis's is essentially not a mystical reading so much as an account of a portrait of an artist. "Traditional mysticism," he comments, "is the surrender of the ego to its creator, in an eventual escape from the limits of names; Whitman's is the expansion of the ego in the act of creation itself, naming every conceivable object as it comes from the womb." Even more arresting is Lewis's earlier (and more fanciful) conception of Whitman in a new/old Eden: "We must cope with the remarkable blend in the man, whereby this Adam, who had already grown to the stature of his own maker, was not less and at the same time his own Eve, breeding the human race out of his love affair with himself. If #5 means anything, it means this: a miraculous intercourse between 'you my soul' and 'the other I am,' with a world as its offspring."[27]

SEXUALITY—MAN

After a sympathetic elaboration of the mystical components Asselineau (1962, 9) concludes that Whitman remains "essentially the poet of the body." Galway Kinnell (223) explains, quite simply, but firmly, "The passage may be about the self and the body and the soul, but to begin with, it is about a man and his lover." While Kinnell leaves the gender of the lover unspecified, Burke (85) sees "reason enough to assume that he is here writing of a male attachment." At the beginning of the century Havelock Ellis (117) asserts that Whitman discovered something "deeper than religion, underneath Socrates and underneath Christ . . . the roots of the most universal love in the intimate and physical love of comrades and lovers."

Avoiding identification of the lover, John F. Lynen (296) views the section as a remembrance of things past. "One can see," he writes, "that all has tended toward this act of memory, that the confused blending of nature imagery and erotic sensations has anticipated the recollected love scene." Martin (1975, 89) refers to "the recollection of a previous sexual experience which is the source of his first knowledge of peace," but unlike Lynen, he consistently delineates a homosexual or Calamus relationship.

The erotic symbolism in the passage and the depiction of fellatio have led to psychological constructions. Gustav Bychowski (237), a psychoanalyst, construes the episode as part of the process of sublimation: "The borderline between the narcissistic and object libido begins to be transcended. The feeling of guilt attached to sex is lifted and libido is recognized as a general force pervading the universe. From here, then, the path leads toward the overcoming of original inhibitions, loneliness and isolation; the path also leads to mystico-philosophical ideas of identity which reaffirm unity and overcome separation anxiety."

Burke (85) observes that the passage may be "complicated by infantile memories of the mother," a point that is elaborated by E. H. Miller (1968, 21):

The scene is played out in regressive sexual imagery. The orality— "plunged your tongue to my barestript heart"—evokes the child at the mother's breast, "heart" being associated with the phallus and the breast. In "going under" Whitman, unconsciously, approximates the child's phallic picture of the mother. The tongue is the means of the child's earliest contact with the world, his bridge, in a literal and figurative sense, to something outside himself as well as a source of physical comfort. At the same time, for we are in the world of a child's associative processes, the tongue like the breast is phallic in its fecundating powers.[28]

Berryman (231, 234) calls the union of the body and soul the "incest passage" of the poem, and then appears to suggest that "peace and knowledge" follow from incestuous consummation. "I cannot avoid remarking," Berryman writes, "what a deeply divided personality created this work."

White (354, 355, 357) interprets #5 as proof of Whitman's bisexuality:

Rather than a joining of body and soul, it was a synthesis of the masculine and feminine within Whitman which caused the mystical vision which inspired his poetry. . . . Actually, Whitman was in love with the masculine image of himself. . . . His primary nature, largely subconscious, is feminine, absorptive, receptive. . . . What he is accepting is the mystical bisexual mixture of his own personality which is for him, like the blade of grass, a microcosm of the benevolent intricacy . . . of nature herself.[29]

Bloom (1976, 256, 257) writes that Whitman "oddly" makes the soul "the active partner, and the self, 'the other I am,' wholly passive in this courtship." Next he argues, "If we translate soul as 'character' and self as 'personality,' then we would find it difficult to identify so passive a personality with 'Walt Whitman, a kosmos, etc.' . . . Clearly, there is a division in Whitman between two elements in the self, as well as between self and soul, and it is the first of these divisions that matters, humanly and poetically. Indeed, it was from the first of these divisions that I believe Emerson initially rescued Whitman, thus making it possible to become a poet." But the mysterious sources and fusions of the creative process, personal, social, and aesthetic, are surely not reducible to the simplification that Emerson is the father of Whitman.

Quentin Anderson (1971, 97–98) considers #5 "a waking wet dream in which one is ravished by the universe," perhaps a facetious observation or an aberration of the "imperial self." Although Tuveson (205–8) subsequently presents a conventional, almost de-eroticized analysis of what he calls one of the "ecstatic conversion visions," he draws attention to the seeming uniqueness of Whitman's "*auto*-erotic" vision. Breitwieser (124–25) notes that "allegorical fellation" precedes "a climax whimsically reprised in the poet's serene notice of the two states of turgidity among the leaves. Let up from the grip, the throat loosed, the poet arises and spreads, echoing the Christian benediction ('the peace that passeth all understanding')," which, to Breitwieser, constitutes "post-coital, post-holocaust calm."

More imaginatively, Hyde (161, 162) construes the oral imagery as "a hunger fantasy," which is introduced when

Somehow—it is not recorded—he gave the soul its bread. It came toward him as a lover then, not as a beggar or beast. It stretched him on the grass and entered his body. His throat opened and it began to sing. . . . It is of little account . . . whether this infusion, this lovemaking between the self and the soul, happened in fact or in imagination. . . . The sequence of events implies that Whitman shared the bread with his soul, and now the soul has given him a return gift, its tongue. . . . In this case, though, the man is a poet and the spirit is a poet's soul. Whitman's account of their commerce constitutes the creation myth of a gifted man.

ART—POET

Section 5 has been characterized as "the crucial moment of the entire poem, the creation of the poetic fetus" (Orth, 17); "the metamorphosis of a conventional, timid hack writer into America's greatest and most courageous 'original'" (E. H. Miller 1968, 20); and Whitman's description of "his birth as a poet" (Cox, 187).

According to James Cox (187–88) it is "a pastoral memory into which the present tense of the poem dissolves. . . . The act of conception and creation in which the disembodied tongue or soul of the poet weds the body is a complete fusion which in turn democratizes and articulates the body. That is to say, the wedding makes every part of the body equal and gives every part of the body a voice." Michael Orth (18) considers the "unconventional use of fellatio rather than copulation as the process of conception . . . daring, but supremely effective. The image of the tongue as the instrument of insemination is particularly apt, for the Soul has been characterized thus far only as an unstructured 'hum,' as a pure sound; in addition, it is significant that the phallic, leaflike tongue, the speaking of the WORD in all religions, here unifies the Body and the Soul."[30]

Waskow (159) ascribes the passivity of the I to the "first stage of the imaginative act—his discovery of the imaginative world into which he will plunge, his seizure by his soul, the spirit of imagination, which will lead to feelings of wholesome relief, repose, content."[31] It is the view of Jean Catel (78) that we "pass imperceptibly from realism to surrealism," that is, to the unconscious. "No one," Catel comments, "has known better than [Whitman] how to fuse the objective outline and the inner image in such a way that everywhere reality unifies the soul while the soul animates reality."

Pearce (1961, 76–77) finds here "the final account of how the soul, turning inward upon itself, discovers its true nature." This "marriage of [the I's] two minds," he says, is a "moment of self-generated apotheosis. . . . Only now— because it is wholly in control of its inner world, can the self begin to turn outward toward its outer world, then surrender and undergo its outward metamorphoses. With its inner stability assured, it now has the strength to do so."

Berryman, as we have noted, calls the union "incest," and Lewis contends that Whitman plays Adam *and* Eve, but nobody, so far as I know, has observed that in giving birth to the poet Whitman has in effect played out a rite such as Erik

Erikson (208) describes: "Mannish man always wants to pretend that he made himself, or at any rate, that no simple woman bore him, and many puberty rites . . . dramatize a new birth from a spiritual mother of a kind that only men understand."

5:77 *Only the lull I like, the hum of your valved voice.*
In this "exquisite line," Berryman (231) explains, "the kind of valve here imagined must be a safety valve . . . : the soul being that which lets the body free a little and then controls it." Gohdes (1954, 584) observes, "The soul is to communicate a pleasurable 'hum,' not formalized, so to speak, into music, verse, instruction, or moral counsel." The soul, according to Tenney Nathanson (122), "is invoked as a ceaseless, pre-linguistic stream of sound. . . . This continuous lull or hum should, of course, remind us of the 'pulsations' of the 'strong base' which 'intermits not.' The soul, that is, is a trope for both the poet's magical voice and the cosmic force that produces all created nature; it serves to suggest their confluence."

To E. H. Miller (1968, 21) "the voice, when the 'stop' is released, is a 'lull' or 'hum,' like the sound of the mother's soothing, wordless lullaby." Lawrence Kramer (224) discovers the "secret" of Whitman's "power" in "the singing voice of the poet's mother, heard in infancy. . . . The primary bond between mother and child, mediated through the mother's voice, becomes the principle of receptivity by which the poet unites with nature. . . . As a woman, the primal singer is the mother of the poet's body; as a voice, she is the mother of his ego, the 'base' (basis/bass) of the 'composition' that is his identity. . . . Whitman recapitulates the birth of his ego from maternal song by becoming a maternal singer himself."

The "valved voice" is to Zweig (252) "a summery *bel canto* without words, rhyme, or 'custom' . . . in effect, a new kind of poetry." Matthiessen (538), on the other hand, attributes "the lull I like" to the influence of Quaker passivity, "which could be of cardinal value to a poet whose strongest desire was to absorb the life of his time."[32]

5:81 *And reached till you felt my beard, and reached till you held my feet.*
Marki (139) finds a parallel to this passage in 49:1287—"I reach to the leafy lips . . . . I reach to the polished breasts of melons." E. H. Miller (1968, 22–23) suggests that the depiction of the union of body and soul takes "the pictorial form of a cross," as Whitman plays a variation perhaps on what Allen (1934, 302) calls a "Christ-drama." Miller continues:

> in one sense the old Whitman dies and a new one is born. . . . The crucifixion also suggests the death of the ancient dualism (body and soul) and the resurrection of a single whole being. The body is reborn without the Judaeo-Christian mortification of the flesh: the soul accepts the entire body, . . . for all organs of the body are equally important and all sensations are equally good. [And so] Whitman resurrects the body, or, to put it another way, makes

the soul sensual again, as it was in the beginning of the child's life before society imposed conscience and "thou-shalt-nots."

Gelpi (181) describes the image as "not of a bearded body and a female soul, as in some of Blake's drawings, but of a bearded body in the woman's position, gripped by a spiritual power that matches the body it mates."

5:82ff. *Swiftly arose and spread around me the peace and joy and knowledge . . .*

Kazin (108) calls this "the great *agnus dei* passage," and F. De Wolfe Miller (12) hears the song of a "democratic messiah." In these "unsurpassable lines," Chase (1955a, 62) writes, "love is at once so sublimely generalized and perfectly particularized." Berryman (231) insists that the New Testament "influenced Whitman's thought even more than his passion for grand opera."

According to A. N. Kaul (255) it is Whitman's "declaration of faith," and he finds a parallel in *White-Jacket,* in which Melville, "too, declares his faith in love and brotherhood, embodying these values in the small maintop community that functions as a human oasis within the otherwise morally sterile world of the *Neversink.*" To Lieber (81), it is "the hero's first vision of cosmic selfhood." "For the first time in history we hear the voice of a prophet," Edward Carpenter (65–66) writes, "who really *knows* and really *accepts* the whole range of human life."

Gelpi (181, 183) maintains that "the lines themselves attest much more strongly to a psychological penetration no less transformative for being internal." Then he adds, "The sense of the body-self at the beginning of the process of coming to consciousness is a development from the child's obliviousness; but it is still closely associated with the unconscious and with the material-maternal order of experience"—a construction that leads him to a restatement of his theory of Whitman's bisexuality.[33]

Allen Ginsberg (238) singles out what perhaps can be called an apotheosis of touch: "out of that one experience of a touch with another person, of complete acceptance, his awareness spread throughout the space around him and he realized that that friendly touch, that friendly awareness was what bound the entire universe together and held everything suspended in gravity."

5:86ff. *. . . a kelson of the creation is love . . .*

Kinnell (224) offers a lovely commentary on the closing lines of the song: "Whitman climbs down the Platonic ladder. The direction is perhaps Blakean, or Rilkean—but mostly Whitmanesque—a motion from the conventionally highest downward toward union with the most ordinary and the least, the conventionally lowest, the common things of the world."

Stephen Adams (9) compares Whitman's "preference for the common approaches closest to a luminist sense of the ordinary bathed in the supernatural splendor of divine light" found in the paintings of Fitz Hugh Lane, Martin Johnson Heade, John F. Kensett, and others.

6:90–121

In 1872 Rudolf Schmidt (244–45) chose this section to illustrate the "greatness" of Whitman's "poetic gifts" of "a power and purity that has seldom if ever been surpassed. There are images that for simplicity and directness remind us of the Homeric pictures, and there are flights of fancy of marvellous grace and vivacity."

Berryman (235) praises the "exquisite transition" from the preceding section: "After the love wrestling of Body and Soul, a child speaks." Despite the "knowledge" achieved in the sexual consummation, now there is "a true instruction: the child's question, and the poet's ignorance and guessings. After the 'peace' achieved [there is] the question of their sundering, of death. With this question, and the enigmatic, magisterial consolation the poet gives, his work really begins." Zweig (252) asks, in a charming parenthetical question, is this the child "born of this marriage"? To the question posed by the child—"What is the grass?"—"the entire poem will be an answer," the grass being "a symbol of the countless varieties of experience that Whitman catalogues on his world-circling journeys."

According to Gelpi (183), Whitman "is able to see the grass as the recapitulation of the whole cycle of life, death and rebirth; it is the symbol of the individual ('the flag of my disposition'), of Deity ('the handkerchief of the Lord'), of reproduction ('the produced babe of the vegetation'), of the new social order of American democracy ('a uniform hieroglyphic'), of death ('the beautiful uncut hair of graves'), and finally of the new form into which death transmogrifies life."[34] But, as Buell (1973, 177) reminds us, this is "a symbolic enumeration, . . . a series of meditations or guesses as to the meaning of a particular image."

Middlebrook (111) deals acutely with the flux of perceptions, of the "guesses" of the poet, and of nature itself:

> The child knows as well as Whitman, for the grass is not known at all except in the mind's transactions, and the changes in the mind confronting it make continual changes in its meaning. All the metaphors for the grass are equally true. At the same time, the grass itself is changing with the light and air, and by sprouting, burgeoning, and dying off, is ever renewed for the mind. Reality washes like waves over consciousness, and what it leaves are regarded as gifts possessed for an instant. While the event of bestowal passes, the soul never loses what was given.

Shelley Fisher Fishkin (47) views the exchange with the child as a game played by a poet with an "experienced eye seeing freshly" who invites readers to participate in the creative experience: "As the poet's imagination 'guesses' out loud, highlighting the whimsical and seemingly off-the-cuff nature of the images it produces, it invites the reader to participate in the guessing game. By playing out a few of the infinite metamorphoses the grass may undergo when appropriated by the imagination, Whitman shows the reader what it means to see and structure reality for oneself."

90–91

Here Whitman writes, Bloom (1976, 249–50) maintains, "firmly within the materialist tradition of Epicurus and Lucretius. Epicurus said: 'The what is unknowable,' and Whitman says he cannot answer the child's question. . . . Poetically, he does answer, in a magnificent series of tropes." Asselineau (1962, 42), however, believes that the question "How could I answer the child?" is an acknowledgment of impotence, "the normal reaction of a mystic who vividly feels the vanity of all attempts at rational explanation. The attitude was natural in him, but it was probably reinforced by his reading—by Carlyle, in particular."

93–95

"The handkerchief of the Lord," Duncan (101) proposes, "may be for some readers a passing sentimental figure, but it may also suggest the concept of creator and creation, of the poet's signature in his own work in a dropped hint, of the idea of signature, gift and memory (*Mnemosyne,* the Mother of the Muses)." Schyberg (90) offers a simpler analogy: "Just as the grass and green turf of 'the handkerchief' the Lord has dropped, so the poet's book, *Leaves of Grass,* is the same thing with his signature in one corner that mankind may pause, wonder, and ask, 'Whose?'"

In Philip Y. Coleman's (46) reading of these lines, "Whitman creates an unusual image of the Lord as coquette with the function of grass as natural symbol receiving metaphorical development in terms of a man-made object. Grass as symbol of Spirit reveals God's ways and purposes to man as a coquette's dropped handkerchief reveals her ways and purposes." Diane Kepner (199) believes that "the flag . . . out of hopeful green stuff woven" is a "spear" that "bends into a 'J' or 'C' shape" appropriate to a "handkerchief of the Lord."

97–100

Maurice Mendelson (128) in his "Soviet View" of Whitman strains the passage about "uniform hieroglyphic" to suit his ideological convictions: "the poet is above all attacking the slavery practices which had been legalized in thousands of acts of legislation and which were stubbornly defended by the government, the church, many newspapers and important public figures."[35]

101–6

Allen (1955a, 159) hears in "uncut hair of graves" a Homeric echo. Burke (87, 88) points out how frequently Whitman "shuttles back and forth along the channel of affinity that links love and death or womb and tomb" and "contrives by quick transitions to go from 'the breasts of young men' to 'mothers' laps.'" This introduces once more the feeding motif that is shortly tied by means of "uttering tongues" to the creative or poetic process, which constitutes a movement "from the nutriently oral to the poetically eloquent." This is part of what Burke (103) terms the "dark mother" theme.

According to Coleman (48), "curling grass" on the breasts of young men "is at once grass-as-natural symbol: hair on the chest which suggests manliness and fertility; and grass-as-poetry: another 'scented herbage from my breast,' the feeling that produces (and is) poetry." "Mothers' laps," Coleman explains, are "sources not only of love (maternal, not necessarily sexual) but also of generation. The life cycle of the grass—out of dying, birth—is manifest in human life as well."

107–9

Marki (128) finds in these lines that the "tongue's transformation from the instrument of the speaker's joyful enlightenment through love" [#5] into the herald of his blinding fear of death dramatizes, then, a tragic clash between impulses and inhibitions. He cannot allay his fears without increasing them, and he cannot satisfy his longing without frustrating it." Rosenthal and Gall (37) point out the repeated use of "dark" in the line beginning, "This grass is very dark": "like the whole drift of the imagery," it "betrays the morbid side of hypersensitive awareness. It is the inevitable price of the volatile imagination that projects such satyr-like joy elsewhere in the sequence."

121

According to Berryman (237), the last line "sounds, surprisingly, not only in assertion but in tone, like another great poet of death, Rilke—to be anti-existential and to be *literally* true, in the following sense: the death a man considers is his own *now*, not his own *then*, when it will actually take place, to himself another man; therefore he can form no just conception of it; and besides—as of the second part of the line—always considers it as the ultimate disaster, whereas in practice for a great part of mankind it comes as the final mercy." Marki (123) insists that the sound of Whitman's lines repudiates his affirmations, a "lapidary stridency" replacing "the early lines' smooth, easy breathing. . . . Who would not want to believe what this speaker is so loudly proclaiming? Yet, listening to him, who can?" Berryman and Marki cannot believe Whitman, but it is just possible that he means what he says, for, unlike Melville, he may have found the "middle way."

7:122–139

Gelpi (184) appears to be closer to Whitman in not emphasizing fear of death but "an immortality of ongoing life." Gelpi finds in the emphasis upon "merge"—"for me mine male and female"—confirmation of the poet's androgynous nature. "If [Whitman] is a Kosmos, his consciousness must incorporate male and female," Tuveson (234) maintains; "he can certainly not be exclusively either. And so must anyone who achieves the cosmic consciousness. This fact is of such central importance that Whitman, if he was to be faithful to his vision and faith, could not slight it." And so although he was aware that this aspect of his poetry would alienate many contemporaries, he was compelled to resort to "images of eroticism."

Marki (124–25) believes that the call to "undrape" is a replay of #5, "except that this time, instead of being subdued, the 'I' moves to subdue. His self-vaunting reassurances, unexpected, and apparently illogical as they are, round this out and frame the sequence that began with his memory of his ecstatic union with the soul."[36] Bedient (32), however, perceives the relationship differently. Whitman, he explains, "exploits the erotics of authority (as he plays the mentor) only by turning the latter into the purest kindness [as in 46:1204–6].... No other writer in English has addressed the reader so winningly, none has taken so much trouble to validate the reader as a dialogic, indeed ontological, force bearing on composition, on faith itself."

8:140–159

140–45

"We see the poet, representing everyman," Griffith Dudding (8) comments, "moving from birth through all the picturesque and grotesque scenes in the American way of life." While Fishkin (32) points out what she terms the "journalistic feel" of these scenes, Tony Tanner (74) views them in a larger perspective: "Birth, love, death: the sequence of glances is not unpremeditated, just as the three visual attitudes change subtly from meditative reverence, to a sort of excited voyeurism, on to almost cold shocked detachment."

Cavitch (1985, 51) points out that in these three descriptions the first line of each "describes a world without Whitman, who materializes only in the second line as a covert presence within the scene"—always, in other words, the outsider or observer—or perhaps a peeping Tom.

Despite the grimness of the description of the suicide sprawled on a blood-stained bedroom floor, Jarrell (108) takes pleasure in Whitman's art. He "has at his command a language of the calmest and most prosaic reality. . . . It is like magic: that is, something has been done to us without our knowing how it was done; but if we look at the lines again we see the *gauze, silently, youngster, redfaced, bushy, peeringly*—not that this is all we see. 'Present! present!' said [Henry] James; these are presented, put down side by side to form a little 'view of life,' from the cradle to the last bloody floor of the bedroom."[37]

146–50

Basil De Selincourt (132) was one of the first critics to delight in "the blab of the pave" and the "resonances" of the urban scenes. "The import of this haphazard envisagement of concrete things," De Selincourt writes, "is in their power of ballast. For the more a man shows us that he has seen what we see, the more we believe him when he professes a new vision."[38] Chase (1955a, 61–62) believes "that more than anyone else, more than Blake or Baudelaire, Whitman made the city poetically available to literature. . . . Such lines as these have been multitudinously echoed in modern prose and poetry, they have been endlessly recapitulated by the journey of the realistic movie camera up the city street. One might argue that Whitman's descriptions of the city made possible T. S. Eliot's *Waste Land*."[39]

In *The Poet and the City* John H. Johnston (118, 124) appears to find a Dostoyevskian or Dickensian dimension and hears in "this remarkably sustained passage . . . an ominous tension; behind the prosaic, ordinary sounds and events of life lurks the unthinkable, ready to erupt in personal crisis or public disaster. Even the sounds Whitman hears—shouts, oaths, groans, exclamations, howls, echoes—seem to issue from some sprawling prison." In Johnston's view both in "Song of Myself" and elsewhere in *Leaves of Grass* Whitman presents only "parts and fragments of a great city poem" because he "simply could not find a satisfactory moral or aesthetic coordinating principle." But only a critic would have such faith in a "coordinating principle" to achieve what may not have been Whitman's intention in the first place.

In the last lines of this passage Duncan (97) cites such "moving" words as "invisible, visible, buried, vibrating, and resonance" and claims that "we are reminded of the felt presence of Life beyond our senses—the individual spermatozoa in its life invisible to us, itself in its own life a *soul.* But now the poem speaks of 'speech,' '*living and buried,*' and the resonance of words become '*soul.*' We begin then to read the poet's '*I come again and again*' with the common sexual meaning of the word *come.*"

9:160–167

In this eight-line stanza the I has moved from the city to rural America, and Kaplan (167n) is reminded of the genre paintings of William Sidney Mount, like Whitman a Long Islander. For Jesse S. Crisler (20) this is the "Whoopee Section" in which the reader "finds relief in laughter" as he "appreciates the beauty of basic, primary experience between man and nature." Buell (1973, 185–86) acknowledges the humor of the scene, but "equally important," he declares, "seems to be the sense of willed innocence in the face of trials, disaster and even death, which has preceded and is certain to follow."

"Stretched atop of the load," the poet, Marki (154) writes, "seems the embodied spirit of the season itself, like Autumn in Keats's ode, which these lines resemble in the delicacy of their diction and the peculiar enchantment of the moment they create." The I as at the beginning of the poem is in a supine position, now atop a load of hay, shortly about to jump and "roll head over heels, and tangle my hair full of wisps," like the young lovers in Sherwood Anderson's *Winesburg, Ohio*, except that the I is once more alone. The loveliness of the

sound of the lines camouflages the reality, which may have been Whitman's intention, conscious or unconscious.

10:168-192

168-82

The I is not floating about in space as he is at the beginning of the great catalogue
later, yet he moves about with extraordinary freedom from a scene in the "mountains," which may evoke Natty Bumppo and his dog Hector: "Soundly falling
asleep on the gathered leaves, my dog and gun by my side." Abruptly he is aboard
a "Yankee clipper," then with clamdiggers, and next observing the marriage of a
trapper and his "red girl" "in the open air in the far-west."

Of this marriage Tony Tanner (81) writes; "His eye moves hungrily from detail
to detail and the effect is to fix an instant in time, immobilizing it in its vividness,
translating it into a tableau, perhaps even turning it into a carnival of gods, unnamed but statuesque." Although Edgeley W. Todd (2) is unable to find among
Whitman's papers or effects a reproduction of Alfred Jacob Miller's painting "The
Trapper's Bride" or any reference to Miller in Whitman's writings, he argues, with
some plausibility, that the passage is "simply a verbal translation of what he saw
in the painting. Not a single detail in the poem is without its counterpart there."

183-92

Of Whitman's treatment of the "runaway slave" Carlisle (184) observes that
the slave "stops at the house of the person Whitman imagines himself to be. The
poet . . . greets him with openness, gives him complete sympathy, recognizes the
slave as a person, but does not project himself into the other man's reality; thus,
he does not really experience that man," as he becomes later the "hounded
slave" (33:834). Black (1969, 224) is harsher as well as perhaps more dogmatic
than Carlisle: "The benevolence of the narrator's liberalism, in this first encounter with the slave, is suspect if compared to the rolling-eyed, gawky stereotype
he transmits. He is altogether too conscious of his tolerance, and the effect
seems to be that he accepts this man only categorically—as slave."[40]

Mendelson (130), on the other hand, is more sympathetic to Whitman: the poet
"discovered heroic deeds in the daily activity of the ordinary supporter of abo-
lition. The hero of the following lines—who is both the poet and one of his
praiseworthy fellow-countrymen—has a 'firelock leaned in the corner' in case he
should be called upon to save the Negro from his pursuers by force of arms."
Mendelson insists that "this is not a symbolic washing of feet," but Thomas
Edward Crawley (92) asserts that the passage evokes "the last supper."[41]

Most commentators have ignored the repetitions in this scene which quietly
provide links in the midst of seeming randomness: the hunter with his dog and
gun by his side; the bridegroom who at his marriage holds the wrist of his Indian

bride with one hand and in the other his rifle; and the I who not only provides the slave with a room "that entered from my own" but also feeds the black at his table, with, as Mendelson notes, "my firelock leaned in the corner." A hunter alone in the wilds, a marriage that is consummated in a hostile environment, and the lonely I who nurses the black for one week before he leaves, probably for Canada, as Whitman perhaps recalls scenes in *Uncle Tom's Cabin,* which shocked American society and the world community on its appearance in 1852.

11:193–210

After a close metrical analysis of this exquisite passage, Sculley Bradley (1939, 456) concludes that it is not only "organically composed" but also becomes "the magnificent parable of the twenty-ninth bather." [42]

Three twentieth-century American poets have bestowed on this portrait of twenty-nine bathers the lovely praise that Whitman's art deserves. "Sometimes," Jarrell (110) writes, "Whitman will take what would generally be considered an unpromising subject (in this case, a woman peeping at men in bathing naked) and treat it with such tenderness and subtlety and understanding that we are ashamed of ourselves for having thought it unpromising, and murmur that Chekhov himself couldn't have treated it better." According to Louis Zukovsky, as reported by his friend Robert Creeley (12), Whitman's poem "constituted the American *Shih King,* which is to say, it taught the possibilities of what might be said or sung in poetry with that grace of technical agency, or mode, thereby to accomplish those possibilities. *It presents.* It does not talk about or refer to—in the subtlety of its realization, it becomes real."

In *The Figure of Echo,* John Hollander (122–23) records these echoes in Whitman's lines:

> Whitman's beautiful fable of the moon becoming moonlight in order to make love to the twenty-eight days, the young men swimming in the ocean, seems strangely evocative when the lunar woman is described. . . . A context of erotic danger for young men is provided by the famous parable of the harlot, Proverbs 7:6–27, beginning "for at the window of my house I looked through the casement, and behold among the simple ones, I discerned among the youths, a young man void of understanding . . . in the twilight, in the evening, in the black and dark night." Whitman clearly identifies himself with the twenty-eight-year-old moon woman behind the blinds, and the separation of narrator and harlot in the biblical passage is reconstituted in his figure of the watcher.

In a discussion of "possible sources" of Whitman's ideas and symbols, Esther Shephard (1953, 74–75) suggests for this passage the Egyptian god Osiris. Sadakichi Hartmann (46) reports that according to one of Whitman's friends, E. C. Stedman, the poet "compared himself with Christ and Osiris," and in the course of his well-documented visits to Dr. Abbott's Egyptian Collection in New York may have become acquainted with the lore surrounding Osiris. In one plate he is depicted as a mummy with twenty-eight stalks of grain growing out of his body. In another plate his son Horus (the sun) is standing next to his father's supine body which is about to revive; and in the third Osiris, again supine, now wearing a mitre, is rendered as an ithyphallic deity. Osiris was also the guardian of the dead ("the nocturnal sun") and was identified with the bull and in Greek mythology with Dionysus.[43]

The number of the naked male bathers, twenty-eight, whom the rich woman joins in fantasy, has led to speculation as to its possible significance. James Davidson (100–1) sums up and then contributes to the discussion:

> It is the cycle of the moon (minus one day), and hence the tide. . . . There are also undertones of reproduction: twenty-eight days is the cycle of the female's fertility. . . . February has twenty-eight days, except in leap year, when it has twenty-nine. 'Dancing and laughing, along the beach came the twenty-ninth bather.' Theoretically, in leap year she can legitimately become the aggressor, and seek her mate. . . . In leap year, as well as in the others, she must remain hidden aft the blinds and under the layers of Victorian clothing.

Or, of course, twenty-eight may be a symbolic or occult number, so far unidentified.[44]

The twenty-ninth bather may or may not be twenty-eight years old, T. J. Kallsen (1967, 88) suggests, but perhaps about forty-eight, "nearing the end of her normal span of childbearing potentiality." If so, there may be a veiled oedipal association to which Kallsen does not refer. Aspiz (1980, 223), however, recognizes "a conspicuous oedipal warp" in the episode. According to his "eugenic" interpretation, the woman is "a tragic, self-indulgent figure who toys with her erotic desires but thwarts her natural mating instincts. . . . For if the lady represents an object lesson in misdirected sexuality, she may also be seen as the central figure of an adolescent and voyeuristic fantasy in which a wealthy and mature female aggressor—or possibly the male persona who has identified with her sexual yearnings and predatory gropings—commits a watery rape upon the passive young men as they float supine in the water."

Reynolds (332, 330) finds the episode confirmation of his thesis that Whitman's "poetry is best understood as an arena for the confrontation of varied, sometimes contradictory cultural forces," specifically in this instance the artist's purification of "the voyeuristic eroticism of the popular sensationalists. . . . Voyeuristic fantasy is stripped of malice and is conveyed through refreshing, baptismal images of nature." Even her masturbation "is adeptly fused with cleansing nature images."

Schyberg (119–20) may have been the first critic to note how frequently Whitman takes "the feminine point of view" and to state that "he is in reality the lonesome young woman watching the young men bathing. . . . we cannot avoid feeling that it is a most deeply personal confession and think of Whitman's own first twenty-eight years, 1819–1847."

Ginsberg (238–39) dwells on "the longing for closeness; erotic tenderness is of course implicit here, his own as well as in empathy," with the spinster lady. Whitman, Ginsberg asserts in his declamatory style, "pointed to that as basic to our bodies, basic to our minds, basic to our community, basic to our sociability, basic to our society, therefore basic to our politics. If that quality of compassion, erotic longing, tenderness, gentleness, was squelched, pushed back, denied, insulted, mocked . . . , then the entire operation of democracy would be squelched, debased, mocked, seen cynically, advantaged, poorly made into a paranoid, mechano-megalopolis congregation of freaks afeard of each other."[45]

E. H. Miller (1968, 94) comments: "Perhaps nowhere else is the pain of separateness and of unwanted sexual chastity depicted so poignantly. And perhaps, too, nowhere else does Whitman, though he transfers the pain to the spinster, sketch so revealingly his own portrait." The woman plays out her fantasy in oral sexuality, which recalls the consummation of the body and soul in #5 as well as the visit of God as the bedfellow. Section 11 culminates in "a bisexual image of the impregnated womb and sexual arousal, a bittersweet conclusion appropriate to the only gratification fantasy permits, autoerotic release."

The "celebrated rape" of the twenty-eight young men becomes another of the catharses that Black (1975, 105) finds in the poem, "a superbly realized psychological penetration into sexual frustration and fantasy: it is fantasy about fantasy. Like the poet himself, the lady confines her sexual experience to her imagination." To Gelpi (198) "the passage displays how divided Whitman himself is; he identifies as much with the lone lady as with the robust young men she lusts for. . . . The division . . . is not just between participation and observation, but, more troublesomely, between actual contact and self-titillation. The understanding of both sides is rendered through the bisexuality, and so the homosexuality, of the poet's perspective."

In what he labels "the notorious eleventh section," Pearce (1961, 78) points out that Whitman, speaking in the third person, "has a woman look for him. . . . it is as though the procreant urge of the self to create and transform itself is not yet quite powerful enough." Martin (1979, 21), from another perspective, cites the "exuberance of this final image"—"all twenty-eight men apparently climax and shower the sky, and their sexual partners, with sperm. . . . The 'spray,' the life force of the twenty-eight young men, . . . becomes a token of the value in multiplicity of the world. Against nineteenth-century medical theories of the conservation of energy, through the withholding of sperm, Whitman proposes a radical redistribution of that energy through the release of sperm. To the 'capitalism' of heterosexual intercourse (with its implications of male domination and ownership) Whitman opposes the 'socialism' of nondirected sex."

John Snyder (60) also dilutes the affect of the poetry: "The sexual union between the lady and the bathers, like the Christian Incarnation and Resurrection, is real only as paradox. The conditions of time and space cannot be broken, yet they are. God cannot be born a man and a man cannot die as God, yet such are the meanings of Incarnation and Resurrection. The rich lady cannot get what she wants and have it; she cannot possess the unpossessible. Her fulfillment would be the death of the young men's freedom, and the death of their freedom would be the death of her desire, which is her life as a woman. Such is the specific paradox of #11."

Although this section has received extraordinary praise, from various perspectives, some admirers of "Song of Myself" have had trouble accepting it as an integral part of the poem. Schyberg (99) fails to find "any connection with what has preceded it other than that the poet has told of an Indian girl's wedding—and of the white woman who has no wedding." De Selincourt (197) perhaps reflects Victorian decorum when he alleges that Whitman "has misrepresented feminine psychology. The young woman would not have cared to see the manly form, but to be seen by the manly eye; her sex would not have driven her to be surreptitious in watching but to be conspicuous in avoiding the bathers."

Matthiessen (610) may have been the first critic to note similarities between #11 and Thomas Eakins's well-known oil painting, "The Swimming Hole," in which five naked young men are sunning themselves in relaxed postures on a rock. Matthiessen believes that Whitman's sketch "approaches the powerful construction of Eakins." Matthiessen does not note that at the edge of the canvas, on the right, we see the head and shoulders of the middle-aged artist who is simultaneously participant and observer. The loneliness of Whitman's poem may be duplicated in the outstretched left arm of the artist—beneath the water—for Eakins like Whitman conceals as he reveals.[46]

Twenty-five years after the appearance of the first edition of *Leaves of Grass*, in *Specimen Days* (*PW*, 1:274–75), Whitman recaptures in prose some of the loneliness of his poem in his description of a large group of bathers at a pier in Brooklyn or New York: "The laughter, voices, calls, responses—the springing and diving of the bathers from the great string-piece of the decay'd pier, where climb or stand long ranks of them, naked rose-color'd, with movements, postures ahead of any sculpture . . . . the frequent splash of the playful boys, sousing—the glittering drops sparkling, and the good western breeze blowing."[47]

12:211–218

From the scene of the twenty-nine bathers Whitman now moves, in fancy, of course, across the American landscape to observe his countrymen in various walks of life. His portraits are actually stereotypical, the emphasis as in genre paintings on movement and color rather than on individuation. Martin (1979, 22) suggests that "Whitman's lines often seem like primitive precursors of Hopkins' meters, and 'lithe sheer' [of the blacksmiths' waists] must strike us now as 'sprung rhythm.'"[48]

13:219–237

Now in a kind of visual ascent we move from the portrait of a butcher-boy sharpening a knife and then dancing "his shuffle and breakdown" and a group of blacksmiths, "with grimed and hairy chests," wielding hammers in their "massive arms," to a "picturesque giant," a black driving a huge dray pulled by four horses. José Martí (252) believes that the black "seems more beautiful to [Whitman] than an emperor coming in triumph," and Orth (19) is reminded of a "primitive nature god." Newton Arvin (38), who is much disturbed by Whitman's often hostile attitude toward blacks, speculates that "in such lines, perhaps, it was the poet's eye and not his philosophy that was at work." John Addington Symonds (91) notes that Whitman is "peculiarly rich in subjects indicated for the sculptor or the painter, glowing with his own religious sense of beauty inherent in the simplest folk."

226–27
Here Whitman characterizes himself as a "caresser of life wherever moving." Carlisle (185) offers this explanation: "In the first instance, he simply wishes to contain everything ('not a person or object missing') in his poem. In the second, however, he points directly to the way he encounters the world in these sections: he watches it and absorbs it into himself. In effect, he removes external reality into the self."[49] Tuveson (216) attributes this absorptive process to hermetic doctrine: "the amalgamation into the individual self is at a more elemental level than intellectual understanding; everything received by sensation, in the proper way, in fact goes to build *another* self, an Over-Self which replaces, for a time, the individual ego." Martin (1975, 84), on the other hand, finds that the line restores to the poem "the total egotism of the child."

228–29
What oxen express in their eyes "seems to me more than all the print I have read in my life," Whitman writes with characteristic hyperbole, which at the same time reflects democratic distrust of aristocratic or elitist art. Hyde (173) offers another interpretation of these lines, a useful one too: "By taking his nourishment through his senses, Whitman comes to have a carnal knowledge of the world. His participatory sensuality [which originates in childhood] 'informs' him in both senses—it fills him up and it instructs."

14:238–256

239
"Ya-honk!" cries the wild gander. The sound, John Cowper Powys (15) declares, is "among the ugly, terrible things, that this great optimist turns into poetry. . . . Others may miss that mad-tossed shadow, that heartbreaking defiance—but

from amid the drift of leaves by the roadside, this bearded Fakir of Outcasts has caught its meaning; has heard, and given it its answer."

253–54

Thomas (1987, 49) offers a sexual and economic construction of "Me going in for my chances, spending for vast returns." "Spend," he observes, "was at this time the popular term for reaching orgasm," and, further, under American capitalism, "Males were assumed to be biologically designed for the strenuous competitiveness of the social life that awaited them."[50]

"Adorning myself to bestow myself on the first that will take me," Bychowski (239–40) interprets as Whitman's feminine "desire to give himself, to surrender. . . . Out of this feminine identification sprung his fervent admiration for manifestations of virility in other men and his constant craving for contact with their maleness. In other words, here we put our finger on one of the essential sources of Whitman's homoeroticism. It would fill pages to quote all the exclamations in which Whitman sings his admiration of virility. At times it seems as though he felt a truly feminine cult of maleness and of the phallos."

Thomas (1983, 7) asserts that Whitman "provocatively represents himself as an easy pick-up," and Martin (1979, 23) extols the poet's "nonselective, divinely promiscuous love."

15:257–325

In the first extended catalogue, of almost seventy-five lines, the protagonist continues to ingest the heterogeneous sights and sounds of democracy. Bubbling over with a rollicking exuberance, he mocks genteel restraints and conventional artistic order and embraces everything with the uncritical eagerness of a child intent upon enjoying, not evaluating, the world he is discovering, as though for the first time. "The pure contralto," introduced in the first line of this section, has her song, Whitman his. She stands "in the organloft," he moves from line to line in space and time, from sound to sound, picture to picture.

The section, Tony Tanner (81) observes in *The Reign of Wonder,* "is paratactical to an extreme degree. And yet as he introduces type after type, person after person, there is a cumulative effect of combination in variety, the 'indescribable crowd' of city and country which is yet one nation, the singularity of individuals which yet adds up to a unity of race. The juxtapositions are not unconsidered or irresponsible, though we are obviously intended to feel, rather than ponder or comprehend, the relevance of the contiguities, the similarities in the differences."

Thomas (1987, 56–57) argues that by isolating the actions of the people "from questions of motive, purpose, and consequence, [Whitman] manages to recreate an idealized form of the comfortably blended urban and rural worlds of his childhood." But Thomas then is compelled by his Marxistic thesis to politicize his point and, worse, Whitman. "Yet the whole panorama is implicitly presented as a celebration of the free spirit of economic liberalism, the laissez-faire capitalism of the mid-nineteenth century. It is of course nothing of the sort. Whitman replaces the pleasure of acquiring and the acquiring of pleasure which was becoming the real business of his time, with the pleasure of simply being and living."

James Perrin Warren (1984a, 36) observes that "the clausal catalogue . . . emphasizes the dynamic, temporal flow of discrete instants, for it is only in flowing that the instants can unite to form an 'ensemble.'" To Jarrell (109), "It is only a list—but what a list! And how delicately in what different ways—likeness and opposition and continuation and climax and anticlimax—the transitions are managed, whenever Whitman wants to manage them," which is indeed a most important point too often ignored.

257–64

"The pure contralto" may be Marietta Alboni (1823–1894), who sang in New York in 1852 and 1853. She was renowned for her performance in *Norma,* and her voice reminded Whitman of a mockingbird.[51] The contralto reminds Kaplan (178) of George Sand's Consuelo "singing Pergolesi's 'Salva Regina' in the organ loft of Saint Mark's in Venice."

Fishkin (37) finds a link between the contralto and the carpenter who appears in the next line: the "tongue of his foreplane whistles its wild ascending lisp": "The timbres may be different, but the vibrations are shown to have something in common. Activities which seem to be distinct and separate are shown, by the fresh and original images and by artful juxtaposition, to be really one and the same." Allen (1961, 48) ties the carpenter's "foreplane" to the spinning-girl who "retreats and advances to the hum of the big wheel."

274–77

Schyberg (121) suggests that the "young fellow" driving the express wagon—"I love him though I do not know him"—is one of the "Calamus-episodes" in the poem.[52] Henry B. Rule (248–49) finds Whitman's picture of "the western turkey-shooting" influenced by George Caleb Bingham's painting "Shooting for the Beef," which was exhibited in New York in 1850 and perhaps for the next two years.[53] Edwin Fussell (412) believes that it is conceivably based on a scene in *The Pioneers* in which Natty Bumppo demonstrates his phenomenal skill with the rifle. Whitman, we recall, categorically and proudly admitted James Fenimore Cooper into the company of *Leaves of Grass* men.

300–6

In these lines Whitman introduces a bride, an opium eater, a prostitute, the President and his cabinet, and "five friendly matrons with twined arms." Tony Tanner (81–82) observes that "time has slowed down," for the bride and the opium eater: "the bride in anticipation of life, the addict in exhaustion of it."[54]

The proximity of the bedraggled prostitute and the President has shocked some readers, which was no doubt Whitman's intention. Thomas Wentworth Higginson

(80), no admirer of the poet, is filled with wrath and morality in about equal parts: "His love is the blunt, undisguised attraction of sex to sex; and whether this appetite is directed towards a goddess or a streetwalker, a Queensberry or a handmaid, is to him absolutely unimportant. This not only separates him from the poets of thoroughly ideal emotion, like Poe, but from those, like Rossetti, whose passion, though it may incarnate itself in the body, has its sources in the soul." Tanner (81) points out that after the reference to the President and his cabinet we are immediately introduced to five matrons: "the fathers of a new nation, the mothers of its necessary men." But are these matrons "with twined arms" mothers or whores, or does it matter?

310
Fishkin (38–39) makes a delightful discovery in the following line—"The floormen are laying the floor—the tinners are tinning the roof—the masons are calling for mortar." In what at first glance may appear to be random activities, she perceives "a subtle and important cohesion": "From laying a floor, tinning a roof, and calling for mortar, a house will result. The mason, as he binds together the farthest parts of the house and turns them into one unified structure, has much in common with the poet who asks, 'Shall I make my list of things in the house and skip the house that supports them?'" [22:465].

324–25
The last two lines Carlisle (186) translates in terms of his thesis, "Whitman's Drama of Identity": "the first line suggests the equality of inner and outer as well as the objective reality of each. The second line emphasizes even more strongly the reality of the outer by indicating that the self achieves meaning only as part of the vast diversity #15 includes. Whitman does not say *it* is part of *him* as he did earlier; rather he is part of it. These are the first lines that clearly focus on the necessary conditions for essential existence. Whitman has not yet experienced full self-awareness, nor has the poem consistently dramatized mutuality."[55] Fussell (412) is less convincing when he fits these lines into his frontier thesis: "'to be' is the equivalent of 'I am.' And so, more or less, it was, in 1855, when Whitman was the West, i.e., the frontier between the American self and its imaginative New World."

The lengthy catalogue ends in a quiet, delicate coda, as city and country, living and dead, aged and young, husbands and wives, and the I merge, diversity momentarily giving way to harmonious union.

16:326–352

347–49
Chase (1955a, 59–60) finds the "characteristic note" of "Song of Myself" in these lines describing the poet's diversity, which, however, has "its place" as do moths,

fisheggs, and visible and invisible suns. "If one finds," he writes, "'Song of Myself' enjoyable at all, it is because one is conscious of how much of the poem, though the feeling in many of its passages need not perhaps have been comic at all, nevertheless appeals to one, first and last, in its comic aspect. . . . it is written by a neo-Ovidian poet for whom self-metamorphosis is almost as free as free association." Bedient (15) prefers to dwell on Whitman's "astonishingly pure feeling for the common idiom": he "knew how to test-thump its words like melons in the street stalls whose local color he so much delighted in."

17:353–364

353–59
In this transitional, recapitulative section Whitman alludes once again to the universality of "the grass that grows wherever the land is and the water is." McMahon (48) seizes upon it in support of his thesis: "The pattern of a marriage between grass and atmosphere might illuminate a reading of Whitman's poem in four ways: (1) local polarities in the different sections take on new cosmic significance, (2) larger structural coherences are brought to light, (3) the poem as a whole can be more firmly placed in the continuing debate about monism and dualism, and (4) the relationship of Whitman's poem to other American poetry can become more clear."

18:365–371

Here Whitman emerges, Cavitch (1985, 52, 53) observes, "as a militant champion of oppressed humanity, playing 'marches for conquered and slain persons' as well as for victors, and heralding a revolution of feelings. His procession is like a triumphal approach to a city that will receive him as a reconciler of age-old conflicts. . . . Yet his commitment to democracy in this poem (as in his family life) is distorted by his authoritarian role. The political stance in 'Song of Myself' implicitly idealizes the benign autocrat, not the common man. Whitman's idea of the fair and good in social terms remains close to the supreme will of a kind, firm parent."

19:372–387

372
"The meal pleasantly set" is the second appearance of what Aspiz (1980, 176) calls "the image of the bread of life" (see also 3:53 and 46:1223), which can be construed as an elaboration of the feeding motif developed by Burke, E. H. Miller,

and, more recently, Zweig. For Crawley, on the other hand, the line evokes the last supper.

377–78

Marki (158) believes that these tender lines on "a bashful hand" and "the float and odor of hair" describe the approach of the twenty-ninth bather to the young men depicted in #11. Here the I also reveals his "darker moods and guilty anxiety," which support Marki's view that the affirmative exterior masks an anxiety-ridden poet.

380

The reference to "the thoughtful merge of myself and the outlet again" produces one of D. H. Lawrence's (177) essentially good-humored but at the same time vituperative passages. "Your mainspring is broken, Walt Whitman," he declares. "The mainspring of your own individuality. And so you run down with a great whirr, merging with everything. . . . Oh, Walter, Walter, what have you done with it? What have you done with yourself? With your own individual self? For it sounds as if it had all leaked out of you into the universe. . . . 'I reject nothing,' says Walt. If that is so, one must be a pipe open at both ends, so everything runs through." Daiches (1955b, 49) attributes Lawrence's outburst to his fierce (and never understated) belief that an ideal relation between two people rests upon "an almost mystical awareness on the part of each of the core of *otherness* in the other."

386–87

Schyberg (109) notes this "strangely engrossing conversational style, in which the poet seems to look up from the book at his reader or to leap from the page into his arms," but warns that later it becomes somewhat of "a mannerism." Berryman (237), on the other hand, has only admiration for this quiet conclusion of what in his partitive structural analysis of the poem constitutes the second "movement." It foreshadows, Berryman writes, "the tone of the conclusion of the whole work. . . . Few poets have ever been able to sound like this, so simple and intimate; though Robert Frost has."

20:388–421

388–89

The greatest of American musical composers, Charles Ives, as idiosyncratic and revolutionary as Whitman himself, set these two lines to music with no elaboration or embellishment, as though he believes Whitman has made a profound statement that requires no ornamentation on his part. Ives's brief song, then, is a gracious bow to and recognition of the other's genius.[56]

Perhaps a comment by Snyder (63) may explain Whitman's statement and

Ives's fascination. Whitman presents "a new variety of lyric communion . . . ('the Falstaffian')," and Whitman now "becomes a jovial, pan-human ('kosmos'). He absorbs all existents in the universe into his 'sweeter fat.'" Or, in the words of a talented undergraduate: Whitman is absorbed in "the physical miracle of the transubstantiation of mere steak and potatoes into the body of Walt Whitman."[57]

Burroughs (1867, 70) offers an elaborate explanation of Whitman's self-portrait, "hankering, gross, mystical, nude": "like the great elk in the forest in springtime; gross as unhoused Nature is gross; mystical as Boehme or Swedenborg; and so far as the concealments and disguises of the conventional man, and the usual adornments of polite verse, are concerned, as nude as Adam in Paradise."

The answer to Whitman's question "How is it I extract strength from the beef I eat?" according to George B. Hutchinson (80) is, "because the cattle eat grass, which grows from soil well-manured by death." Or, in the words of Zweig (256), "We know now what he's been eating—the very world—and we will learn shortly who he is. Meanwhile, . . . we hear the boastful American voice that Whitman extracted from the booster journalism of his day, from the tall stories and the folklore."

390–92

To the next question, "What is a man anyhow? What am I? and what are you?," the answer is, according to Myers (244): "A man is not something small, contained within an impermeable shell, and set off against a world order. . . . Who is Walt Whitman? He is infinite; he is of the past and of the present and future, of the old and of the youth. . . . He pervades everything, becomes everything. . . . He will admit no limitations."[58]

We are now according to Berryman (237) at the beginning of "triumphant explorations of experience" which are distinguished by "two series of answers . . . to the question that he has asked, what a man is: first, answers that are given as of the *Self;* second, answers that are given as *not* of the Self. Most of the famous passages occur in the first series, but the most intense reality, as a matter of fact, is experienced by him in the second series. *Both* series become *intolerable,* and have to be abandoned (he has been trying . . . a series of experiments on himself—two series—to see what he is)."

John Updike (34), who does not share Berryman's view of a tormented poet, arrives at another conclusion: Whitman's "egotism—the egotism of this persona not contained between his hat and his boots—is companionable; he urges it upon others; the 'you' of his poem is as important, as vivacious, as the 'I.' . . . His egotism is suffused and tempered with a strenuous empathy."

399–400

Anderson (1971, 104–5) offers a significant comment on this witty passage: "Whitman's narcissism was a communicated delight in the fat sticking to his bones; it was very far from a lapse into a solipsism. The culture had found no voice for it earlier; a delighted self-absorption was in theory reserved to God, but hadn't been emotionally realized in the world of art or practice." Wallace (60), who places Whitman among the inspired clowns of our literature, discovers a parody of "the language of science. . . . Whitman humorously deflates the experts by beating them with their own language."

401–2

These lines are important in the argument of Myers (246) that the poem describes (in a witty use of the vernacular) a "spiritual democracy": "with Whitman equality is much more than a political ideal; it is an *eternal fact* in the real world of unlimited personalities; it is a great first principle. . . . Equality of this kind . . . is discovered only by piercing through the coverings and turmoils to the insides of beings." Hugh l'Anson Fausset (122), however, will have none of this: "The flaw in this dream of a natural democracy was that it presupposed a society formed of men and women who remained at this comparatively primitive stage of development and engaged in manual tasks. No society, perhaps, can be healthy which is not solidly based upon such men and women. But a society exclusively composed of them would be a limited and static one."

408

In the "child's carlacue cut with a burnt stick at night," J. E. Miller (1962, 139) makes a delightful discovery, that "a meaningless, whimsical abstraction," which glows in the night, "signifies life as it would appear were there no purpose pervading the universe."

419–21

Symonds (31–32) reads these lines as a noble statement of Whitman's confidence in the universe. "The secret of Whitman, his inner wisdom," he explains in an eloquently Victorian statement of faith, "consists in attaining an attitude of confidence, a sense of security, by depending on the great thought of the universe, to which all things including our particular selves are attached by an indubitable link of vital participation. This religion corresponds exactly to the Scientific Principia of the modern age; to the evolutionary hypothesis with its display of an immense unfolding organism, to the correlation of forces and the conservation of energy, which forbid the doubt of any atom wasted, any part mismade or unaccounted for eventually."

The striking depiction of the poet "tenoned and mortised in granite," with its mixture of carpentry and sculpture, evokes the "picturesque giant . . . poised on one leg on the stringpiece, . . . His glance . . . calm and commanding" (13:220–24).

21:422–450

424–25

After the quiet reiteration that the I is the poet of the body and the soul, which foreshadows another scene or fantasy that will replicate #5, the I proceeds to redefine heaven and soul. "As in Blake's heaven-hell marriage," Martin Bidney

(38) writes, "Whitman admits no disjunction, no mutual exclusion; both entities are changed to fit a new myth of psychic integration. Heaven is psychologically grafted onto the poet's present awareness; hell is also fully accepted and incorporated, after being translated 'into a new tongue.' . . . As in Blake, 'hellish' energies, namely the passions or fiery energies, are translated out of the language of narrowly religious negation into the new tongue of affirmation, the language of creative contraries."

Asselineau (1962, 53), however, believes that Whitman's affirmations rest on enduring personal conflicts: as "a mystical pantheist" (if he is a mystical pantheist), Whitman is deeply troubled that "God should be evil, that evil should partake of God." He is also "sometimes horribly tormented by troubled desires which society reproved and which he had to hold in check."

426–28

Tuveson (213) emphasizes the significance of Whitman's reassertion that he is the poet of "the woman the same as the man" as indicative "of the comprehensive bisexuality characteristic of the divine Self," which the poet as "the counterpart of the divine being" shares. Where Tuveson reads the passage from his mystical perspective, Updike (35) offers another point of view: "This translucence, free of personal miasma, is possessed, I believe, by the noblest literature always, and is what leads us to turn to it out of the petty depressions and defeats of our lives. We feel it in the tone of words more than in their content—in the simplicity of the assertion." In establishing the equality of the sexes, the I gives precedence to women, especially "the mother of men" (line 428).

429–48

As the poem now gradually rises in a Wagnerian erotic crescendo—"Press close barebosomed night! Press close magnetic nourishing night!"—the I, no doubt unconsciously, evokes the craved mother-child relationship or bond. The aggressive chanter of "a new chant of dilation or pride" assumes the longed-for passive protective relationship, as he does in #4 and again in #11, although in the latter he is (in fantasy) both the aggressive female and the passive male bathers.

Sculley Bradley (1939, 455–56) analyzes these lines and the evocation of "barebosomed night" in terms of the varying rhythms and the organic structure. "It is a passage," he comments, "in which subtle patterns are embroidered upon each other in a manner comparable to that of great symphonic music." Lenhart (203) also draws a musical analogy, that Whitman's "repetition of a word around which the phrases cluster is like a single repeated note with variations," and then adds, "The parallelisms that had delighted the Beowulf poet also delighted Whitman."

According to Catel (83), "We have here the action of the ego, but, as it were, its negative action, which is quite characteristic of the nature of Whitman. The night, the sea, two infinite mediums in which his soul dilates in sterile exaltation, sterile as regards practical life, but on the contrary productive of beauty. . . . One

may say that Night and the Sea are symbols in which Whitman has best expressed his soul. Wrapped up in them, his soul has conquered its supremacy."

Aspiz (1980, 149) explains the "human and celestial coupling" in terms of
nineteenth-century medical and occult discussions of sexual electricity:

> the cosmic persona, identifying with the masculine moon ("he that walks
> with the tender and growing night") embraces the "voluptuous" and "prodi-
> gal" earth and the "magnetic nourishing night" with "unspeakable passionate
> love" like "the bridegroom" embracing "the bride." Since female electricity
> was said to be magnetic, we may assume that the womb of the "nourishing
> night" is entrusted with the precious vitellus and that the cosmic sexual em-
> braces of the persona, enacting the role of the electro-deific "Male and
> Lover," spark the creation of that matter of which the universe is formed.[59]

449–50

The section culminates in a graphic depiction of intercourse. According to
Tuveson (213) "we have an elucidation of the sense, in #5, of the 'true self' eroti-
cally nuzzling the poet." Martin (1979, 23–24) views the scene as homosexual
consummation: "The 'thruster' is an unmistakable image of the male lover, and
the simile of the second line indicates a deliberate comparison with heterosexual
love. . . . Whitman makes use of the male marriage metaphor in order to suggest
his closeness to experience and his role as a passive receiver of inspiration. . . .
At the same time, he is both giver and receiver ('we hurt each other'), as an artist
imposing an order upon the experience that he receives."

In 1867 in the fourth edition of *Leaves of Grass* the two lines were excised as
Whitman moved to his new role as The Good Gray Poet.

22:451–482

451–56

In Black's (1975, 106) psychoanalytic emphasis upon catharsis, Whitman "projects himself into a symbolic love affair with the maternal sea, an unmistakable
though disguised Oedipal fantasy. In this respect the episode differs from earlier
cathartic experiences in its metaphorical form and in the extent to which the
poet initiates catharsis. Previously he has believed himself wholly passive, but
now he declares that he and the sea 'must have a turn together . . . . I undress.'"
Yet the I appears to regress to a more comfortable passive state: "I resign myself
to you," "Cushion me soft . . . . rock me in billowy drowse," which would seem to
evoke the fetus in the womb.

Fiedler (21) speculates that Whitman "may never have held in a final embrace
a human lover," and then adds, "the sea, embracing him, taught him to love, and
he responded with love." Surely loving the sea has little in common with the
complexities of human relationships and maturation.

Nathanson (121) calls attention to "images of flooding" in Whitman's poem which "almost always have such cosmological implications. They often serve to signal the welling up of nature's creative power within individual creatures; rightly incarnate or rightly apprehended, the objects created by the flood of *natura naturans* share its qualities. So Whitman's lyrical visions of a redeemed natural world typically figure it as filled and animated by a flood that dissolves the surfaces of individual objects."[60]

465
Again Fishkin (39) draws attention to Whitman's repeated use of house-building imagery: "Like the mason, the poet binds together the farthest parts; a unifier of opposites, he plays marches for the victors and for the slain and joins living and dead, body and soul, now and eternity. It is the enigma of how one can be many and many can be one that has given rise to the central preoccupation of both the poet and the poem."

467–71
Discussions of "the poet of goodness" and "the poet of wickedness" almost inevitably lead to dubious extrapolations about ethical values and philosophy—Symonds (44), Smuts (75), and Tuveson (214)—although "Song of Myself" as a lyric deals with such matters only superficially, unless one is determined to view Whitman as prophet or teacher or both, and to be swayed by what are frequently fuzzy pronouncements.

"Foofoos" (line 468) apparently derives from the highly successful plays of the 1850s dealing with Mose—"buffoon, champion, and guardian angel of the Bowery," who became a national favorite with his uncouth slang and uninhibited comments. "Foofoos" are "outsiders 'wot can't come de big figure,' i.e. three cents for a glass of grog and a night's lodgings." Mose, the freckled and bearded epitome of nineteenth-century masculinity, easily bests such phonies. Whitman eliminated the line in 1881. Chapter 17 of Mark Twain's *The Prince and the Pauper* (1882) is titled "Foo-foo the First."[61]

472–73
Aspiz (1984, 383–84) provides a helpful gloss on the I's act of moistening "the roots of all that has grown" based on nineteenth-century medical practices and lore: "The euphemistic moistening exemplifies the scattering of the spermatic persona's fertilizing seed; the earth's immunity to scrofula (akin to the consumption that was often attributed to too-frequent pregnancies and to sexual excess) complements his 'unflagging' sexual prowess. Like the literature of genetic reform, which generally assumed that the laws of plant and animal breeding were applicable to humans, *Leaves of Grass* tends to associate sexual and agricultural concepts."

The sea has dashed the I with "amorous wet" in what perhaps may be construed as a bisexual image, and the I is then able, in a striking economic image, to repay his debt and, it would appear, to give birth to himself, metaphorically. Once more the imagery of #5 hovers over the poem.

23:483–498

Quietly we as readers have been hearing the endless motion of an amorous sea, the rhythms of sexuality—impregnation, conception, and birth—occurring in a time continuum that fuses past, present, and future. The poem like the kosmos itself is also in motion, as Whitman reminds us of the "Endless unfolding of words of ages!"

488–94

The I utters "a word of the modern": "Hurrah for positive science!" J. E. Miller (1962, 109) considers this Whitman's "complete and unreserved acceptance of science," although shortly the poet is to say that the "facts" of science are "useful and real . . . . they are not my dwelling." As Frederick W. Conner (95, 96) points out in *Cosmic Optimism*, the influence of science on Whitman "was never more than skin deep. . . . What he believed in and what he required any theory of the universe to vindicate was the ordering of all things by the same kind of mental and moral nature that he found in himself, and this vindication Darwin not only did not supply but in his role of scientist had no interest in. . . . what Whitman was concerned to do . . . was to pour the old wine of divine purpose into the new bottles of evolutionary 'process.'" Or in the words of John T. Irwin (22): "The physical fact is not the dwelling place because for Whitman the physical is the path to the metaphysical ('path' not in the sense that the metaphysical is located elsewhere, but in the sense that the metaphysical is a radically different way of experiencing the physical)."[62]

Aspiz (1980, 59–60) identifies the lexicographer, chemist, and the man who "works with the scalpel" as Dr. Henry Abbott, Dr. John Wakefield Francis, and Dr. Edward H. Dixon, editor of *The Scalpel*. Irwin (20) offers the following gloss on "a grammar of the old cartouches": "A cartouche is an oval ring used in hiero- glyphic writing to set off the characters of a royal or divine name. The earliest examiners of the Rosetta stone had noticed that a group of characters enclosed in an oval appeared at a point in the hieroglyphic inscription corresponding to the place where the name of the pharoah Ptolemy Epiphanes occurred in the Greek inscription."

497

The section culminates in as rollicking and Rabelaisian a line as one can find in American literature, except for a few passages in *Moby-Dick*. "[I] make short ac- count of neuters and geldings, and favor men and women fully equipped" is a considerable improvement over an earlier version, "see here the phallic choice of America, a full-sized man or woman—a natural, well-trained man or woman"

(*NUPM*, 4:1305). Again the I is abandoning what is "not my dwelling," that is, an emasculating environment and society, and creating in fantasy his own version of Eden. The sexual imagery which has built from one crescendo to another, again perhaps in the Wagnerian manner, now climaxes in the greatest act in the poet's life and in American literature—the birth of Walt Whitman, "fully equipped," but formerly Walter Whitman, perhaps as a journalist and a bit of a hack, one of the neuters and geldings, too fearful to acknowledge publicly the demands of an overwhelming libido.

24:499–561

499

"Like Odysseus crowing his name to the blinded Cyclops," writes Paul Zweig (257), his exuberance almost out of control, "Whitman's singer has made a name for himself. . . . the name 'Walt Whitman' enters literature." James Thomson (26) is no less exuberant, as he draws upon the hero-centered Elizabethan world-picture: "With such measureless pride, as of Marlowe's Tamburlaine the Great, [Whitman] announces himself from the first in his poem." Then Holbrook Jackson (255) reclaims Whitman, who "is American in attitude and idea: the quintessence of the United States; more American than the Declaration of Independence, more characteristic than Abraham Lincoln, more western than Mark Twain: as American as a Sky Scraper or a Wisecrack. . . . *Leaves of Grass*, nearly a hundred years after its birth, is still America's most native literary production."[63]

The poet's characterization of himself as "one of the roughs" was deleted in 1867 after he undertook the transformation into The Good Gray Poet. In the 1850s when in an inexplicably mysterious fashion he discovered himself and his poetic genius, he took pride in linking himself with Manhattan's roughs, as in this passage in his jottings (*NUPM*, 4:1304): "And again the young man of Mannahatta, the celebrated rough, (The one I love well—let others sing whom they may—him I sing for a thousand years!)." Or at least until he lost his nerve. The disciple who effected according to plan the transformation of the rough into a more acceptable image, William D. O'Connor (Allen 1955b, 7), sought to fuse the appearance of a rough with the majesty of an overman: "a man of striking masculine beauty . . . powerful and venerable in appearance; large, calm, superbly formed; oftenest clad in the careless, rough, and always picturesque costume of the common people . . . head, majestic, large, Homeric, and set upon his strong shoulders with the grandeur of ancient sculpture." Van Wyck Brooks (1947, 181) asks, "When Whitman called himself 'one of the roughs,' was he not thinking of Emerson's 'Berserkers,' who were coming to destroy the old and build the new? Emerson had looked to Jacksonism, the 'rank rebel party,' to root out the hollow dilettantism of American culture?"

The "rough," Reynolds (463, 512) maintains, originates in the "b-hoy figure" of popular humorous literature and represents "the attempt of the radical-democrat imagination to reconstruct human value on the ruins of a civilization viewed as rotten to the core." Whitman seeks "to preserve the best qualities" of the type, which he achieves "most notably" in the I of "Song of Myself": "Whitman's boy was swaggering, cocksure, indolent, wicked, acute, generous, and altogether lovable."[64]

Both Dudding and Tuveson suggest the appropriateness of Whitman's self-characterization. "On the one hand," Dudding (5) writes, "the reader must view Whitman as 'one of the roughs,' an integral part of Whitman's reality; and on the other hand, the reader must adjust his focus to see Whitman as 'the kosmos,' a man encompassing the metaphysical truths of existence and imparting his message with Promethean pain." Tuveson (236–37) puts it this way: "If the poet is cosmic, there must be represented in him the destructive, the 'fierce and terrible,' the volcanic elements of nature. His emphasis on his being one of the 'roughs,' certainly not one of the 'douce' people, is the principal expression of this side of his being."

Contemporaries sputtered when Whitman introduced himself at his birth or baptism as "a kosmos." Detractors still sputter. Leo Spitzer (274–75), however, provides a justification: Whitman "felt himself to be a microcosm reflecting the macrocosm. He shares with Dante the conviction that the Here and the Hereafter collaborate toward his poetry, and as with Dante this attitude is not one of boastfulness. Dante felt impelled to include his own human self (with all his faults) because in his poem his Ego is necessary as a representative of Christendom on its voyage to the Beyond. Walt Whitman felt impelled to include in his poetry his own self (with all his faults) as the representative of American democracy undertaking this worldly voyage of exploration."[65]

In many ways John Kinnaird (30), writing in 1958, provides one of the most perceptive attempts to delineate the self-portrait, or the myself:

> The first of these faces we may readily identify as the Whitman of Manhattan, the democratic ideologue of the Preface; the second we recognize as his compensatory masculine image of himself—the cocky, indolent young workingman of the anonymous daguerreotype frontispiece . . . ; while the third, the "kosmos," is the most functionally mythical aspect of the *persona*—the furthest from worldly ego and the closest to his dream life—the fantastic, serio-comic mask of godhead whereby Whitman resolved in imagination the contradictions of his conscious identity into a divinely free and conventionally lawless unity of opposites. This cosmic "self" suggests, of course, his debt to Emerson; but the stylistic life of Whitman's "kosmos" suggests also a rebellious conspiracy against the romantic transcendentalism from which it derives.

Yet perhaps the brilliant intellectualizations dilute somewhat the braggadocio and sensuality of the lines. In "The Primer of Words," Whitman (*DBN,* 3:739) writes: "Kosmos-words, Words of the *Free Expansion of Thought, History, Chronology, Literature,* are showing themselves, with foreheads muscular necks and breasts.—These gladden me!—I put my arms around them—touch my lips to them.—I am mad that their poems, bibles, words, still rule and represent the earth, and are not . . . superceded [sic]. But why do I say so?—I must not,—will not, be impatient."[66]

500

To Tuveson (220) "Disorderly fleshy and sensual" is "the ultimate democratization of hermeticism. . . . the truly kosmic being must not be priestly, aloof, 'refined'; he cannot exclude." Jerome Loving (150) maintains that behind the verbalization of a sensual being lie the repressions of "an unwanted but unavoidable sense of chastity." But Aspiz (1984, 385) believes that the "spermatic attributes form a link with the cosmos" and lead shortly to the utterance of "the password primeval."

502–3

After the poet dares "to name himself—as though the self had now earned, through its loving transaction with its world, a right to take on such substantial being as it could create in that transaction," Pearce (1961, 79) states, Whitman utters "the great, joyous, comic pronouncement—one of the great moments in the history of the American spirit." After writing these lines, E. H. Miller (1979, 90) comments, Whitman "must have guffawed and danced about uninhibitedly as he does in Max Beerbohm's affectionate caricature which recaptures the child-like narcissism of a bearded poet. . . . [Whitman] is happy and contented in a kosmos of his creation, which in turn is happy and contented with him."

For Bloom (1976, 258) this passage is the beginning of an "astonishing chant that as completing synecdoche it verges on emptying-out metonymy, reminding us of the instability of all tropes and of all psychic defenses. Primarily, Whitman's defense in this passage is a fantasy reversal, in which his fear of contact with other selves is so turned that no outward overthrow of his separateness is possible. It is as though he were denying denial, negating negation, by absorbing every outward self, every outcast of society, history, and even of nature."

507

Robert G. Ingersoll (261), the nineteenth-century freethinker of great oratorical powers, expands on "the password primeval" and "the sign of democracy": "This one declaration covers the entire ground. It is a declaration of independence, and it is also a declaration of justice, that is to say, a declaration of the independence of the individual, and a declaration that all shall be free." Unlike Ingersoll, Paul Elmer More (249–50) finds no answer in Whitman's poetry to "the problems confronting the actual militant democracy. . . . even more than Emerson's his philosophy is one of fraternal anarchy, leaving no room for the stricter ties of marriage or the state." According to More, the meaning of the "password primeval" is "Camerado!" or, to use Whitman's phrenological jargon, adhesiveness.

Burke (90) caresses the line of "the password primeval" with one of his felicitous verbal analyses:

The more familiar we become with Whitman's vocabulary, the more condensed this line is felt to be. Identity is proclaimed quasi-temporally, in the word "primeval." Such firstness is further established in terms of the poetic I as spokesman for a public cause. But the more closely one examines the word "sign" in Whitman, the more one comes to realize that it has a special significance for him ranging from signs of God ("and every one is signed by God's name, / And I leave them where they are" [48:1279–80]) to such signs as figure in a flirtation. . . . "Password" is notable for merging one of his major verbs with the term that sums up his own speciality (elsewhere he has "passkey").

Chase (1955a, 68) suggests that "the threat of madness, crime, and obscenity is to be allayed by the curative powers of that Adamic world where wisdom consists in uttering 'the password primeval,' 'the sign of democracy.'" Fausset (121), writing during World War II, believes that Whitman's "prophetic claim has sinister implications, and mass credulity and dementia and uniformity are more apparent than social co-operation." F. D. Miller (13) hears here and in the following lines "the idiom and authority of the Sermon on the Mount, bald and bold, an open plagiarism."

513–14

Whitman, Aspiz (1980, 149) suggests, presents an "analogy between his creative sexuality and the operation of the celestial spheres. . . . The electrical and spermatic 'threads' connecting the stars seem to be a projection of the persona's sexual and visionary powers. Just as the 'fatherstuff' represents the electrical source of human life, so the stars represent the electrical sources of universal life."[67]

517

T. O. Mabbott (item 43) finds a hidden meaning in this somewhat perplexing line: "Beetles rolling balls of dung have a double significance. All readers will see in them typically despised forms of life, but . . . the Egyptians saw in the beetle rolling a ball of dung (supposed to contain an egg) a life symbol, and had the myth that a giant beetle rolled the great ball of the Sun across the heavens."

518–20

These "veil-lifting metaphors," according to Reynolds (322), illustrate Whitman's ability to draw upon sensational (or, in his terminology, "subversive") popular literature, mired in prurience and ugly innuendo, and to "transfigure these themes into something new by ridding them of both guilt and prurience." "Clarified" and "transfigured" are then key words in the passage and in Reynolds's thesis. J. E. Miller (1962, 94) believes that the clarification and transfiguration occur in #28–30, "in which sexual ecstasy and fulfillment lead to a 'new identity,' granting a deeper perception. Thus the poet inverts the traditional mystical pattern: he purifies the senses not by mortification but by transfiguration and glorification."

526–46

"Divine am I inside and out," Whitman writes at the beginning of a passionate passage venerating the body. Most recent critics agree with Gelpi (191) that it is "one of the masterful passages of the poem," in the words of Rosenthal and Gall (33), "a paean to the 'luscious' all of him, in exclamations that parallel those of the paean to nature [#21]." For Zweig (258–59) "These lines . . . contain all of Whitman's humor and sensuality and outrageousness. He sings out about 'worship' and 'prayer'—the language of churchgoing—but also about 'arm-pits,' . . . the wind's 'soft-tickling genitals.' Whitman's church is his body. Aroused from head to toe, he describes himself as a well-fed and bearded erection, so deliciously happy that the trees, the fields, and the winds have become his lovers."[68]

Karl Shapiro (67) does not consider Whitman in this passage "either narcissistic or egomaniac; he [is] trying to obliterate the fatal dualism of body and soul." Fausset (118–19) cites "a morbid preoccupation with the physical. . . . The self-conscious man who affirmed the flesh with a false relish was as much tied to it by perverted appetite as he who recoiled from it in disgust." Lewis (1955, 43–44), however, describes it as a moment of "Adamic narcissism," which is at the same time "an act of turbulent incarnation." Kinnell (222, 223) proposes that "Whitman feels his way back into an infant's joys in the body," but that "the infantile narcissism opens outward" finally in line 544: "Hands I have taken, face I have kissed, mortal I have ever touched, it shall be you." For Cavitch (1985, 57) the line supports his argument for the significance of the mother in the poet's life: "His greatest pleasure culminates in a child's sexual response to a *mother*, who is 'ever' the *mortal*: older and inaccessible."

Jarrell (106) reminds us that when in lines 545–46 Whitman writes, "I dote on myself . . . . there is that lot of me, and all so luscious," "we should realize that we are not the only ones who are amused."[69]

551–61

The lovely line, "A morning-glory at my window satisfies me more than the metaphysics of books," Matthiessen (614–15) observes, "might easily have gone on Wordsworth's title page as an epitaph. But beyond any specific similarities both exemplify the dominant trend of art during their century. They both represent man and nature as deeply interrelated, for reasons given by [Alfred North] Whitehead's explanation, in *Science and the Modern World,* of the origin of romanticism."

The following line of exquisite simplicity—"To behold the daybreak!"—Zweig (126) likens to a "celebration of sunrise" in a nineteenth-century luminist painting.[70] "The passionate, beautiful love-scene," according to R. P. Adams (134), "is Whitman's description of dawn and sunrise. . . . At sunrise the earth achieves a sexually described union with the sky, and the speaker, now strongly identified with the earth, participates in the affair. If it were not for the previous identification, he intimates, he might be overwhelmed by the power of this cosmic union."[71]

Anderson (1971, 143, 153) points to "a familiar mythological motif" in the "solar character" of the soul: "Here Whitman and sun are twinned powers neither physical nor psychic, but both at once. A marriage which counters that of the sky and earth has been consummated between Whitman's soul and the daybreak scene. . . . the contention in which he masters the sun made him 'complete.'"

Cavitch (1985, 58–59) advances a Freudian and speculative interpretation of the passage: "These lines suggest an episode, remembered or invented, in which the child Whitman is abruptly ousted from his morning of bliss by a frightening and powerful father claiming sexual union with the mother, who was cuddling and rousing the child. Apparently humiliated and mocked by a jealous father, the child is driven away with blame and mockery. . . . His initial sexual defeat leads him to compensate by an imaginative triumph in which all the sexuality in the world is expressed by his fantasies."[72]

The line "Seas of bright juice suffuse heaven" Aspiz (1984, 386) construes as follows: "The up-spurts into the interstellar spheres of his mystic semen, possibly reflecting his self-induced orgasm or the workings of his vivid imagination, are hyperbolical expressions of the persona's generative force, his powers of utterance, and his quenchless spirit. In keeping with the spermatic trope, the sexual climax is transformed into vocalism: the phallic utterance of the persona's semen becomes the seminal utterance of the poet's words [lines 566–70]." The passage evokes the twenty-eight bathers who "souse with spray" (11:210), and foreshadows, as Chase (1955a, 68–69) perceives the situation, the appearance of traitors and the red marauder in #28.

Now the "moving world at innocent gambols" gives birth to another sunrise. But the sun rises in the east with a "mocking taunt, See then whether you shall be master!" The taunt Mendelson (201) likens to Ahab's challenge: "I bring the sun to ye! Yoke on the further billows; hallo! a tandem. I drive the sea!"[73] There may be a conflict between the I and the sun as "a symbol of God" (Berkove, 34)— a kosmic conflict—but at the same time there is the inner conflict of the I.

Of "Whitman's enchantingly libidinous knowledge of sunrise," Bedient (28) remarks, "this trio of self, personal body, and world, is Whitman's province and glory. Whitman is the supreme poet of consent. Consent happily confuses the Cartesian dichotomy between matter and mental 'substance.' Its knowing is sportive, infantile, deathless—what Lawrence called knowing in togetherness."

25:562–583

562–65

Lawrence Berkove (34 and 37n) proposes that "'Sun-rise' can also mean *son*-rise, i.e. procreation, or *Son*-rise, the rise of man to godhead." "As an alternative dawn," Bloom (1982, 133) explains, "Whitman crucially identifies himself as a voice, a voice overflowing with presence, a presence that is a sexual self-knowledge." Aspiz (1984, 386) offers an interpretation that confers divinity perhaps upon the poet: "Like a primordial god, he has projected his semen into the womb of the universe, and the magnificence of his voice harmonizes with the music of the spheres." Hyde (171) arrives at essentially the same explanation but from another rhythmic and internal base: "In sympathy the poet receives (inhales, absorbs) the embodied presences of creation into the self; in pride he asserts (exhales, emanates) his being out toward others. As with any respiration, this activity keeps him alive." As Martin (1975, 92) points out, the orgasm evokes the union of body and soul on a June morning in #5.[74]

According to Berryman (238) the passage "if heard aright is thoroughly ominous"; it foreshadows 26:606–8, which concludes, "my windpipe squeezed in the fakes of death," where "the pleasure is rendered as pure pain." That passage in turn anticipates #28—"a wild one."

In a detailed analysis of this section Berkove (34–35) singles out "a series of Biblical allusions to God as Creator. . . . [A]lthough the power of creativity familiarly symbolized by sun-rise is seen as a dynamic and insistent force which would kill if not released, the attributes of natural sun-rise . . . are duplicated in the poet in intensified and over-matching form." In the line "in the calm and cool of the daybreak" Berkove hears an "echo" of Genesis 3:8, "And they heard the voice of the Lord God walking in the garden in the cool of the day." This, he explains, "refers to Adam and Eve who . . . are about to be expelled from the Garden of Eden. The poet's use of 'we,' therefore, seems to be an apotheosizing of Adam and Eve as the symbols of humanity and a fusion and incorporation of them into the 'I' of the poem. As if in defiance of the God who caused Adam and Eve to descend from the garden, the 'we-I' of the poem ascends and assumes godhead."

566–71

Berkove (35) believes that in the line "My voice goes after what my eyes cannot reach" "a contrast is established between the voice of the poet, a divine attribute, and his human eyes. The voice is divine because it expresses creativity; sight, however, is only human because it is limited to perceiving what already exists to be seen." Whitman uses "encompass" as a synonym for "create," and the biblical parallel appears in Proverbs 8:27: "When he prepared the heavens, I was there: when he set a compass upon the face of the depth." "God's act of physical creation," Berkove concludes, "is thus duplicated by the poet-creator's tongue which creates, through words, 'worlds and volumes of worlds.'"[75]

Sydney J. Krause (1957, 715) explains the passage in terms of Whitman's interest in music. "Sound," he writes, "is a method of 'seeing,' and the insights developed from sounds of opera music, for example, lead to a knowledge of the spirit of life and poetry."

In a rare instance of dialogue (imaginary, of course, since Whitman is talking to himself), speech "says sarcastically, Walt, you understand enough . . . . why don't you let it out then?" It is the interpretation of Pearce (1961, 79) that "the words announce the completion of the creative transaction between the self and its world; what has emerged is a man, a poet—no longer just a force, but now a substantial being, a means and an end."[76] Thomas (1983, 6) believes that "'Let it out then' could be the motto of *Song of Myself.* Whitman likes to represent his openness, his 'giving out,' as a form of liberality and of frankness." At that moment the I replies (to himself), "Come now I will not be tantalized . . . . you conceive too much of articulation." According to Berkove (35), the last sentence involves a play on the words "conceive" and "articulation," and recalls the "miraculous vision" recorded in Ezekiel 37:1–14, the meaning of which is that "Words may speak of the principle of life, but they do not contain it; only the Deity has within Him the creative essence."[77]

572–77

In "Waiting in gloom protected by frost," Schyberg (76) alleges, Whitman refers to "his own long gestation during his twenties and thirties."

"The dirt receding before my prophetical screams," Catel (78–79) says in a complex reading of Whitman's symbolism, "is related both to the image of the seed emerging from the ground and to the notion of the errors which the poet dispels with his work. . . . the image of the seed loses its reality and becomes in the next line the abstract idea of 'Cause,' which possesses enough universality to embrace the real and the spiritual. Hence the apparently metaphysical statement: 'I underlying causes to balance them at last,' in which one can recognize a memory of the theories of substance, but in which the main thing is the imaginative content."[78]

Bloom (1982, 132) offers a subtle construction of "keeping tally with the meaning of things." "Tally," he writes, "may be Whitman's most crucial trope or ultimate image of voice. As a word, it goes back to the Latin *talea* for twig or cutting. . . . The word meant originally a cutting or stick upon which notches are made so to keep count or score, but first in the English and then in the American vernacular, it inevitably took on the meaning of a sexual score."

578–83

The last six lines of this section are not without ambiguities that the critical commentary has not resolved. Berkove (36) proposes that "My final merit I refuse you . . . . I refuse putting from me the best I am," "means both 'I will not reveal myself' and 'I will not put *away from* myself my essence.' The latter reading seems more likely because the 'I' already has revealed that knowledge is his essence. But it is a conceiving, not passive, knowledge in an active, not a static, universe." "What he really is," Lieber (98) explains, "will be in a process of becoming and will always be unfinished and finally unknowable." In the words of Zweig (184), "When Whitman recoils from the trap of language, he writes his reticences, and his silence becomes a condition of his poem." Which may or may not shed light on the passage.

The poet is now ready for a "second great adventure, the long journey . . . toward *godhead,*" as Lewis (1965, 14) interprets the poem. He will undergo "a second ecstatic experience" during which his sanity is threatened.

26:584–610

584–96

Gratified after sexual release, still presumably in the supine position, which as we have seen is his characteristic posture, the I retreats again to the role of a passive listener, incorporating sounds he both hears and imagines. "Let sounds contribute toward me," he exclaims with wonderful aptness, while he passively-actively accrues.[79] This new catalogue of sounds recalls 8:146–59 as well as 15:257–325. Thomas (1987, 49) is reminded of the chapter on "Sounds" in Thoreau's *Walden*, although it is hardly likely that either Thoreau or Whitman is, as Thomas alleges, "orientating himself by reacting against the kind of active, acquisitive individualism which was so admired, produced, and promoted by his society."

The sounds the I hears waver uncertainly between those that please and those that foretell death and disaster. He hears at one moment the "recitative" of fish and fruit pedlars but also "The angry base of disjointed friendship" as well as "the faint tones of the sick." A judge pronounces with "shaky lips" a death sentence, while stevedores sound their "heave'e'yo," and in the distance are "the cry of fire,"[80] "the solid roll of the train," and a "slow-march" played over a corpse. Gradually, and quietly, then, Whitman is sounding a dirge as sexuality and death inevitably merge. The "sweet-flag, timorous pond-snipe, nest of guarded duplicate eggs" (24:536)—or male genitalia—are transformed into "flag-tops . . . draped with black muslin" (26:596).

597–610

The allusions to music ("recitative" and "slow-march") now take on greater significance, the "violincello" being linked to "man's heart's complaint" and "the keyed cornet" becoming "the echo of sunset." Chase (1955a, 69–70) observes that sounds here "amplify into a symphonic orchestration" that will mount into a crescendo and then a "dying fall" at the conclusion of the section.

In the *New-York Evening Post* on August 11, 1851, Whitman (*UPP*, 1:256) describes a performance of Donizetti's *La Favorite* at Castle Garden: "a sublime orchestra of a myriad orchestras—a colossal volume of harmony, in which the thunder might roll in its proper place; and above it, the vast, pure Tenor,—identity of the Creative Power itself—rising through the universe, until the boundless and unspeakable capacities of that mystery, the human soul, should be filled to the uttermost, and the problems of human cravingness be satisfied and destroyed?" The tenor he heard was Alessandro Bettini and the aria "Spirito Gentil," which requires, in the words of William Ashbrook (446), "the utmost vocal refinement and security of technique" as well as the "ability to cast a spell over the audience so that he holds them suspended and silent, alive to every expressive nuance."[81]

"The orbic flex of [the tenor's] mouth is pouring and filling me full," the I exclaims, and "*when* he is full enough," Berryman (231) comments, "a valve will open. The valve notion, sense of outlet, is crucial to the poem." Berryman cites

"Through me many long dumb voices" (24:509) and "I act as the tongue of you, / It was tied in your mouth . . . . in mine it begins to be loosened" (47:1244–45).[82]

The most detailed analysis of these lines, musically as well as emotionally, appears in Lawrence Kramer's *Music and Poetry* (141–42):

> These lines trace the step-by-step dissociation of the poet's identity as his response to the music intensifies. The most striking feature of this process is the continuous sexualization of musical response, and more particularly the juxtaposition of images that displace erotic feeling from instrumental to vocal objects and back again—for instance by identifying the cello with the young man's heart's complaint, then turning to the openly phallic cornet. . . . Though the music seems to lure, even to seduce the ear by eliciting an aroused and arrogant vitality—"this indeed is music—this suits me"—its primary effect is to thrust the listener into an erotically charged passivity, most tellingly so when it "fills" him with the tenor "large and fresh as the creation." Disorientation and self-estrangement follow in the form of unsuspected "ardors" and a phantasmagoria of place. Finally, in rapid succession, the music wounds, lulls, and kills the ego. . . .
>
> The exultant perversity of being thus "steeped amid honeyed morphine" is redoubled by the suggestion of oral sexuality in the "orbic flex" of the tenor's mouth.[83]

Robert E. Abrams (613) characterizes the images as "hallucinations": the poet "becomes lost in surrealistic nightmares—'bad trips' of the sort that plague opium-eaters and users of psychedelic drugs." Law (96) singles out the I's feeling of suffocation—"my windpipe squeezed in the fakes of death."[84] Warren (1984a, 38) proposes that the imagery evokes "strangulation and rape," which he explains as the effect of "an uneasy balance between the active outer world of sounds and the static inner world of the poet."[85]

Jarrell (107) takes a fellow poet's delight in Whitman's sheer mastery in these lines. "One hardly knows," he writes, "what to point at—everything works. . . . no wonder Crane admired Whitman! This originality, as absolute in its way as that of Berlioz' orchestration, is often at Whitman's command."

Irwin (108, 109) approaches the passage through Nietzsche's construction of tragedy. The "Apollonian/Dionysian interplay is represented," he proposes, "in the distinction between the operatic chorus and the lead singers (tenor and soprano)." Whitman goes under, as he experiences "an ecstatic brush with death," which leads to "a joyous affirmation of the eternity of the will [that] seems to parallel Nietzsche's interpretation of the ultimate meaning of tragedy."

Bloom (1982, 134) supplies another construction of the passage:

> This Sublime antithetical flight (or repression) not only takes Whitman out of nature, but makes him a new kind of god, ever-dying and ever-living, a god whose touchstone is of course voice. The ardors wrenched from him are operatic and the cosmos becomes stage machinery, a context in which the whirling bard first loses his breath to the envious hail, then sleeps a drugged

illusory death in uncharacteristic silence, and at last is let up again to sustain the enigma of Being. For this hero of voice, we expect now a triumphant ordeal by voice, but surprisingly we get an equivocal ordeal by sexual self-touching.

Hutchinson (84), however, believes that Whitman draws upon his "opera-going experience," but only "to help express a true ecstasy of shamanic type, combining erotic climax, the speaker's passivity before the possessing forces, physical suffering and laceration, symbolic death in an entranced state ('amid honeyed morphine'), and finally reemergence. The astonishingly quick movement to cosmic and finally ontic awareness owes much of its success to the libidinal appeal of the language that joins the disparate qualities of the experience, for, as the final lines suggest, the ecstatic experience penetrates the riddles that cannot be fathomed in the ordinary state of mind."

27:611–617

Now Whitman confirms, "in the outstanding understatement in American poetry," in the words of Rosenthal and Gall (37), that "Mine is no callous shell"—which is perhaps an attempt to justify his tactile sensitivity, although Whitman had no reason to consider his sensitivity unusual or abnormal: it was part of a lifelong hunger for "contact," but he had no way (nor has anyone else) of discovering what the norm is.[86]

Some commentators, however, have thought otherwise. Mark Van Doren (1935, 282) insists that Whitman "was one of a small class, the name of which is erethistic, and the nature of which is sufficiently indicated by the Greek word meaning 'to irritate.' Whitman was one of those persons whose organs and tissues are chronically in a state of abnormal excitement, who tremble and quiver when the rest of us are merely conscious that we are being interested or pleased. Or so, here, he represents himself as being." Asselineau (1962, 13, 26) uses for much the same conclusion the term "hyperesthesia," "which explains the chronic nature of his mysticism and which is perhaps connected with the repression of his sexual instincts. [Whitman] appears constantly to feel the need of rubbing himself, in his imagination, against things and against people, probably because he could not satisfy his desires otherwise. . . . His position might be defined by that formula of André Gide which parodies Descartes's *cogito:* 'I feel therefore I am.'" Edmund Reiss (81, 83) attempts to relate Whitman's tactile sensitivity to such contemporary fads as hypnosis, mesmerism, and animal magnetism, the body being "a potent generator of magnetic or electric power."[87]

Bychowski's (235, 236) psychoanalytic analysis is far more empathic than Van Doren's theory of erethism. According to Bychowski, Whitman

recreates the craving for a love companion through the sense of touch. . . . This extremely sensitive poignant tactile perception helps the poet to maintain the contact with reality for which he hungers with all his soul, yet the libidinization is so strong that the ego . . . has to defend itself. . . . There is in these lines a poignant, almost pathetic description of the submission of the ego which became overwhelmed by libidinal sensation and surrendered to them with a characteristic passive-masochistic delight. Here the autoerotic element struggles with the imperative desire to transcend the boundaries of the ego, since the ego is unable to contain so much delight.

Daiches (1955a, 111) focuses on "the use Whitman makes of this quality in his poetry . . . as a means of intensifying contact to the point of identification," particularly in "Song of Myself," in which "Whitman strives most obviously to establish his inclusive and representative status."

28:618–640

Section 28 is, in the words of Karl Shapiro (59), "one of the greatest moments of poetry." "The famous auto-erotic dream" (Chase 1955a, 70), however, has often proved an embarrassment to readers and critics alike, because of personal and cultural inhibitions surrounding sex and especially masturbation. Bloom (1982, 133) breaks through the reticences to declare that the I "achieves both orgasm and poetic release through a Sublime yet quite literal masturbation."[88] Other critics, however, emphasize the I's guilt and fears of censure, one going so far as to speak of Whitman's "slavery" to his senses in "a tragic paradigm of original sin" (Snyder, 74).[89]

J. E. Miller (1957, 20), in elaboration of the poem "as an inverted mystical experience," proposes that the poet is quivered "to a new identity," "purified by a purgation not of the senses but of the illusion of the senses as vile."[90] Allen and Davis (129) regard the episode as the "second mystical experience, this one induced by the chorus of human voices around the poet," which follows the fusion of body and soul delineated in #5 and anticipates the fusion of the I and the kosmos in 49:1290ff. Hutchinson (86) asserts that "masturbatory fantasies . . . must be subordinated to the more overt indications that spiritual agents induce the climax," the "provokers" being "demonic, aids to a 'red marauder.'"

Middlebrook (57, 59) fits the section into her Coleridgean interpretation, "as rendering a threat to what Coleridge calls the 'reconciling' influence of imagination, its power to incorporate the reason in images of the sense, and to organize the flux of the senses. . . . the Real Me reveals himself to feel separated from the body of the man. Myself, the 'tallying' faculty mediating between sensation and thought, has temporarily been replaced by a new identity who is only erotic." She also points out, but perhaps not convincingly, that the I has become preoccupied in his "delighted exploration of masculinity as one resource of imagination," which limits "the power to identify with the 'female' in his human nature [which] is half the creative power of the Real Me. Becoming all man, the speaker loses the Universal Man in himself."[91]

Berryman (238) characterizes this section as "a wild one . . . about his senses as sentries who become *traitors.*" Reading it perhaps as a version of Henry James's "The Jolly Corner" or Conrad's *Heart of Darkness,* Marki (162) refers "to a confrontation with his arch-fear: the horror in the ecstasy." The "sentries" desert the I and leave him "helpless to a red marauder" who proceeds to rape him (Gelpi, 204). The I talks "wildly," and experiences "temporary insanity" (Buell 1973, 328), as he approaches orgasm. As Fussell (410) interprets the episode the "red marauder" is "the attacking Indian," and "so, once again, the American Indian is also the American poet."[92] A more plausible source may be a sensational tract entitled *Night Side of New York* (New York: J. C. Haney, 1866): "rough-looking men" seated in dance houses or drinking at the bar "are red shirted fellows who probably make their living in some way as longshoremen, while some . . . are pretty well known by the police as river thieves" (30).

Martin (1975, 93) believes that "This most extraordinary passage is almost certainly a depiction of anal intercourse, in which Whitman has turned the entire physical experience into mythic proportions and sees himself reborn as he takes into himself the seed of the unnamed lover," and he concludes, "the orgasm is followed by passages of philosophical summary and visionary perception of unity."[93] According to Black (1975, 108–9) this is Whitman's "most powerful cathartic experience" and "an example of narcissistic autoeroticism," as the I "wards off the threat of actual sexual relations and reverts to masturbation." Black like Fiedler is among those critics who believe that Whitman never experienced a sexual relationship except in fantasy.

Interpreters are almost unanimous that the "wild" scene ends in a "new calm" as "all the sensual elements fall into place" (Rosenthal and Gall, 33). In Berryman's (238) words, "a sort of coda" follows in #29, "to stabilize the tone of the poem." Or, as Chase (1955a, 70) puts it, "This act of restoration is accomplished through love, natural piety, pastoral and cosmic meditations, symbolic fusions of self with America," which in effect provides a kind of summary of the rest of "Song of Myself." Tapscott (69–70) suggests that #28 and #29 "recall the ritual death and resurrection of Osiris. . . . Whitman recasts the ritual as a personal experience of his sensually divine Self."[94]

The following trial lines for this passage appear in Whitman's notebooks (*NUPM,* 1:75–76):

> A touch now reads me a library of knowledge in an instant,
> It smells for me the fragrance of wine and lemon-blows,
> It tastes for me ripe strawberries and melons.—
> It talks for me with a tongue of its own,
> It finds an ear wherever it rests or taps,
> It brings the rest around it, and enjoy them[?] meanwhile and
>   then they all stand on a headland and mock me
> The sentries have deserted every other part of me
> They have all come to the headland to witness and assist against me.—
> They have left me helpless to the torrent of touch

I am given up by traitors,
I talk wildly I[?] am surely out of my head,
I am myself the greatest traitor
I went myself first to the headland /

Unloose me touch you are taking the breath from my throat
Unbar your gates—you are too much for me.—

29:641–646

641–42

This six-line stanza Binns (1905, 99) calls "an obscure, erotic dithyramb on the ecstasy of touch, the proof of reality, for we understand everything through touch." Though we may wish to qualify his last clause, as perhaps even Whitman himself would, Binns is probably close to the truth.

Rosenthal and Gall (38) point out the "power, weight, and deliberation" of "Blind loving wrestling touch! Sheathed hooded sharptoothed touch!" "carried rhythmically by the overwhelming presence of nine stresses in a twelve-syllable line." They offer an attractive reading that the context does not sustain. The first half of the line, they state, "is an excellent image for a man's sensual experience of a woman," and the second part "for the woman's of the man. . . . [It presents] both sides of love-experience. And either partner could ask wistfully, tenderly, and proudly: 'Did it make you ache so leaving me?'"[95]

According to Middlebrook (59–60), "Touch is perceived to be not some external stalking predator but a 'blind' and 'sharptoothed' potential within the self." Like Middlebrook, Gelpi (196–97) offers an internal reading: "Whitman's experience combines within the individual as well active and passive responses, violence and victimization, maddening desire and maddening fear—in short, the double drive to possess and be possessed. In the imagery of the passage phallic aggressor and raped woman merge."

According to Cavitch (1985, 62, 63) "Whitman's masturbation at this midpoint crisis of the poem dramatizes the apocalyptic experience of love from which he dated the emergence of his true identity. He is pierced by a love that wounds and possesses him, like the divine arrows that pierced Saint Teresa. The force of the tongue that 'plunged . . . to my barestript heart' in #5 assails him again in #29. . . . Delighted to find the germination of his poetic self in a sexual act, he is wonder-struck over the spiritual dimensions of masturbation."

643–44

Catel (80) provides an explication of the next two lines, the theme being, in his judgment, "creation" or "procreation," which Whitman "does not distinguish. 'Parting tracked by arriving' indicates by means of a familiar image the continuity of life in sexual intercourse. This idea is *immediately* . . . expressed by a new image: 'perpetual payment of the perpetual loan,' whose obscurity is cleared up only by the context (a further proof that Whitman builds the whole and each image is merely an 'indirection'). The idea of richness potentially contained in this image is taken up again in the next line: 'Rich showering rain, and recompense richer afterward.'" Middlebrook (59–60) is of Catel's school in arguing that after the "fear" and "horror" of the sexual fantasy, "the unifying power of imagination returns, infusing sense data with the understanding, which organizes and interprets them. The recompense of surrender is insight into the creative process. The crisis mellows into metaphors that identify fertility in nature with just such surrender and recovery as the Real Me has mentally undergone in 28."[96]

645–46

Now, according to Catel (80), Whitman's "image is extended: it is no longer a spear of grass or even a plant or tree which germinates and grows. It is 'a landscape,' a synthesis of lines and colors; it is the world of external things with its splendor and power." The far more esoteric and mystical construction of Kennedy (1926, 190–91) drains the lines of erotic potency: "The allusion . . . is either to the lingam with its divine zoa,—the gate, avenue, curb, prolific and vital,—through which are carried forward all the precious results of civilization and art, or to the yoni, which is equally the gate of the soul. The second line is philosophical, and hints that the sexual apparatus of flowers or animals focuses the creative power of the universe, the power that projects upon the screen of eternity the many-colored landscapes of the worlds of space."

Matthiessen (601) also approaches somewhat timidly one of the great phallic images in our literature—"Landscapes projected masculine full-sized and golden": it refers, he observes, directly to "the forces of nature." Matthiessen apparently finds no delight in an utterance worthy of a megalomaniac like "crazy" Ahab. Or in the words of Anderson (1971, 115–16), "This is no adolescent Rousseau lurking in an alley to show his penis, but . . . a penis splendidly shown, a body 'published,' to use Emerson's term." Or Bloom (1982, 135): "the most productive masturbation since the ancient Egyptian myth of a god who masturbates the world into being." Or, more soberly, Aspiz (1987, 5): "Those vital 'sprouts,' the product of his spermatic essence . . . may be interpreted, in terms of Whitman's public voice, as the idealized poetic race who will inhabit the golden landscapes of the future, unified by the 'omnific' lesson of love, or, more abstractly, as the persona's poetic utterances—his own creative/spermatic essence translated into words."

Trial lines for this passage appear in Whitman's notebooks (*NUPM*, 1:77):

> Fierce Wrestler! do you keep your heaviest grip for the last?
> Will you sting me most even at parting?
> Will you struggle even at the threshold with spasms more delicious
>   than all before?

Does it make you ache so to leave me?
Do you wish to show me that even what you did before was nothing
   to what you can do
Or have you and all the rest combined to see how much I can endure
Pass as you will; take drops of my life if that is what you are after
Only pass to some one else, for I can contain you no longer.
I held more than I thought
I did not think I was big enough for so much exstasy
Or that a touch could take it all out of me.
I am a Curse:
Sharper than serpent's eyes or wind of the ice-fields!

30:647–661

In the I's fantasy the landscape is an extension of himself as inseminator, perhaps, as Bloom suggests, recalling an Egyptian deity or a Greek god of fertility.
The poem again becomes quieter as the I recovers from the quivering agitation
preceding ejaculation, and he perceives the kosmos in the sexual afterglow that
corresponds to the state of repose and contentment following the union of body
and soul in #5. Or, to put the passage in a musical framework, the ardor and
throbbing gradually subside, as in a Wagnerian decrescendo. The I no longer
talks "wildly" but reflectively, cradled as it were in a (momentarily) benign and
maternally protective universe.

647–51
"All truths wait in all things," Whitman writes, which, Catel (79) says, evokes another passage, "Waiting in gloom protected by frost" (25:573): "Just as the poet
waits in solitude and silence for the fatal moment when he will sing, the germ of
truth waits for the moment which will certainly come, for 'They neither hasten
their own delivery nor resist it.'"

652–55
In a century of spellbinding orators and preachers—Webster, Channing, Beecher,
for example—Whitman scoffs at their excesses, although he too is sometimes
victimized in prose and verse by his own taste for oratorical virtuosity, and
once again asserts the supremacy of feelings. In the line "The damp of the night
drives deeper into my soul," Whitman "uses a vivid, visual, and sensuous image,"
J. E. Miller (1962, 139) writes, "to describe the poet's somber emotional state.
The dominant, driving d's underscore the depth of the feeling."

656–61
Continuing in this relaxed, contented state, the I declares, "A minute and a drop
of me settle my brain." This Aspiz (1984, 387) finds "one of the most puzzling

lines in the entire poem," and then offers a perhaps overcomplicated explanation: "Sexual experts . . . generally held that the loss of semen would result in debility and mental derangement unless sufficient semen has been conserved to maintain physical and mental well-being. . . . Apparently, the 'prurient provokers' [28:622] who threaten to rob the 'udder' of the Whitman persona's heart of its 'withheld drip' have failed; he has retained enough of his semen (in Pound's phrase) to 'super-think.' Perhaps the persona was only fantasizing the sensations of sexual ecstasy while conserving the flower of his blood in order to conjure up these 'full-sized' and 'golden' visions [29:646]."

31:662–683

With the recovery of what Aspiz (1984, 387) terms his "spermatic balance," Whitman composes one of his piercingly eloquent and deeply moving passages, beginning, "I believe a leaf of grass is no less than the journeywork of the stars," in another of his glorious unions of democracy and the kosmos, chauvinism and self-aggrandisement. We hear in the background, "And that a kelson of the creation is love" (5:86), as Whitman extols the miracles of "the pismire," "the cow crunching," and "a mouse." In eight lines we move from a kosmic picture of the "stars" to a genre painting or a Currier and Ives print of "the farmer's girl boiling her iron tea-kettle and baking shortcake." Would any other poet of the century wittily juxtapose the stars and shortcake? Updike (34) describes the Whitmanesque moment this way: "The perfect democracy of stimuli . . . gives Whitman's tireless catalogues at their best a beautiful surprisingness of sequence, and an unexpected tenderness of precision as the love freely focuses now here, now there."

Symonds (89–90) approaches the famous passage from the nineteenth-century intellectual's thinly veiled search for certitude in an era of mounting doubt and anxiety: "Whitman expels miracles from the region of mysticism, only to find a deeper mysticism in the world of which he forms a part, and miracles in commonplace occurrences. He dethrones the gods of old pantheons, because he sees God everywhere around him. He disowns the heroes of myth and romance; but greets their like again among his living comrades. What is near to his side, beneath his feet, upon the trees around him, in the men and women he consorts with, bears comparison with things far off and rarities imagined."

Beach (385–86) admires Whitman's concreteness in such passages, especially the "startling" sense of wonder that renews the enduring life of the commonplace. "The logic of transcendentalism," Beach writes, "Whitman carries much farther than any philosopher or poet . . . and being somehow free from the ethical prepossessions of most nature-poets, he can give it a more complete and startling illustration than they. . . . He retains that sense of wonder whose loss in our day Carlyle considers the cause of our unfaith."[97]

670–73

In a "beautifully witty" passage, Jarrell (103) writes, Whitman depicts himself now in the act of swallowing or incorporating the world, like a child discovering the big world, which he fearlessly embraces and absorbs: "I find I incorporate gneiss and coal and long-threaded moss and fruits and grains and esculent roots." It is Whitman's "most famous passage on geology," according to Joseph Beaver (101) in *Walt Whitman—Poet of Science.* "The poet," Alice L. Cooke (1935, 104) comments, "traces his own origins back to the First Nothing, identifying himself thereby with all creation, not by the old philosophical doctrine of identity, but by the scientific doctrine of the unity of nature."

In commenting on Whitman's seeming ability to incorporate everything in the kosmos, Thomas (1983, 5) evokes Kronos, that devourer of children who seeks to protect himself from the inevitable successors, his sons, and therefore another Kronos, who "has a benign aspect, corresponding to that pristine impulse in man of which rampant possessiveness is the ugly, dangerous and sadly common perversion. 'Song of Myself' is itself written by such a latter Kronos: a 'primal god' who 'incorporates gneiss, etc.' as well as human beings and living things." Breitwieser (128) prefers to view Whitman here as "the ecosphere he elsewhere was terrified by. He is large, prolific, indifferent to instances of life, able to produce satisfactory duplicates if whim so chooses."

In a wonderful line, "And am stucco'd with quadrupeds and birds all over," which might almost be a description of Queequeg, Mendelson (200) finds more "fantasy" than in Cooper's depiction of Leather-Stocking or in Melville's delineation of Captain Ahab.

674–83

In this ten-line passage, nine of which begin with the words "In vain," the seemingly passive I asserts his incredible powers of absorption as well as his shared origin with primitive societies and primitive forms of life. Free of space and time, he acquires, in Hutchinson's (82) words, "a fluid identity; he has the power of self-transformation and of penetrating all things." At the same time it is a reassertion of his sexual potency: "I ascend to the nest in the fissure of the cliff," to the timeless womb. Or perhaps he is once more a fetus. Cavitch (1985, 65) construes the line as substantiation of his oedipal interpretation of the poem.

32:684–708

684–91

Whitman toys with the prospect of living with "placid and self-contained" animals (the adjectives somehow conjuring up the poet himself). These animals "in a prelapsarian condition," according to Hutchinson (83), are not tormented by doubt, sin, "duty to God," or "the mania of owning things." "By listing all of the things animals aren't and don't do," Wallace (60) maintains, Whitman "exposes all of the negativistic things people are and do"; and he finds a parallel in James Thurber's world, where "animals are always happier than humans, and when animals take on human characteristics they get into bad fixes, the moral being 'If you live as humans do, it will be the end of you.'" Thus Wallace sees "Song of Myself" "as a grand comic correction."

Havelock Ellis (114) draws another conclusion from this passage in his comment: "Whitman is lacking—and in this respect he comes nearer to Goethe than to any other great modern man—in what may be possibly the disease of the 'soul,' the disease that was so bitterly bewailed by Heine. Whitman was congenitally deficient in 'soul'; he is a kind of Titanic Undine."[98]

692–95

The animals bring the poet "tokens," which, he speculates, they may have "negligently dropt . . . untold times ago." Hyde (174) provides an unusually sensitive interpretation of the passage: "Natural objects—living things in particular—are like a language we only faintly remember. It is as if creation had been dismembered sometime in the past and all things are limbs we have lost that will make us whole if only we can recall them. Whitman's sympathetic perception of objects is a remembrance of the wholeness of things." Donald E. Pease (137) appears to elaborate on Hyde's insight: "Just as the person develops a personal memory through the use of signs, so, Whitman suggests, the things signified can develop a memory of the person who gave them up for signs. That is why the things in nature can recollect mankind. They are prior developments of mankind waiting to recollect man back into them."

696–708

The I now moves about in space at will—"moving forward then and now and forever"—which is part of what E. H. Miller (1979, 89) calls the choreography of this poem, reminiscent in its way of a ballet by Balanchine: endless configurations in space seem to achieve a resolution, only to unfold again. Finally, the I chances upon "my amie, / Choosing to go with him on brotherly terms," as he evokes, "And I know that the spirit of God is the eldest brother of my own" (5:84), and perhaps the loved-feared "red marauder" (28:634).

The brother is the "gigantic beauty of a stallion, fresh and responsive to my caresses," as the I now becomes the aggressor. J. E. Miller (Miller, Shapiro, and Slote, 125) finds in the stallion "the same symbolic meaning" that Lou finds in D. H. Lawrence's "St. Mawr": "a great, burning, instinctual life that springs from the deepest, mysterious sources of the blood. Lou seems to be saying with Whitman, 'I think I could turn and live with animals.'"[99] To Hutchinson (144) "This passage strongly suggests the common shamanic motif of the horse that either carries the shaman to the spirit-world or is sacrificed at the beginning of the ecstatic ascent." Whitman may be evoking Pegasus, whose friendship with Bellerophon is the subject of one of the adaptations of classical tales in Hawthorne's *A Wonder-Book,* which became a children's classic in 1851.[100]

After the I dominates and pleasures the stallion—"His nostrils dilate . . . . my heels embrace him . . . . his well built limbs tremble with pleasure"—he has no more to prove and abandons the horse. For his imagination can "outgallop" the animal, and so Whitman is ready to unfold the greatest of his catalogues and undertake another journey—"placid and self-contained," at least for a time.[101]

33:709–863

In the longest and most dazzling of the catalogue recitatives, the I soars, sails, floats, "afoot with my vision," and is often in the supine position in which he observes "a spear of summer grass" (#1), or is "impregnated" by his divine "loving bedfellow" (#3), or lies on a June morning before body and soul fuse in intercourse (#5), or is "stretched atop of the load" of hay surveying the rural landscape (#9), or is one of the young men floating on their backs (#11), or rocks "in billowy drowse" (#22), or in his bout with the sun lies in his bed and sends "sunrise out of me" (#25).

As John Bailey (144) observes with enthusiasm: "both the rush and range of it all are such as it would be hard to parallel elsewhere; and many, a great many, of the lines are not more astonishing in the exactness of the thing seen than in the felicities both of phrase and of rhythm which convert the fact into experience and make the poet's feelings our own."[102]

Tony Tanner (82, 83) fumbles to find some sort of "hidden organization" in this section, only to posit eventually that there may be "a sort of deliberately inchoate form which nudges things together," and to conclude: "The whole section requires the closest attention to see what hidden currents manipulate the surface drift; to discover the relentless purpose in the random air. Of course the poet must not appear to have a sequence in mind; all must occur as discovery, all must be noticed as for the first time."

Jarrell (114–15) has no patience with Tanner's critical hesitations or the objections of harsher critics than Tanner: "Whitman is a world, a waste with, here and there, systems blazing at random out of the darkness. Only an innocent and rigidly methodical mind will reject it for this disorganization, particularly since there are in it, here and there, little systems as beautifully and astonishingly organized as the rings and satellites of Saturn."

709–12
The "emotional feeling" of confidence and gratification with the self and the world is confirmed, in J. E. Miller's (1957, 22) interpretation, by "the image of the balloon, its ties and ballasts cast off, ascending above the world. But this image merges immediately with that of a giant self, whose 'elbows rest in the sea-gaps'

and whose 'palms cover continents.' The one image suggests upward movement or flight, while the other suggests immense power; together the images imply greater physical sight, symbolic of the greater spiritual insight that has been attained."

Miller imaginatively absorbs the I's flight into his depiction of the "inverted mystical experience" of one who must be "awakened and purified" to apprehend "Divine Reality." Middlebrook (65) believes that the I turns from the exploration of the "autocosmic boundaries of his own body (#20–30) . . . to the theme of the macrospheric boundlessness of space and time," but her terminology and intellectual approach perhaps dilute the visceral immediacy of the experiences about to be recorded and the rich concreteness and earthiness of Whitman's listings.

Steven Foster (382) admires Whitman's depiction of "an inward voyage where he steers by imaginative points of geography. He is a creature of being, a vehicle in motion." Buell (1968, 337) delights in the "beautiful eighty-line list of places visited by the singer . . . and the tremendous sense of vitality conveyed by running these and many more epiphanies together—a vitality made more intense by those phrases within individual lines whose sounds slide and bounce into one another."

The Soviet poet Kornei Chukovsky (70), who at seventeen purchased his first copy of *Leaves of Grass* from a sailor furtively, "as if the book were a banned one," experienced a shock of recognition from which he apparently never fully recovered, since in maturity he recreates his adolescent excitement:

> Never before had I read anything like this. Clearly it had been written by an inspired madman who, in a state of trance or delirium, fancied himself absolutely free of the illusions of time and space. The distant past was to him identical with the present moment and his native Niagara Falls was neighbour to the millions of suns whirling in the void of the universe.
>
> I was shaken . . . as much as by some epoch-making event. . . . I seemed to have climbed to dizzying heights from which I looked down upon the ant-hill of human life and activities.[103]

715–43

Because of the wealth of materials and the exquisiteness and incisiveness of the detail, few critics have taken time out to enjoy—criticism, after all, is a serious matter—the unending movement in space and time, the indefatigable energy, and the endless inventiveness of the I's associations and suggestiveness, all of which are part of his self-generated electrical state.

Tony Tanner (82) notes the juxtaposition of a steamship that "trails hindways its long pennant of smoke" and "the ground-shark's fin [that] cuts like a black chip out of the water" (lines 742–43)—"suggesting the vigour and movement alive in a new continent, in the air, on land, at sea." If we include the preceding line, "Where the she-whale swims with her calves and never forsakes them,"

then, within three lines Whitman introduces birth and mothering in a watery setting, the emergence of an industrial society with the creation of Fulton's steamship *Clermont,* and the recurring threat of the fin or "black chip," the unknown.[104]

744–77

Whitman's camera roams freely to capture scenes with superb detail and brevity:
the mockingbird sounding "his delicious gurgles," the laughing-gull scooting "by
the slappy shore," the katydid working "her chromatic reed on the walnut-tree
over the well." We are momentarily in Audubon's world, as the I gathers sights
and sounds. Repeatedly he tells us he is "pleased," like God, at what he has
recreated.

778–89

At one point Whitman recreates his youth when he looked "in at the shop-
windows in Broadway the whole forenoon . . . . pressing the flesh of my nose to
the thick plate-glass" (line 778). A few lines later with a gigantic leap in space
and time he walks in "the old hills of Judea with the beautiful gentle god by my
side" (line 789). As Symonds (29–30) observes, Whitman captures "the charm
of that nomadic life in Galilee, that 'sweet story of old,' as the children's hymn
expressed it, . . . [in] this mood of loving comradeship with Christ, the brother of
rejected persons, the sufferer for others, the gentle God." Symonds overlooks the
lines preparing us for the introduction of "the gentle god": the trio, the I in the
middle, his arms "round the sides of two friends" and the I "Coming home with
the bearded and dark-cheeked bush-boy" (lines 780–81). Here Whitman also
seems to evoke our memory of God as "a loving bedfellow" (3:52).

790–96

From Judea we are soon "speeding through heaven and the stars," as Whitman
refers, Cooke (1935, 99) writes, "to two astronomical revelations of the day,—
namely, the discovery of Neptune by [Urbain Jean Joseph] Leverrier in 1846 and
the discovery in 1850 of the inner ring of Saturn. . . . National pride had been
stirred by the part American scientists, particularly Benjamin Peirce of Harvard,
had taken in the discovery." Beaver (55) offers a lovely gloss on line 793, "Carrying the crescent child that carries its own full mother in its belly": "'Carrying' is a
metaphorical expression of the earth's gravitational force holding the moon in its
orbit; 'Carrying' modifies an unstated 'earth'; 'crescent' refers to the phase of the
moon (new), and also suggests the position of the foetus in the womb."

797–800

Beaver (60) offers another happy suggestion that these lines may "have as their
basis Whitman's imaginary concept of himself as a comet. . . . The metaphorical
comparison of the life of celestial bodies to ripening fruit is a novel one, which
could have been derived from another contemporary scientist."[105] Dutton (70)

assumes that "This passage provides yet another example of Whitman's use of language as a force similar in its potency to sex—'a knit of identity'—and equally able to unite the physical and homely with the spiritual."

Bloom (1976, 264, 265) observes that in "this audacious mounting into the Sublime . . . Whitman's angelic flight breaks down the distinction between material and immaterial, because his soul, as he precisely says, is 'fluid and swallowing.' . . . Whitman's ego, in his most Sublime transformations, wholly absorbs and thus pragmatically forgets the fathering force, and presents instead the force of the son, of his own self on, in Whitman's case, perhaps we should say of his own selves."

"The fluid and swallowing soul" leads Zweig (255–56, 174) to characterize the catalogue in #33 as an "impressionistic journey and gargantuan menu, . . . the world enters the maw of the awakened self. . . . Whitman's singer is not ecstatic solitary; he is not solipsist or idealist. The world exists for him as food, and he devours it with his song. . . . the poem is also a body feeding itself indiscriminately with all its senses." And so we observe "a hungry self traveling through an edible world which it learns to know . . . by digesting it."[106]

814–27

Continuing "the flight of the fluid and swallowing soul," the I now records multiple experiences and assumes many forms. "A free companion," he turns "the bridegroom out of bed" and tightens the bride "all night to my thighs and lips." This kind of passage led Thomas Wentworth Higginson (in Giantvalley, 18) to censure "the somewhat nauseating quality" of Whitman's handling of sex: "Whitman's love, if such it can be called, is the sheer animal longing of sex for sex—the impulse of the savage, who knocks down the first woman he sees, and drags her to his cave. On the whole, the condition of the savage seems the more wholesome, for he simply gratifies his brute lust and writes no resounding lines about it."

Following this scene of "nauseating" lust, the I answers the "voice" of another wife and "the screech by the rail of the stairs" is his/hers, as neighbors "fetch my man's body up dripping and drowned." Thus, as in #8, sexuality is followed, almost inevitably it appears, by death, for Whitman relates how a brave skipper went to the rescue of a stricken ship, the story of which was "graphically" reported in the *New-York Tribune* on January 14, 16, 1854 (Goodale, 203 n).

The tragedy at sea culminates in two of the most famous lines in the poem:

All this I swallow and it tastes good . . . . I like it well, and it becomes mine,
I am the man . . . . I suffered . . . . I was there.

Here, Jarrell (115) exclaims, "Whitman has reached—as great writers always reach—a point at which criticism seems not only unnecessary but absurd: these lines are so good that even admiration feels like insolence, and one is ashamed of anything that one can find to say about them. How anyone can dismiss or accept patronizingly the man who wrote them, I do not understand." The passage is "as memorable as that of any poet who ever lived, and in a different way," Mary M. Colum (300) writes.

James Wright (167) considers the line beginning "I am the man" "Virgilian . . . , one of the noblest lines of poetry ever written . . . because it is not a boast but a modest bit of information, almost as unobtrusive as a stage-direction or perhaps a whispered aside to the reader." Daiches (1955a, 110) is reminded of the biblical "In all their affliction he was afflicted." Berryman (239) believes that the "superb" line "probably includes an allusion to 'Ecce homo' and so another Christ-identification, but this is incidental to its compendious report of what the artist is up to. The Self, of course, has disappeared, been put aside; the 'I' is now Soul only, the imagination."

Denis Donoghue (29), however, objects rather strongly to Whitman's too fluent response to "the pains of others" and his identification with sufferers: "It is one thing to suffer and it is another thing to sympathize with the suffering of others, and these experiences are not identical, no matter what Whitman's equations say."

828–39

In this second appearance of a fugitive slave, Carlisle (193–94) believes that a more empathic I has gradually emerged: "he no longer absorbs the world to himself, nor regards others as simply extensions of himself." For Frederic I. Carpenter (44) the passage is also evidence of Whitman's "imaginative power of transforming himself into another person." Black (1975, 93), however, avers that, as in #10, the poet "is more preoccupied with his own sympathies than with the slave [who] still exists only as an idea by which the poet measures his humanity," which is more or less Donoghue's position. But how does one determine Whitman's or for that matter any one's sincerity, and why should the critic make the determination?

His ire ablaze, D. H. Lawrence (188) attacks Whitman on other grounds: "This was not *sympathy*. It was merging and self-sacrifice. . . . If Whitman had truly *sympathised*, he would have said: 'That negro slave . . . has wounds, but they are the price of freedom. . . . I will not take over his wounds and his slavery to myself. But I will help him fight the power that enslaves him when he wants to be free, if he wants my help. Since I see in his face that he needs to be free. But even when he is free, his soul has many journeys down the open road, before it is a free soul." [107]

840–63

Since Whitman's "poetic pores were oddly open, as were Melville's," Lewis (1965, 14) writes, "to the grand or archetypal patterns common to the human imagination," he now begins "the familiar [Jungian] descent into darkness and hell." And "Agonies are one of my changes of garments," as he becomes "the mashed fireman" lying "in the night air in my red shirt" surrounded by "the pervading hush." This may even be a replay in another key of the erotic fantasy of the "red marauder" related in #28.

Finally, Whitman reaffirms the "perpetual present," to quote Berryman (239), when he writes:

> Distant and dead resuscitate,
> They show as the dial or move as the hands of me . . . . and I am the
>   clock myself.

The I (again Berryman) "assumes the functions of Time."[108] "By becoming the clock," Carlisle (194) explains, "Whitman measures himself and his existence by a mythic or human time rather than by chronometric time. In effect he humanizes time and he skirts space. He clearly is not confined to a particular realm, for he experiences a world . . . through his awareness."

The pictures the I summons appear to mock the seeming order implied in the resuscitation of the "distant and dead." As the "hounded slave" the I's "gore dribs [drops]" flow. As "the mashed fireman" in a "red shirt," he lies in the night air surrounded by "White and beautiful" faces. As an "old artillerist" he observes an ambulance "trailing its red drip." Grenades explode, and he sees and hears "The whizz of limbs heads stone wood and iron high in the air." As the long section comes to its conclusion, he witnesses and hears another tragedy: "Again gurgles the mouth of my dying general," who waves his hand "furiously" and ineffectually. And so "the fluid and swallowing soul" in its identification with the general "gasps through the cot . . . . Mind not me . . . . mind. . . . the entrenchments."

34:864–889

The description of the massacre of Texas soldiers at Alamo on March 27, 1836, is based on the accounts of survivors.[109] Tony Tanner (83) has summed up admirably Whitman's quiet understatement, the antithesis of his oratorical excesses and his self-styled "barbaric yawp": "This is far more effective and shocking than any plangent invocation to outrage could be—it is a method which Hemingway was at some pains to perfect. It is a prose which confronts only the essential facts."

35:890–917

In 1855, Pearce (1981, 96) notes, both Herman Melville, in *Israel Potter,* and Whitman wrote of the triumph of the *Bonhomme Richard,* under the command of John Paul Jones, over the *Serapis:* "Only where Whitman had brought himself to live with the invocation by understanding it as an overmastering 'fit,' Melville transformed the episode into an appendage (or introduction) to a grotesque joke."

Bucke identifies the source as John Henry Sherburne's *Life and Character of the Chevalier John Paul Jones* (1825), but Emory Holloway (24) claims that most of the details come from J. T. Headley's *Washington and His Generals* (1847). David Goodale (203–4) finds borrowings from one of Jones's letters to Ben Franklin.[110]

36:918–932

Now Whitman turns from the heroism and greatness of Jones to another deeply empathic description of the toll of battle, the human suffering. Here he recreates the historical experience with the kind of physical and intellectual identification that historians rarely achieve. "There are faults in this passage," Jarrell (112) writes, "and they *do not matter:* the serious truth, the complete realization of these last lines make us remember that few poets have shown more of the tears of things, and the joy of things, and of the reality beneath either tears or joy."

According to Berryman (240), in the depiction of the "magnificent, dreadful aftermath" Whitman comes "closer and closer into the experience" of the dead sailors, particularly in the line "The cut of cordage and dangle of rigging . . . . the slight shock of the soothe of waves." Bailey (124) notes the "vivid reality and tender sincerity. It has not much music and little power of suggesting anything beyond what it says. But there is a genius in the almost physical closeness of its embrace of the scene which the greatest poet in the world might envy."

Richard R. Adicks (19) provides this gloss on the last three lines of the section, singling out the acoustical or musical effect that Whitman creates with unerring tact and delicacy: "The onomatopoeia in these lines grows out of the silence, beginning with 'hiss,' rises to a crescendo in 'short wild scream,' and subsides in 'long dull tapering groan.' The last line ['These so . . . . these irretrievable'], returning to the prevailing calm, articulates the fullest sense of loss and pain."

Rosenthal and Gall (40) praise the movement of this section from "the breathtaking image" of "Two great hulls motionless on the breast of the darkness" to "one of the simplest and most powerful indictments of war. . . . There is an absolute agony of war that nothing can expiate, and all of Whitman's affirmations of the positive meaning of death must be measured against this passage and the accumulated power of the last line."

Whitman seems to hesitate before he puts down on paper the frightening word "irretrievable," a word that Berryman (240) suggests "mediates between two facts for the poet: that they *are* retrievable (he retrieves them) and that they are *intolerable,*" as the lines in the next section reveal.

Some of the critics are apparently on the verge of what Whitman later calls "the usual mistake." For while he graphically depicts suffering, at the same time he reaffirms the procreant urge, the eternal continuum of renewal. Without firsthand knowledge of war in 1855, Whitman somehow perceives and hears the irony every sailor (or soldier) learns—wracking human pain, voiced and unvoiced, and the hissing sound of crude medical instruments against "the soothe of waves." The I breathes in, absorbs, the odor of "stacks of bodies" and the "Delicate sniffs of the seabreeze."

37:933–954

As in #28, the I appears to be threatened by enemies or, more probably, by internal conflicts that he momentarily is unable to resolve. Whitman "finally recognizes," Carlisle (196) writes, "how he has slipped . . . , but he cannot yet control the dying, the suffering, and the victims crowding in on him." In #28 "he reaches an orgasmic peak; here he falls into impotent depression."

Fiedler (183–84) also emphasizes the "terror" that the I experiences: "The images of pain by which he has asked to be possessed are too much for him." But the terror is to be lifted after he sees himself "as the crucified Christ, then as Christ resurrected." Wallace (68, 74), who considers "Song of Myself" an exposure comedy, argues that Whitman's "boastful egotism" is exposed "to a kind of ritual death or grand comeuppance in #34–37," and he becomes "a comic Christ figure," crucified but "self-resurrected" in #38 "as a god powerful enough" to bid corpses to rise.[111]

If Wallace perhaps overstates, so too does Stephen E. Whicher (6–7), who like Berryman tends to read Whitman in terms of a vision of the twentieth century as a waste land, which no doubt reflects his own pessimism and despair. Whicher states categorically that "the demonic recessive . . . shows its teeth everywhere in 'Song of Myself,' something like one-fifteenth of the whole being of this character. It touches with its threat the key passage on the meaning of the grass; it creeps in intermittently to darken the catalogues; and in the central sections it seizes control of the poem altogether and hammers at the poet with image after image of agony and defeat ('O Christ! My fit is mastering me!') until, cuffed and stunned, he wins a moment's respite and in that interval the transcendental vision sweeps back 'replenished with supreme power.'"[112]

Now Whitman, like a cholera victim perhaps,[113] becomes a beggar, which Berryman (240) terms "this terrible, almost funny, deeply actual, final humiliation to the poet's dignity and independence." It is true that at the close of the section the I (in fantasy) is a beggar, his hat held in outstretched hand, temporarily inarticulate and unable to extend his hand in blessing. But the text reads, significantly, "I project my hat," and we hear faintly in the background 29:646: "Landscapes projected masculine full-sized and golden"—Whitman in his phallic splendor as a fertility god. Whitman is not about to give in to despair or self-pity: "I rise extatic through all, . . . / The whirling and whirling is elemental within me." Once again he is about to re-experience rebirth and renewal, in harmony with the "elemental within me."

38:955-973

Not without difficulty, however. For as the poet rises he feels "stunned." He needs "a little time" to recover his equilibrium: "I discover myself on a verge of the usual mistake." He rebukes his arrogance: "That I could look with a separate look on my own crucifixion and bloody crowning!" Now he remembers: "I resume the overstaid fraction."

J. E. Miller (1957, 25) explains "the usual mistake" as "the exclusion of the Divine, the Infinite. What seems lost is not, as the poet had thought, 'irretrievable.' The hell, the despair, the shame are illusion, false reality; genuine reality may be perceived by union with the Transcendent, out of time, out of space. Such union results not in identification with the lowly, the degraded, the sinful and suffering, and acceptance of them on their own terms, but in infinite sympathy and tenderness and granted power for them."

According to Schyberg (88–89), the "mistake" is "denying Him." For a time the I's "sight is strangely obscured" until "suddenly" he recognizes his "own crucifixion." Now Whitman articulates, Schyberg continues, "for the first time this modern American's attitude toward the Christ-figure. Strongly influenced by Elias Hicks and his Quakerism, he pictures the *human* Christ and confidently places himself at His side." Or in the words of Dutton (71): the I has stood apart "from the activities of the world," and now learns that "Jesus was, above all, involved." Writing from the premise that the Christ-symbol is the most significant one in *Leaves of Grass* and permeates "Song of Myself," Crawley (64) terms the reference to "my own crucifixion and bloody crowning" as the "climactic" passage in which "the poet identifies himself and all men with the crucified Christ."[114]

Both Anderson and Bloom read the passage as a commentary on Emerson's view of "historical Christianity." The "separate look" of the I, Anderson (1971, 130) observes, is "the danger" man faces in betraying "his supremacy by pinning him to a role." Bloom (1976, 259–60) comments: "Emerson had prophesied a Central Man who would reverse the 'great Defeat' of Christ, insisting that 'we demand Victory.' Whitman, more audacious even than his precursor, dares to present himself both as a repetition of the great Defeat and as the Victory of a Resurrection: 'I troop forth replenished with supreme power, one of an average unending procession.' What are we to do with a hyperbolic Sublime this outrageous?" What indeed!

Waskow (180) approaches the passage from the perspective of Whitman's imagination: "The 'usual mistake' is to stay too long in the poetic night—to assume that the self is so healthy and whole that it can exchange identities endlessly, without injuring itself, or the process. The preoccupation with scenes of suffering and death suggests that Whitman senses the mistake even as he commits it; but his triumph now is to state that mistake." The "mistake" in the view of Carlisle (195) is the I's assumption that agony is his only change "of garments" (33:840).[115]

Jarrell (104) maintains that change of tone evident in the line referring to "the usual mistake" is "the essence of wit." Wallace (71), however, believes that the mistake "seems also to include the loss of comic spirit." Becoming "less the jolly one there, and more the silent one," (37:947); Whitman has temporarily aligned himself "with the quiet questioners and mockers who see life tragically rather than comically."

Wallace's reading of the "mistake" is similar to E. H. Miller's (1968, 106) explanation of "the overstaid fraction": the I "has been preoccupied with pain, which excludes or minimizes joy; he has been preoccupied with defeat, which excludes victory; tragedy, of 'my own crucifixion,' has absorbed him in the separateness of pain and self-pity and has momentarily eclipsed the comic vision of men united in joy and love."

At the conclusion of the section the I goes forth "replenished with supreme power" in an "unending procession." "Whitman here," Couser (91) claims, rescues "himself from his predicament by a rather literal *deus ex machina*." "The poet becomes," for Lewis (1965, 14), "a divine figure. Just as, by the poetic act of creating a world, the man had previously grown into a poet; so now, by experiencing and . . . melting into the world's totality to its furthest width and darkest depth, the poet expands into a divinity." Middlebrook (70, 71) considers the episode a drama of Whitman's "identity crisis" by "a reawakening of intelligence. . . . To be successful [the poet] must 'forget' something of the actual suffering his art seeks to reveal."

And Faner (169–70) "almost" hears "a strong baritone voice proclaiming these words, his ringing tones punctuated by heavy, crashing chords in the orchestra."

39:974–983

"Friendly and flowing savage" is, according to Strauch (605), a "pivotal" phrase: "it not only refers to the immediately preceding evolutionary interpenetration but it also shoots forward into the announcement of the Superman, which is given us in #40 and #41. . . . The Superman brushes aside the old gods, for god is in all." Elaborating on Strauch's conception, J. T. F. Tanner (89) attributes to the Superman "five general attributes: (1) he is athletic; (2) he is arrogant; (3) he is affectionate; (4) he is invincible; and (5) he is scholarly."

J. E. Miller (1957, 26) believes that at this point the Christ figure merges with the "friendly and flowing savage," in both instances God becoming man: "He does not conform to man's law but to divine or Nature's law. . . . The savage, man in his primitive original state, becomes the symbol of the divinity that civilized man has lost. The poet has had to strip away the errors and delusions of civilization in order to achieve his union."

The savage has been characterized simply as "divinity" (Lewis 1965, 15); "noble savage, a beloved primal being" (Pearce 1961, 80); "the American Indian" as "the American poet" (Fussell, 410); and the "native of the New World, who moves among his fellow men bestowing forms of selfhood" (Middlebrook, 75). Aspiz (1980, 157) alleges that the savage exercizes "mesmeric powers" here and in the following section, and "appears to become a primal energizer": "Electricity emanates from his body, his fingers, and his breath. The electricity of paternity charges his loins. His will is exerted to heal the souls and bodies of all sufferers. . . . As his healing powers merge with his electric love and his electric clairvoyance, he becomes the peer of all the gods."

The savage, Asselineau (1960, 66) writes, is "no other than himself." Because "Men are prone to see God in their own image," J. T. F. Tanner (90) agrees, "it is only natural that Walt Whitman should equip his future Supermen with one of his own personal traits. Whitman's 'homosexuality' was almost a way of life with him; and, certainly, he saw 'the true love of comrades' as the thread which would hold together future society, the society of Supermen." Perhaps another way to say this would be that the conception of the Overman satisfies vicariously, that is, poetically as well as personally, the longing that Whitman reveals everywhere in "Song of Myself" for acceptance, approval, tactile relationships, for, in short, "a loving bedfellow" (#3). Whitman is compelled to voice his own need through indirection in the deeply felt line (979): "They desire he should like them and touch them and speak to them and stay with them." It is a moment of shattering poignancy.

On the basis of the references to "words simple as grass" (980) and "the odor of his body or breath," as well as the power of "the glance of his eyes" (983), Middlebrook (75) concludes that the figure is "a self-projection of the Real Me, one which incorporates his discovery that his role in culture is to serve in the national destiny." Black (1975, 99) states somewhat unsympathetically that Whitman "seeks to create imaginatively an identity for himself that derives partly from the grab-bag of myths and ideas that constituted his higher education: some noble savage, some *Übermensch,* some Emerson, some Orientalisms, some evolutionary biology, some Yankee pragmatism."

Hutchinson (88–89) introduces a reservation. While the "poet is *such* a savage," Whitman is not referring "specifically" to himself at this point, but rather is providing "the audience with an appealing 'aboriginal' model . . . associated not with Manhattan but with any region of the country—and, ultimately, abroad, as the American message will become universal."

40:984–1014

"The orator 'I,'" as Marki (173) characterizes Strauch's Superman, now "resumes his greeting, and if his extravagant promises can bring to mind a huckster hawking his wares, one cannot help admiring him all the same, for his 'spiel' is superb—comic, unusual, invigorating, and irresistible."

"Flaunt of the sunshine I need not your bask . . . . lie over" reminds Robert H. Woodward (48) of one of the most famous stories attributed to Davy Crockett, who is in turn Woodward's candidate for the "friendly and flowing savage": "the time 'the very day-break froze fast as it war tryin' to dawn'—'the sun had got jammed between two cakes o' ice under the wheels, an' thar he had bin shinin' and workin' to get loose, till he friz fast in his cold sweat,' Crockett loosened the earth's axis with hot bear greese, gave 'the airth's cog-wheel one kick backward,' and 'got the sun loose.' Then he lit his pipe by the blaze of the sun's 'top-knot' and walked home, with a piece of sunrise in his pocket."[116]

After a witty beginning—with a flourish worthy of Ahab, if he had had a sense of humor, "Say old topknot! what do you want?"—the speech of the Overman changes abruptly. He confesses, somewhat vaguely, his inability to articulate his love and admits to "pinings" and "the pulse of my nights and days." Soon he voices a grandiose fantasy of himself in the role of a savior. In what Schyberg (94–95) calls the "baroque" section of the poem the I encounters an "impotent" into whose "scarfed chops" he blows "grit," assuming for himself now the role of the tenor described in 26:600–1. The I brags that "I start bigger and nimbler babes, / . . . jetting the stuff of far more arrogant republics": he sees himself as a divine impregnator or seedman and gabs about his omni-potency. This is "the compensatory *imago* of the 'rough,'" according to Kinnaird (31). In this "act of phallic boldness" Whitman takes the "'oath of procreation,'[117] that becomes the metaphor of his 'language experiment.'" But perhaps more important than the "language experiment" is the life experiment or wish fulfillment.

The I sees himself in the role of a rescuer—or savior (F. D. Miller, 13)—who ejects physician and priest from the house of the dying. To the "despairer" he offers his "neck": "Hang your whole weight upon me," he cries. The I now fills "every room of the [imaginary] house" with "armed force" or "lovers of me." And so his fantasy is played out: he embraces those in physical and emotional stress with "the family kiss" of mother-father. The orphan of the poem has created a family! At the same time the I exposes his own need.

To explain the line, "I dilate you with tremendous breath . . . . I buoy you up" (1009), Aspiz (1980, 158) suggests that the I "appears to engage in a sort of mesmeric breath therapy. His breath is no idle wind: it is a charge of his own electrified energy or the operation, through him, of the universal deific electricity." It is as if the I, Black (1975, 111) writes, "has now become the 'loving bedfellow' that impregnated him in #3 and started him off on his journey." While Black finds the I still locked in his "narcissistic world," Reiss (83) calls attention to the power of the I's "finger" or touch and the widespread belief of the nineteenth century in the miraculous "magnetism which supposedly exuded from the Great Healer's hands." Coleman (53) construes the "life-giving" as "an act of poetic communication—the gift of will and hope and insight to a defeated man" as well as suddenly to "'you,' the reader."

Perhaps not surprisingly since Whitman himself supervised the writing and publication of John Burroughs's biographical study (1867, 13), the description of the poet in the Washington hospital wards during the Civil War is an instance of life confirming art: "His magnetism was incredible and exhaustless. It is no figure of speech, but a fact deeper than speech. The lustreless eye brightened up at his approach; his common-place words invigorated; a bracing air seemed to fill the ward and neutralize the bed smells. I beheld, in practical force, something like that fervid incantation of one of his own poems."

41:1015–1049

Section 41 "explodes," Snyder (94) writes, as Whitman extols "every typical American virtue," and upon the "rough deific sketches" of the ages delineates Christ as "the triumphant American imperialist" and "the militant Westerner," which is one (perhaps strange) way of summarizing its contents. Whitman's friend, Robert G. Ingersoll (274), puts it somewhat differently: "Whitman keeps open house. He is intellectually hospitable. He extends his hand to a new idea. He does not accept a creed because it is wrinkled and old and has a long white beard. He knows that hypocrisy has a venerable look, and that it relies on looks and masks—on stupidity—and fear."

1015–33

At the time Whitman was preparing the first edition of *Leaves of Grass* he was also dabbling with a prose work that he called "The Primer of Words" (published posthumously as *An American Primer* [DBN 3:755]). His earlier jottings are more restrained than his sweeping attack on "the old hucksters" whose "rough deific sketches" are not equal to "a spirt of my own seminal wet": "The old theory and practice of classical education is to give way, and a new race of teachers is to appear. I say we have here, now, a greater age to celebrate, greater ideas to embody than any thing ever in Greece or Rome—or in the names of Jupiter, Jehovah, Apollos, and their myths."[118]

Symonds (18), like Ingersoll, defends what to the orthodox is indefensible: "This passage, though it may sound irreverent, is nothing more than an expression of the belief that theology is the subject of comparative study, and has to be considered from the point of view of historical development. There is no finality in any creed, nor can there be, because man's place in the universe is but a speck of cloud in an illimitable sky, a fragment of straw afloat upon a boundless ocean." Yet Whitman himself deleted the reference to his "seminal wet" after the Civil War when he paid more attention to the thinking of orthodoxy as he sought respectability and popularity in the somewhat sanitized role of The Good Gray Poet. Even a sympathetic commentator such as James Thomson (36) acknowledges that Whitman's credo "is a religion without God (though it often uses His name), and without any creed or with all creeds indifferently."

When Whitman claims a place for "a framer framing a house, . . . with his rolled-up sleeves, driving the mallet and chisel," above that of "the old cautious hucksters" of religion and philosophy, is he perhaps celebrating himself as a former Brooklyn carpenter and housebuilder who now with the force of his pen assumes heroic and mythic proportions? Is he perhaps also thinking of his father carpenter whom he is displacing here as well as in #40, when he reconstitutes the family?

1034–47

Commenting on Whitman's discovery that "a hair on the back of my hand" is "just as curious as any revelation," Robert Louis Stevenson (67) writes: "His whole life is to him what it was to Sir Thomas Browne, one perpetual miracle. Everything is strange, everything unaccountable, everything beautiful. . . . He makes it his business to see things as if he saw them for the first time, and professes astonishment on principle."

In successive lines New York firemen become "gods of the antique wars," a "mechanic's wife" is elevated to the status of the Virgin Mary, men wielding scythes are "lusty angels," and "the snag-toothed hostler . . . redeeming sins past and to come" apparently assumes the role of Christ.

Of the firemen Symonds (89) says, "The heroic lies within our reach, if we but stretch a finger forth to touch it" (perhaps like Michelangelo's God); and Schyberg (121) includes the firemen among the "Calamus-episodes" in the poem.

Jarrell (104) considers the "mechanic's wife" "another Breughel," while for Dutton (71) the woman as well as the farmers with the scythes "could have been subjects for Piero della Francesca or Verrochio." Both Maynard Shipley (387) and Murry (133) believe that in the creation of a modern Madonna we are close to the essence of Whitman's thought, although they may forget that on her first appearance Hester Prynne is "the image of Divine Maternity."

Symonds (94) ranks the three reapers with the "resplendid manhood" of Michael, Gabriel, and Raphael: "Do what we will, our imagination cannot transcend the stalwart strength of thews and sinews. . . . the beautiful, strong body of the man remains the central fact for art." Even more interesting, and perhaps significant, is the picture of the repellent or frightening "snag-toothed hostler with red hair," who may be a reincarnation of the "red marauder" (#28) with "sharptoothed touch!" (#29), who, in turn, may be related to the divine "loving bedfellow" (#3).

Here Whitman fulfills one of his prose jottings of the 1850s (*NUPM*, 1:67): "I will not descend among professors and capitalists,—I will turn up the ends of my trowsers around my boots, and my cuffs back from my wrists, and go with the drivers and boatmen and men that catch fish or work in the field. I know they are sublime." According to Wallace (71), Whitman "triumphs over mortality by an absurd belief in his own salvational powers." Wallace, perhaps, underestimates Whitman's self-awareness, his ability to free himself from quixotic illusions: he only *appears* to be carried away by his fantasies, or, put another way, the self-styled "furtive hen" may also be a shrewd rooster.

1048–49

With comic exuberance in the last two lines of the section Whitman proclaims himself "a creator" with the aid of his "life-lumps!" Even phrenology serves his affirmative and aesthetic posture as he anticipates here the aesthetic epiphanies of the democratic age. J. E. Miller (1962, 138) believes that the "ambushed womb" refers to "the day of his fruition" as a creator. According to Miller's construction, "ambushed" juxtaposed to "womb" "connotes a *potency* . . . of such force that it will not be denied its time of fulfillment," although the phrase "of the shadows" introduces "the uncertainty of the future."

Perhaps Whitman is referring to his own beginning as a poet, with the publication of *Leaves of Grass* in the printing shop of the most famous phrenologists of the age. At the same time he is restating his image of "the procreant urge," of which Everyman is a part, and "the shadows" may refer to the unconscious or demonic sources of art as well as to future "uncertainty."

42:1050–1091

After a witty affirmation of his creativity, the I (or perhaps the "friendly and flowing savage," another figment of his fantasy) assumes the role of an orator-father, his voice like the tenor's, "orotund sweeping and final." Paternally he addresses "my children," yet almost at once seems to lose both authority and purpose, perhaps because of the almost inevitable reaction, and guilt, following the grandiose claims of one who appears to avoid fatherhood. "Folks are around me," he admits, "but they are no household of mine." As at the beginning and at the end too, the situation will be no different: like the woman in #11 he is alone, without a "household" or a dwelling, except what his fantasy supplies. Almost as though to reassure himself, and to place himself in the continuum, he invokes "the procreant urge"—"Ever love . . . . ever the sobbing liquid of life"—but personal fulfillment, it appears, eludes him.

Bedient (13) takes a more optimistic view, from an essentially comic perspective: "Here, as head, priest, and musician of his American household, Whitman comically evolves so fast and far that he hears the hymning (but non-churchified) spheres themselves and fails to recognize the strange, equally evolved folk around him."

Now the I surveys the modern city, not with the eyes of the astonished child who revels in its sounds and sights, but as an adult who sees people, in an image almost out of Bosch, "with dimes on the eyes walking, / To feed the greed of the belly"; the indictment anticipates "Democratic Vistas" and the Gilded Age. Yet the I acknowledges that he shares the uncertainties of "the duplicates of myself": "Every thought that flounders in me the same flounders in them."

He speaks of his "egotism" and "my omnivorous words, and cannot say any less," because he "would fetch you whoever you are flush with myself." According to Blasing (122), the "'omnivorous' poet devours the world and transmutes natural energy into *Leaves of Grass,* his words are recycled into natural energy, inscribed in the grounds as leaves of grass underfoot." But throughout this section he appears to vacillate. "He has passed," he claims, "his prelude on the reeds within," probably meaning that he has learned self-reliance and wants to inculcate the lesson. But his "words are words of a questioning, and to indicate reality." Only "questioning," and what does "reality" mean to one who appears to live vicariously?

Asselineau (1962, 92–93) avers that Whitman has no clear conception of himself as "rival and model" of Jesus. But then does anyone except possibly a madman?

43:1092–1132

1092–1108

Whitman now inventories religious rites and practices of Africa, Asia, Greece, and America, moving back and forth in time from the phallic processions of early Greece to the drab processions of seventeenth-century American puritans. Such are his powers of identification that he relives—or so he professes—the emotional turmoil of the practitioners—"Ranting and frothing in my insane crisis"— once again almost out of control emotionally and intellectually, as he is during the rape fantasy ("I talk wildly . . . . I have lost my wits" [28:637]) and after his lengthy account of historical and contemporary tragedies ("My fit is mastering me!" [37:933]).

As Beaver (86) observes, Whitman regards himself as one of "that centripetal and centrifugal gang," which is "a collective noun for all religionists of all times" who have "a common goal," and "come from a common motive or source"—"Belonging to the winders of the circuit of circuits." George L. Sixbey (178) suggests that Whitman "synchronized and embodied in himself many creeds and theologies" in order "to approximate Hegel's Absolute Idea."[119]

1109–19

Whitman admits that he understands and shares the experiences not only of the believers but also of the doubters with their "unspoken interrogatories." According to Asselineau (1960, 68, 70), the "strange dissonances" in the poetry prove that Whitman has "not always possessed the faith and certitude" that he is shortly to reaffirm. Asselineau, further, suspects that "the joy which uplifts his poems has a secret corollary in moments of depression that, he claims, are without cause. It is clear that [Whitman] had never learned to analyze himself." But should we—or can we—draw this conclusion? It appears to rest on the assumption that Whitman is intuitive in his artistry and despite his reflectiveness not insightful, yet he unveils the moods and emotions of the I—which is surely a self-portrait—with extraordinary acuity and self-awareness.

1120–32

Now Whitman vaguely promises amelioration in the future while he asks people to set aside their doubts. But at once he presents a list of singularly troubling tragedies and failures. At one point he refers to a man "in the poorhouse tubercled by rum and the bad disorder," which Aspiz (1980, 57) says may be an allusion to the Kings County Hospital, part of a complex that included a penitentiary, a poorhouse, and a lunatic asylum. "The implication," Aspiz writes, "that drinking rum causes tubercles (ulcerations resembling those produced by syphilis) may seem antic, but the ulcerative nodules covering the pauper's face and body are grim evidence of his secondary-stage syphilis." Next Whitman refers to the vicious rites of "the brutish koboo" and to "the sacs merely floating with open mouths for food to slip in"—one of the ugliest pictures in the poem in which the mouth, no longer with the "orbic flex" of the tenor's, suddenly assumes a terrifying role.

44:1133–1168

1133

The time has arrived, Whitman declares, "to explain myself," and he and his listeners at his request "stand up," to complete more or less formally a celebratory rite that begins in a quiet meditation concerning a "spear of summer grass." This is a line, Anderson (1971, 218) writes, "in which the association of movement with a deliverance of the total intention is not in the least inconsequent. [Modern cant] is replaced by the imaginative project of conveying just such feelings with as much of their fullness as the poet can muster. There is no hint of the objective correlative, only the direct effort to induce inconclusive sensations and penumbras of awareness."[120]

"The reader," Foster (382, 377) imagines, "leans forward expectantly. The poet intends to participate in a divination.... As the 'unknown' unfolds, no doubt remains that this is a rough but clear approximation of Bergson's 'metaphysics of process,' ... perceived as ceaseless motion by intuition ..., the seed of [Bergson's] nonmaterialist philosophy." Or in the words of Schyberg (91), "Continuity, development, evolution receive homage ... [as] the poet philosophically looks back throughout the epochs to the first, infinite Nothing, where his wandering began."

1134–56

Smuts (61) heralds the passage beginning "I am an acme of things accomplished" as "a matchless account of human evolution." "In one of his sublimest flights of imagination," Symonds (37–38) comments, "Whitman describes the evolution of man out of primordial elements. He has absorbed the results of modern scientific speculation regarding planetary development and the gradual emergence of life through its successive stages on our globe. The picture is dashed in with broad touches from 'the huge first Nothing' to the emergence of a conscious human soul." But "dashed" seems an inappropriate word to describe Whitman's architecture and the delicacy as well as the grandeur of his lovely mosaic.

Beaver (71–72), the most exhaustive commentator on Whitman as "Poet of

Science," avers that the poet "makes genuine poetic use of the nebular hypothesis. . . . This is Whitman at his poetic-scientific best. Nowhere does he achieve greater success in depicting the vast waste stretches of time involved in the nebular formation. The 'trillions of winters and summers' is restated in the magnificent figure, 'On every step bunches of ages, and larger bunches between the steps,' the infinitely slow progression is captured by the device of time (the mounting of the stairs) and of space ('Afar down I see the huge first Nothing')."[121]

M. Beck (15) points out the similarity to the "joyous affirmation of life" in Nietzsche's *Thus Spake Zarathustra,* and Zweig (161) finds the passage an illustration of "cosmic comedy; a form of boasting, of frontier arm flapping with a broad wink and a shuffle. This Daniel Boone cohered out of a nebula; his development required 'trillions of winters and summers.'" (One of the wonders of Whitman criticism may well be the variety of responses and allusions, as here to the claims for Dionysian, cosmic, and frontier humor.) As Carlisle (200) notes, Whitman, released "from the limits of a realm or a particular place and from chronometric time . . . lives in the continuity of mythic time, yet he lives simultaneously 'on this spot,' at a particular place in history, as a self-in-the-world. He assuredly does 'have the best of time and space' [line 1198]!"

1157–68

When the poet looks down from the height into "the huge first Nothing, the vapor from the nostrils of death," he is not overcome by horror or despair, for he also perceives the fetus in the universal womb, part of the "procreant urge," which he celebrates in #3. The embryo will be aided, as he has been, he affirms, by "Faithful and friendly" arms, protecting, sheltering, and loving. Emerson writes of the "nine-months' astonishment"; Whitman writes of eternal astonishment in the eternal procession.

In the passage beginning, "Cycles ferried my cradle, rowing and rowing like cheerful boatmen," Thomas (1987, 60) proposes that Whitman gives "a new twist . . . to a very familiar American story. The providential view of a human history, in which America has been chosen to play the leading modern part, is here neatly translated into pre-Darwinian evolutionary terms." The prehistoric environment that Whitman recreates is one of wonder and love in which "Monstrous sauroids transported [his embryo] in their mouths and deposited it with care," which contrasts markedly with the "sacs" described in 43:1129.

To illuminate this passage Thomas (62) draws upon the psychoanalytic theories of D. M. Winnicott, who asserts that a creative child achieves a feeling of omnipotence "when the mother (or surrounding environment) has so empathized with the child as to anticipate its every instinctual and emotional need, so providing its fragile ego with maximum support. Consequently, it appears to itself to be the satisfier of its own needs—the creator, as it were, of its own world. This habit of confidence then forms the primitive basis of all the subsequent creative functioning which alone can produce a personally meaningful world."[122]

Cavitch (68) sums up the passage this way: "Protected against obliteration and nurtured through the ages by an adoring nature that never pushed him aside . . . Whitman at last enjoys perfect familial security in a setting free of Oedipal conflict. The limits of the universe bend closer to shelter the small but cherished figure of Whitman standing firm in the company of his 'robust soul'" (revised line 1168).

45:1169–1197

1169–79

Suddenly, after one of his "most powerful lyric flights," Schyberg (91, 120) writes, Whitman "becomes himself, positively and definitively—the personal Ego takes possession in a lyrical, musical, erotic hymn which introduces the poem's finale. Here again, as in the opening section, it is the poet personally and only he who speaks of himself and his book and defines precisely its nature and significance." "'My lovers suffocate me,'" Schyberg explains, "contains the seeds of *Calamus*," only vague intimations of which, he claims, appear earlier in the poem. Again the autoerotic fantasy of #28—the poet passive, the lovers active, the feeling of suffocation ("my breath is tight in its throat" [639])—is relived but this time with lovers and beloved harmoniously united. But, of course, it is only fantasy. Fausset (123) insists that this is "hardly the language of 'Manhood balanced and florid and full', of men and women who fulfilled their instincts in marriage and parenthood and were too healthily absorbed in the labour of life to indulge emotional hungers."

Middlebrook (76) may limit the resonances and meanings of the passage by construing it from an Emersonian perspective. "The Real me," she declares, "ushers his human subjects into himself with a gesture of delight, admitting them through the porches of every sense . . . on the basis of his Emersonian perception that mankind is actually One Man, an 'elastic' compendium of life at every stage from the 'span of youth' to 'Old age superbly rising!'"

1180–96

William Kingdon Clifford (2:269), a nineteenth-century philosopher-scientist, whose writings were edited by Leslie Stephen, father of Virginia Woolf, draws upon this passage in an article entitled "Cosmic Emotion" (1877), in which he admits Whitman into the company of scientists. "The old cosmos had a boundary space in space, a finite extent in time," Clifford writes. "But now the real universe extends at least far beyond the cosmos, the order that we actually know of. The sum total of our experience and of the inferences that can fairly be drawn from it is only, after all, a part of something larger. So sings one whom great poets revere as a poet, but to whom writers of excellent prose, and even of leading articles, refuse the name."

1197

In 1867, after the coming of The Good Gray Poet, the conclusion of this section
was altered to read as follows:

> My rendezvous is appointed—it is certain,
> The Lord will be there, and wait till I come, on perfect terms;
> (The great Camerado, the lover true for whom I pine, will be there.)

In Couser's opinion (92) Whitman's "final union with God" is presented "in
images that legitimize, by spiritualizing, his homoerotic impulses." J. E. Miller
(1957, 30) finds the description of the "great Camerado" as "the lover true" suggestive "of the symbolism of the 'Mystical Marriage' with which, as Evelyn Underhill has noted, many mystics describe their union with the Absolute." Schyberg
(93) recalls "the Persian [Jalal ad-Din ar-] Rumi[123] who also described his reunion with a friend (his real friend Shamzi Tabriz) as symbolic of his union with
God. . . . Whitman used as a conclusion for his pantheistic vision the very same
lyrical imagery as the Persian poet, that of a friend into whose arms he falls to be
united finally and completely with the Infinite and Whole."

"In bounden duty toward Whitman," Symonds (35) feels compelled to "make
this personal statement; for had it not been for the contact of his fervent spirit
with my own, the pyre ready to be lighted, the combustible materials of modern
thought awaiting the touch of the fire-bringer, might never have leapt up into the
flame of life-long faith and consolation. During my darkest hours, it comforted
me with the conviction that I too played my part in the illimitable symphony of
cosmic life."

46:1198–1230

1198

Now Whitman voices simply and unequivocally his affirmation of life and the self,
and at the same time reminds readers that he is a self-contained enigma. Whitman, Hyatt H. Waggoner (158, 159) explains, "is thinking of himself . . . as *the*
Emersonian poet, not just as a poet who accepts the general outlines of the ideal
poet Emerson had described. . . . he could find himself justified, and not only justified, exalted, in the ending of Emerson's 'The Poet.' . . . Along with the other
essays of Emerson, it made it possible for Whitman to *become* a poet."[124]

1199–1206

"I tramp a perpetual journey," Whitman declares with sonorous emphasis, as he,
in Hutchinson's words (91), "takes on the role of master of our initiation. The
page acts as the surface of the dream he penetrates to make contact. The sense
of his being with us yet being dead, of his hiding in the leaf of paper as a timeless
being emerging in time, controls the reader's experience from here to the end of
the poem." Whitman admits that he has "no chair, nor church nor philosophy"

when he leads man or woman not to a library or church but to "a knoll," with the "left hand" round the waist. "His contact is made as usual," Middlebrook (79) comments, "by way of touch. But this is the touch of secondary imagination, the power of form-finding; it invests the mind with articulate intelligence. In the company of the Real Me the mind moves to an elevated perspective—here a knoll—from which small particulars may be perceived in terms of their relation to each other in a larger whole." Instead of "secondary imagination," Daiches (1955b, 35) calls it "a symbolic gesture . . . which brings into one relationship the three factors of individual identity, love, and 'landscapes of continents.' Whitman's most memorable utterances," he adds, "are all symbolic gestures—of embracing, pointing, hailing; devices for joining the unique and mystical identity of the self with the world of his fellow men, of the other unique and mystical identities."

1207–21

Adopting the democratic vernacular, the poet directs the other—the you—to shoulder his duds and begin the journey that will lead to a hill where "we become the enfolders of those orbs," in a passage that may evoke Bunyan's allegory. "To Whitman," Schyberg (92) explains, "any moment seemed as little worthy of the plea, 'Verweile dich, du bist so schön,' as to Faust; there is immeasurable space, unmeasured time, and infinite joy beyond each instant. . . . As with Goethe, the wanderer can never pause for a permanent love affair."

1222–30

The poet sits at the end of the day with the "wayfarer" and offers him biscuits and milk, as he becomes "the dispenser of the bread of life: literally, he is the Lord." This is the third appearance of what Aspiz (1980, 176) calls "the image of the bread of life," and Whitman's "dream journey reaches its outermost limits."

The next morning the I, in the dual role of father-mother, wakens the wayfarer—"Now I wash the gum from your eyes"—and "will[s] you to be a bold swimmer, / . . . and rise again and nod to me and shout." In Black's construction (1975, 115) the disciple must let go "of Father Walt's plank, [and] he makes that disciple do what the teacher cannot, submit to immersion in the maternal sea. The fantasized disciple will therefore do what grants the master vicarious gratification (while it simultaneously justifies the poet, whose pupil outswims the teacher)." Black believes that the "fantasized disciple is a part of Whitman himself, split away from the central Oedipal constellation in order to permit some gratification of instinctual urges through fantasy."

But such a psychoanalytic explanation appears to overexplain and to limit reverberations. "Laughingly dash with your hair" evokes perhaps the last line of #11—"They do not think whom they souse with spray"—with the result that at this moment of Whitman's greatest affirmation, or greatest reiteration, he candidly acknowledges without despair the inevitable coexistence of joy and sorrow, union and separateness, fantasy and reality.

47:1231–1261

1231–33

In "I am the teacher of athletes," Bailey (46) hears "the great words of Augustine. . . . It is freedom and life, more and more abundant, that he gives to those who come to him." But one may have some question as to the Augustinian analogy. Here and elsewhere in his writings Whitman (*I Sit and Look Out*, 55, 106) insists that "teachers themselves should be athletes," as muscular as the farmers and blacksmiths he venerates in "Song of Myself." "Here, in this young, vigorous country," Whitman states with emphasis, "we want no spoonies and milk-sops—better have a little too much of the animal physique, . . . than to be narrow in the chest, shaky in the legs and pusillanimous in self-defense and self-assertion!"

1240–42

Schyberg (97) finds in these lines "the essence of the poem and its magic, that confidential tone of direct conversation establishing personal communication between the poet and the reader, which more than anything else is responsible for the peculiar effect . . . that even the unsympathetic reader finds almost irresistible." Schyberg, of course, is referring to the teasing, seductive lines that conclude memorably, "My words itch at your ears till you understand them." But as this gathering of interpretations illustrates, Whitman's words still "itch" at our ears without producing agreement as to what the words say or mean.

1244–45

In one of his most daring and enigmatic images, Whitman claims, "I act as the tongue of you." The justification for his claim "to act as the spokesman for all," Bucke observes, is "his prophetic role as 'Chanter of Personality.'" The explanation of Cox (188–89) takes into account the "growing political division and paralysis" of the age. Whitman "managed to create a poetic personality which would recognize the diversity of the national self, include all its aspects, and finally contain that self. . . . the tongue of the poet expanded itself in successive invasions upon experience in an attempt to contain America by expressing the self." Middlebrook (102) believes that the passage is tied to Whitman's attempt "to create an exemplary American hero, on the democratic assumption that all men were really poets if only they knew it."[125]

Charles Feidelson, Jr. (18–19), contributes a perceptive explication of the lines: "Indeed, no distinction can be made between the poet and the reader. . . . His new method was predicated not only on the sense of creative vision—itself a process which renders a world in process—but also, as part and parcel of that consciousness, or the sense of creative speech. The 'I' of Whitman's poems speaks the world that he sees, and sees the world that he speaks, and does this by *becoming* the reality of his vision and of his words, in which the reader also participates."

The tongue may recall 5:80, "And parted the shirt from my bosom-bone, and plunged your tongue to my barestript heart." It functions as a motif—orally and, above all, sexually, by means of displacement—providing a unity that quietly and consistently, perhaps even insistently, often eludes readers unaccustomed to Whitman's "faint clews & indirections."

48:1262–1280

1262–65

Of Whitman's summation, or reiteration, Daiches (1955b, 38) writes: "The complete self is both bodily and spiritual, and Whitman is emphatic in declaring that both aspects are equal. . . . To be capable of the proper kind of imaginative expansion, the self must not deny any of its aspects." Bidney (38) draws an analogy with Blake. "Both poets," he writes, "aspire toward a poetic-psychological model of Human Form Divine. . . . The self that is meant here, however, is no narrow ego but a soul-body hierogamy, a marriage of energy and order brought about by the creative psyche and capable of so transforming the poet that he is no longer 'contained between' his 'hat and boots.'" Black (1975, 116), however, avers that, having "neither resolved conflicts nor resolved ambivalences," Whitman "determines to keep in suspension a conflict between the superego (soul) and the instinctual drives (body)."

D. H. Lawrence and Tony Tanner focus on the line referring to the person who makes the journey through life "without sympathy." Lawrence[126] accommodates the passage to his theory of "Supreme spiritual consciousness, and the divine drunkenness of supreme consciousness. It is reached through embracing love. . . . And this supreme state, once reached, shows us the One Identity in everything, Whitman's cryptic One Identity." Tanner (75–76) draws a comparison with Huckleberry Finn, whose "great virtues are his capacity for wonder and natural reverence, and the endless spontaneity of his sympathy. This is not to force a genealogy but rather to indicate a family likeness, since Huck also is the adopted naive vernacular mask of his creator."

1269–70

In commenting on "the wheeled universe," Beaver (73) observes, "the existence of other universes comforted Whitman. A hubbed wheel is a fairly accurate way to describe the shape of the galaxy, and it is Whitman's favorite figure. A more accurate comparison would be to a grindstone."

1271–75

"Be not curious about God," the I in the role of teacher-prophet commands, but his use of the word "curious" and his biblical parallels may reveal that despite his command he has not put his own curiosity about God to rest. Carlisle (201–2) comes to another conclusion: "he is not curious about God and does not

seem to anticipate an ultimate state of being with God. . . . His call, in other
words, comes from existence; and he responds to it through his dialogue with the
world. . . . The 'Lord' remains as problematic in 'Song of Myself' for the reader as
he no doubt was for Whitman." Anderson (1974, 24–25) uses the passage for a
cogently argued critique of Whitman's glorification of what Anderson calls the
"imperial self."

> The concern about God ties us to a primal story or plot; to be concerned
> about God is to ask ourselves what is going to happen to *me?* What part do I
> have to play? This immediately subjects us to something outside ourselves
> [and] makes us immediately dependent on other people for our sense of our-
> selves. What will he, she, or they do in this or that event, what role am I to
> play? These questions are fatal to the Whitman consciousness. If I treat any-
> one as an eminence, or a "character," in the sense of someone strongly
> marked by his personal traits, I immediately subject myself to the idea of his
> existence, and I am limited by the fact. In the Whitman universe the strong-
> est emotion is reserved not for someone I love, or hate, or envy, it is reserved
> to the widest possible span of attention to things, an attention in which
> other persons appear as representatives of the "divine average," not as dra-
> matic figures.

1276–80

Cowley (xxiii, xxii) finds in Whitman "a kinship in thinking and experience" with
Indian mystical philosophies, "based on conceptions that have been shaped and
defined by centuries of discussion." Whitman, he suggests, "might be an older
brother of Sri Ramakrishna (1836–1886), the nineteenth-century apostle of
"Tantric Brahmanism and of joyous affirmation."

C. Carroll Hollis (1986, 15–22) believes that in this context of "letters from
God" Whitman is saying that "we all waste too much time and spiritual energy
searching for God, for something beyond life, instead of participating and enjoying life itself, where God is revealed in everything we experience." Then Hollis
offers a new explication, that here Whitman is talking about "horse-droppings":
"His horse-bun theology was doubtless meant to be a shocker to the sancti-
monious." But this kind of wit seems more Melvillean than Whitmanesque.

49:1281–1298

1281–89

In this exquisite chant Whitman writes of birth and death, the opening and closing of gates, the endless motion of an eternal rite, of fetuses and the manure of
corpses. At the same time he may be describing the birth of his poem, himself as
the midwife, which reiterates the masculine-feminine fusion in his person and
art. There is also another delicate instance of the Whitmanesque sound system:
the "accoucheur" at the beginning and "debouch" in the final line.

As Hyde (179) observes, "The 'accoucheur' is a midwife or obstetrician, so these 'doors' are both an entrance to the grave and an exit from the womb. . . . The poems appear in the frame of the flexible doors, and they themselves are the leaves of grass, threshold gifts uttered from the still-point where life both rises and falls, where identity forms and perishes." [127]

Aspiz (1987, 6) characterizes this section as "the hauntingly proto-Roethkean harrowing of hell" in which the I "undergoes the ultimate experience. Couched between two sexually charged French words—'accoucheur' (the term by which many professional obstetricians in Whitman's day preferred to be called) and 'debouch' (with its suggestions of both verbal utterance and birthing)—the persona descends into the primal ooze and undergoes the entire cycle of death, decay, and spiritual rebirth."

According to Burke (87, 88), "associations, taking their lead from the vital connotations of the participle 'growing' [at the end of line 1286], shift into quite a different order: 'I reach to the leafy lips . . . . I reach to the polished breasts of melons.' And do we not find tonal vestiges of 'leafy' in the two similar-sounding words of the next line: 'And as to you life, I reckon you are the leavings of many deaths'?" The melons evoke for Burke the passage referring to "baskets covered with white towels bulging the house with their plenty" (3:53). For E. H. Miller (1968, 112), "This evocation of the child at the breast of the eternal mother brings to our eyes and ears once more a line in #5: 'And reached till you felt my beard, and reached till you held my feet.'" [128]

His ears attuned to Whitman's latent wit, which escapes many readers, Chase (1955a, 71) cites the line, "I recline by the sills of the exquisite flexible doors," as rivaling in "rococo refinement . . . anything that Congreve's Millament might say to Mirabell." At the same time Whitman appears to draw upon the house or dwelling motif to evoke, quietly and complexly, construction of a building and a poem, which in turn summon up Walter Whitman, Sr., and Walt Whitman, as well as the womb ("flexible doors") and death.

1290–98

In the references to "the turbid pool" and "the moaning gibberish of the dry limbs," Whicher (6) finds that, "though no longer with power to alarm, a breath of nightmare returns and the poet must reconfirm his victory." Rosenthal and Gall (41–42) believe that here Whitman "reaches through to what he was preparing for—the realm of continued existence beyond death, a rebirth of a kind in the cold and lonely cosmos. Nothing here—although the passage does affirm—is cheerful or sentimental."

Carlisle (202) arrives at another construction on the basis of the line, "I ascend from the moon . . . . I ascend from the night": "Whitman sees death and life, darkness and day, the moon and the sun as parts of a single, seamless reality—and only in that sense are they the same thing." Beaver (53) presents a subtle, careful explication both of imagery and meaning: "The moon, a cold dead satellite . . . , is associated with earthly death—there is even the suggestion of the chemical phosphorescence of decay in 'the ghastly glitter.' . . . But as Whitman achieves perspective . . . he perceives that what appears to be death, what appears to be the moon's ghastly glimmer and extinction of life, is in reality a form of life. Implicit here is the concept of the conservation of matter . . . and of the sun as the physical source of life."

50:1299–1308

The sexual and birth imagery of the last section—accoucheur-debouch and the descent and ascent of the moon and the poet who is giving birth to a self-portrait as he reasserts his faith—continues. Something in the poet struggles to emerge: what it is he doesn't know. At last he sleeps "calm and cool" for a long time—a night or possibly a century, it matters little since he speaks in past, present, and future time—until he is wakened by the "embracing" of a friend, who may or may not be the "loving bedfellow" of #3 but who expresses a need or hunger never fully satisfied.

And now the summation of life as the pursuit of happiness folding out of and expressing "form and union and plan"[129] toward which Whitman has been leading readers from the first line. "No poet," writes Holbrook Jackson (256), with Whitmanesque hyperbole, "has voiced such unqualified approval of life, if not since *Genesis* was written and the work of creation declared to be good, at least since the canticle *Benedicte, omnia Opera* rejoiced in the splendour of the world. Whitman is Nature's 'Yes man', the personification of the Everlasting Yea." Gohdes (1960, 655–56) finds a "clue" as to the meaning of the passage in Whitman's essay, "Carlyle from American Points of View" [*PW,* 1:257–58]: the poet "is concerned with mystical intuition, the 'soul-sight' which for Whitman was indeed the 'root-centre for the mind.' What he says about this unifying intuition . . . conforms very well with the ineffability and the noetic quality considered to be characteristic of mysticism."

A recent critic, Mark Bauerlein (12), writing from and employing Derridean perspectives, reaches another, but unconvincing, conclusion: "The separations and distances of written discourse, the mediations inherent in the writing and reading processes, tend to rob language of its immediate power, oracular or otherwise. What Whitman wanted most he could not have. And he knew it. For 'Song of Myself' ends not with a mystical joining of speaker and listener but with an anticipation of 'form and union and plan' finally realized . . . well, 'somewhere'—but not in writing."

Taking into account the Calamus-like reference to "the friend whose embracing awakes me," Martin (1975, 95) attributes Whitman's "poetry of vision" to "the euphoria of the satisfied lover. . . . Its need fulfilled, the body expands to encompass the world, through its physical embodiment of the lover, who in his role as 'other' is the world."

Beaver (84) suggests that the line, "Something it swings on more than the earth I swing on," "is hardly comprehensible without an appreciation of Whitman's frequent identification of himself with astronomical bodies. Here Whitman apparently likens himself to a satellite revolving about and controlled by the central mass (the earth)."

In a reading that supports his interpretation of the poem as a "family romance," Cavitch (69) argues that as he "again faces the worrisome possibility of disintegration," Whitman appeals to his "brothers and sisters" "for intuitive sympathy that will perpetuate among his readers the family relationships he has integrated in his poem." But "integrated" may be somewhat unrealistic as a characterization of what is a lovely dream as well as a lonely fantasy.

51:1309–1320

The "Listener up there!" is, according to Coleman (57), "a reader looking down at a book. . . . this elusive 'I' has hidden again in the basic leaves pun [as] he reminds us once again that he lives in the book, however elusive he seems to be." But Coleman's reading hardly does justice to one of the loveliest lines in the poem that unveils (once more) one of Whitman's deepest, unfulfilled needs, "Look in my face while I snuff the sidle of evening." With unerring empathy as well as concern for linguistic delicacy, Burke (100) asks: "Does not 'snuff the sidle' here suggest the picture of a youngster nosing against the side of the evening, as were the evening an adult, with a child pressing his face against its breast? In any case, 'fold' [line 1310] is a notable word in Whitman, with its maternal connotations obvious in the line ['Unfolded out of the folds, man comes unfolded, and is always to come unfolded,'] where the syllable is repeated almost like an *idée fixe*."

Whitman himself asks a question, "Do I contradict myself?" and Alfred H. Marks (100) elaborates on the poet's answer with wit: "Although I may seem to contradict myself, there are so many circumstances mitigating those contradictions within me that within my size and complexity they are resolved and synthesized." According to Carlisle (204), Whitman "indicates more than a Romantic's confusion, his own diversity, or even a poet's ironic sense that he is a poet, not a philosopher. . . . Whitman accepts the illogicalities and contradictions in reality in order to find that new way . . . of dealing with the multiplicity and crises of existence."[130]

Now we are present at a virtuoso performance almost without parallel in American literature, except perhaps in Ishmael's tragicomic "unbuttoning" in *Moby-Dick* ("A Bower in the Arsacides"), a work with which "Song of Myself" has many affinities, usually overlooked. With immodest ribaldry Whitman proclaims his prophetic role. For a moment he may even sound like "crazy" Ahab except that his mockery is devoid of gnawing self-hatred, although he is, as we have seen, not without doubts. He goodnaturedly flaunts his equality with the "Listener" and by indirection once again attacks the dogmas of the "cautious hucksters." Writing in the tradition of Montaigne and Emerson, Whitman honestly avows his lack of logic and consistency. The admission, however, may be proof of his confidence in himself and his art, or he may be, as Burke says of Emerson, simply "whistling in the dark." But what whistling!

Quietly and with great subtlety—his elusive complexity is easy to overlook—the I waits "on the door-slab" for the companion who "will soonest be through with his supper." The I is outside of the house, alone, like the woman in #11. Despite the seeming self-confidence evident in preceding lines, he asks, somewhat anxiously perhaps, "Will you speak before I am gone? Will you prove already too late?" And so with the verbal optimism there is still uncertainty, for Whitman is compelled to state as well as to face reality. And so it is the last meal of the dying day, as the poet evokes and at the same time summons up recurrent imagery—houses, gates or doors, arriving and departing, food and hunger, and oral needs. The door is open, the feast is ended, and the road lies before him. The music of the song will rise in a final crescendo and then gradually fade into a barely audible decrescendo.[131]

52:1321–1336

In what Updike (35) calls "the surreal beauty of his farewell," Whitman avoids "the generally grandiose nineteenth-century melodrama of love and death." "Where else," Chase (1955a, 62–63) asks, "shall we find anything like the delicate precision of these incomparable lines?" Dutton (72) provides an answer: the final vision, "typically composed of the 'now' and the 'beyond,'" is "expressed in that all-including language which is also characteristic of Shakespeare at his most mature, language not nervous of being familiar and exalted at the same time." The close of the song "affects" Berryman (241) "like some of the late, great songs in (Schubert's) *Winterreise* and above all 'Leiermann.'"[132]

1321–23
Constance Rourke (141) was perhaps the first to recognize the humor of the spotted hawk's attack on Whitman's "gab," or "my barbaric yawp," which, she says, "might have been shouted by the gamecock of the wilderness, even though the image belongs to the cities. . . . Whitman joined in the classic comic warfare between the backwoodsman and the Yankee. Half gravity, half burlesque, in its swift slipping from the foothold of reality the poem is not far from the pattern of the tall tales or from the familiar extravagant form of mock-oratory." D. H. Lawrence also recognizes the wit behind Whitman's daring at the conclusion of his great poem to mock his pretension and aspirations, although he perhaps mocks the epic tradition as well as his own arrogance in the first line. In "The American Eagle" Lawrence's eagle

> . . . was growing a startling big bird
> On the roof of the world;
> A bit awkward, and with a funny squawk in his voice,
> His mother Liberty trying always to teach him to coo

> And him always ending with a yawp
> *Coo ! Coo ! Coo ! Coo-ark ! Coo-ark ! Quark !! Quark !!*
> YAWP !!! [133]

In a perceptive, but strangely neglected article entitled "Whitman's Yawping Bird as Comic Defense," Sydney J. Krause (1964, 349, 353–55) suggests that the final song shares "the poignancy" of #11—"a frustrated yearning and an unreturnable passion." The "spotted hawk" is in Krause's interpretation a *Doppelgänger*, Whitman immediately identifying with it since both are expressing their love to an "unresponsive mate," the hawk to a mate, Whitman to you or the public. The hawk is actually not a "spotted hawk," but "a nighthawk, which belongs to the family of ('goatsuckers,') . . . , a name given them because of the legend that with their enormous mouth (called a 'yawning trap' by some) they were thought to have sucked at the paps of goats." The male nighthawk, according to Krause, apparently gives

> an ardent and amorous performance. . . . At more or less regular intervals he swoops down often within a few yards of his mate. Just as he seems about to dash into the ground he makes an abrupt upward turn, the vibrating primaries producing the well-known boom. From that point he descends and begins a comical dance before the largely passive female, spreading his tail and wagging it while he gives his body a peculiar rocking motion and utters "guttural croaking notes." The boom can be heard for a considerable distance, and one popular ornithologist has described it—in a way Whitman would have appreciated—as coming rather close to the "Bronx Cheer." [134]

1324–28

It is twilight, the shadows lengthen over the "wilds," projecting no doubt the I's shadowy presence in the uncertain light. The poety is unmatchable: "The last scud of day holds back for me, / . . . It coaxes me to the vapor and the dusk." If for a moment the hawk mocks, the I now soars beyond the bird, as earlier his imagination bestows on him a power and freedom beyond the capacity of the magnificent stallion. Here, according to Beaver (62), the reference "is to the phenomenon of atmospheric refraction of light from celestial bodies, particularly when these are near the horizon. Sun, moon, stars, and the comet Whitman imagined himself to be, have a 'true' as well as an 'apparent' position, due among other things to the fact that light from these objects is bent as it goes through the earth's atmosphere. . . . because refraction is greatest at the very rim of the horizon, objects appear to hang momentarily on the horizon and then drop suddenly." [135]

1329–30

Abruptly the I returns from his transcendent flight to "bequeath" himself "to the dirt to grow from the grass I love." Now, as Tony Tanner (78) notes, Whitman evokes "the soft bed of sensual love" in the opening lines of the poem as well as the grass in #6 as "the symbol of the fertility of death." McMahon (45, 52) puts it this way: "the grass . . . enjoys a copular bond with an appropriate spouse," the air, upon which the "ending lines set a final seal."[136]

1331–36

As J. E. Miller (1957, 34–35) interprets the poem, the hawk and the meteor images "relate to the mystical experience from which the poet has emerged. . . . More important than the pantheism on the surface . . . is the suggestion that every man has easily within his grasp, his for the taking, the means for his own mystical journey. The poet is under the 'bootsoles' only in the sense that the clue to what he has hinted at is there for each man to discover for himself." According to Carlisle (204), the "dominant ego-centric presence," the poet, "disappears for good at the end by planting himself to grow from the grass he loves. Instead of presenting the reader with an immensely inflated Romantic hero, the poet leaves him with a more genuine and complete self—a self living in-the-world."

For Bloom (1976, 262) the poem fulfills "Emerson prophecies of the Central Man." "An effective conclusion," Middlebrook (85) writes, "derives too from the poem's ideology. To the extent that 'Song of Myself' is an allegory of imagination, Whitman is here acknowledging that the self projected in the poem is an abstraction from life, vulnerable to the claims of life. . . . The poet 'dies' back into reality as the poem ends."

It is Black's conclusion (1975, 90) that "the development of 'Song of Myself' occurs in the changes of attitude toward recurring issues and ideas. . . . his poetic method taught him to value the process of poetic exploration as much as any vision of order yielded by the exploratory journeys. By writing 'Song of Myself' Whitman learned that psychological fluidity may be more viable than any particular set of defenses."

Law (96) cites the repetition in this final section of what he calls "the soil-air-respiration-nourishment images," which are introduced in #1 and #2: "And Whitman's earlier generous invitation to the reader to 'Stop this day and night with me' [2:25] has become a timeless, godlike offer because through the interpenetration and the spiritual elevation which are symbolized in the ascendant movement of the poem, Whitman has become part of eternal existence, a generator in the universe."

As Fiedler (17) observes, "'Song of Myself' begins with the word 'I' but ends with 'you,' a 'you' believed in though never possessed. . . . It is, then, a poem of faith, its doubts incidental and repressed." The poem, Tony Tanner (79) writes, "ends on a note of sunset and death which is yet a note of calm ecstasy. For the poet has seen in death not an end but the secret of all beginnings: with perfect rightness the last line is in the present tense, and in the first edition it rightly refuses the finality of a full-stop."[137] "But the grass," Zweig (261) in effect adds, "will continue to grow, the singer will be waiting for you; the cycles of death and resurrection, like the cycle of day and night, will continue. The poem's end will not be a true ending, merely an articulation of endlessness."[138]

Rarely do we remember that *Moby-Dick, Walden,* and "Song of Myself" have in common the appearance of a hawk toward the conclusion. Melville's hawk on the last day of the chase carries off "a red flag flying at the main-truck," and is the harbinger of Ahab's death. Thoreau's "night-hawk" sports "with proud reliance in the fields of air; mounting again and again with its strange chuckle. . . . It appeared to have no companion in the universe,—sporting there alone,—and to need none but the morning and the ether with which it played. It was not lonely, but made all the earth lonely beneath it. Where was the parent which hatched it, its kindred, and its father in the heavens?"[139]

Like Natty Bumppo's majestic "Here!" at the conclusion of Cooper's *The Prairie,* "I stop some where waiting for you" is affirmation and elegy—or, in Whitman's words, "Good-bye—and hail! my Fancy." The sound of the poet's voice fades into a very faint but most seductive pianissimo, a whisper that itches at our ears.

Epilogue

The collective explorations of the readers of "Song of Myself" have yielded a rich harvest of interpretations for our understanding and pleasure, and, even when limited, are often "delicious," to use one of Whitman's favorite words. The last word will never be said, and *the key* will probably never be found. Whitman himself saw to that! The poem like the poet will always be "waiting for you."

Whitman's Catalogues

In a letter in 1856 to Thomas Carlyle, Emerson (1964, 509) characterizes *Leaves of Grass* as "a nondescript monster which yet has terrible eyes & buffalo strength, & was indubitably American," a witticism that confirms what was to become a lifelong ambivalent relationship with Whitman's book: "after you have looked into it, if you think, as you may, that it is only an auctioneer's inventory of a warehouse, you can light your pipe with it." Many years later, in 1871, Emerson is reported to have said, "I expected—him—to make—the songs of the Nation—but he seems—to be contented to—make the inventories."[1]

Whitman's catalogues have been mocked and parodied ever since. They have been likened to telephone directories, Sears Roebuck catalogues, the "untouched" records of "a surveyor's clerk or a compiler of statistics for a county council" (Bailey, 5), "market reports gone wrong" (Maxwell, 192), or "his price-current list of poetic materials" (Willard, 178–79). Instead of assuming, as Anne Gilchrist does, that Whitman knew what he was doing, which might have led to insight and understanding, some critics have apparently taken delight in cutting a poet with a gigantic ego down to their own pygmy sizes.

Even such a consistently hostile critic as Amy Lowell (505), reluctantly no doubt, concedes that Whitman will be "read centuries hence for his lists of occupations," but, of course, she finds them "Flat, flat, flat, seldom a pregnant word, scarcely a relieving gesture." Van Doren (1955, 21–22), generally a far more sympathetic critic than Lowell, believes that no one can read through them. "Somehow the review is not impressive," he comments; "it can even be ludicrous, with its suggestion that if Whitman had not come along to love these things they would have felt neglected." Even an unstinting admirer such as Schyberg (97) has trouble with the "long reiterations in which Whitman did not succeed in animating his phrases, so that they are no more than cold, uninspired prose."

Jesse Bier (387) comes to the conclusion that Whitman meant his catalogues "to be taken quite seriously, but, then, they always go on too long and encourage the expectation of deflation. . . . We await mock heroics or anticlimax, out of normal commonsensical experience." This profundity appears in a book discussing American humor.[2] Martin Green (426) not only misses the point but also plays foul: "Even his catalogues are of things he had read about, not seen and heard himself. In a word, he does not tell us the truth. Quite often, he tells lies; he says he has felt and seen things which he has not. Again and again, he makes a fool of himself; having invited us into his mind, with our keenest expectations aroused, he appears before us in a tatty series of road company spangles, cutting capers he's never properly practised."

Wellek and Warren (195) characterize Whitman's "poetic method as an analytic spreadout, an itemized unpacking, of certain large, parallel categories. . . . he is dominated by the desire to present details, individuals, parts as parts of a whole. For all his love of lists, he is not really a pluralist or personalist but a pantheistic monist; and the total effect of his catalogues is not complexity but simplicity. First he lays out his categories, and then he copiously illustrates them." But the complexity of the seeming simplicity as well as the inventiveness seems to escape the two critics.

Whitman replied during his lifetime at least twice to his critics, particularly to Emerson's comment to Carlyle. Bucke's biography of the poet (1883, 188–89) contains the following passage: "The book is doubtless open to a charge of the kind. Only it is as if the primary Creator were the 'auctioneer,' and the spirit in which the lists are made out is the motif of all vitality, all form. Or, a new Adam, in a modern and more complex Paradise, here gives names to everything—to mechanics' trades, tools—to our own days, and their commonest objects." We now know that the poet himself wrote this passage.[3] In a conversation with Horace Traubel (6:132–33), Whitman comments: "Do you know, of all the charges that have been laid at my door, this has affected me least—has not affected me at all, in fact. I have gone right on—my bent has remained my bent,—everything remained as it would have remained otherwise. . . . the *physiological* Leaves of Grass—the Leaves of Grass nursed in these native occurrences, facts—the occupations, habits, habitats, of men."

That the catalogues—sometimes called lists, enumerations, inventories, or litanies—have received a great deal of attention is understandable not only because of their novelty in the nineteenth century and Whitman's implicit rivalry with Homer and Milton but also because of their length and frequency in the poems written between 1855 and 1860, particularly in "Song of Myself." (After 1860 they appear less often and eventually disappear.) According to the compilations of R. P. Adams (129) "more than a third of the poem's length" consists of catalogues—#8 through #16 and #31 through #36. Even if we exclude short lists and consider only the two well-known and extended catalogues, #15–16 and #33, almost twenty per cent of the poem is accounted for.

In recent decades in the midst of the vast proliferation of Whitman criticism have come deeper insights into the significance of the catalogues, aesthetically, psychologically, and philosophically. This positive approach has paid rich dividends.[4]

Daiches (1955a, 112) points out that despite the indebtedness to tradition, "in tone and purpose they are unique and essentially Whitmanesque, vivid camera shots of a nation at work in all its variety and multiplicity, expert montage to project the picture of civilization. Once the poet has established the stature and function of the 'I' in his poem, he can achieve epic effects by lyrical methods." Here Daiches elaborates on Muriel Rukeyser's recognition that Whitman, like Thomas Eakins and Eadweard Muybridge, anticipates the modern world of motion in which the movie camera plays a major role in our perceptions. Rukeyser (85) explains: "Whitman, writing years before the invention of the moving picture camera, has in his poems given to us sequence after sequence that might be the detailed instructions, not to the director and cameraman only, but to the film editor as well. The rhythm of these sequences is film rhythm, the form is montage; and movies could easily be made of these poems, in which the lines in the longer, more sustained speech rhythms would serve as sound track, while these seemingly broken and choppy descriptive lines would serve well as image track."

E. H. Miller (1970, 60) finds a parallel between the radical visions of Whitman and Jackson Pollock, perhaps the most influential of twentieth-century American painters: "The endless gyrations of Pollock's over-all canvases are the visual counterparts of Whitman's verbal transitoriness. Just as Whitman's catalogues move the eye and the mind from one object to the next without regard to the usual similarities or familiar rational relationships, so Pollock's restless lines of paint ignore the four corners of the canvas and refuse to fall into the customary patterns of representational art."

Faner (168–69) suggests that operatic recitative has "the straight line, unvaried pitch, chanting effect" of the catalogues, and then illustrates by placing a passage from Verdi's *Ernani* next to #37. Lenhart (179) likens Whitman's expansion of a single idea "through many facets of human experience" to what happens in a symphony, "where a musical theme is first plainly stated and then treated by the various instruments, though with few melodic and rhythmic changes." Buell (1968, 330), however, believes that the catalogues may produce "rudimentary paeans or chants like litanies from the *Book of Common Prayer.* But often enough both tone and structure are more complex, creating tapestries of imagery and rhetoric which are fine by any standard."

Wright Morris (57), the novelist, believes that in the catalogues "the very act of celebrating himself becomes an act of transformation, not of himself, but of the world of artifacts along the road where he passes, yawping his barbaric yawp. This counting of heads, this effort to assess the raw-material resources of the continent, becomes an act of poetry, an act of possessing all that he sees." According to Karl Shapiro (67), Whitman "is the only modern poet who has the courage to meet the crowd." Daiches (1959, 34–35) believes that by means of the catalogues you "cultivate a kind of awareness of other people so complexly developed that your own stream of consciousness while you are in the act of contemplation takes you outside of yourself and achieves a new kind of relationship between your ineradicable self (which remains the core and centre of all Whitman's poems) and the external world." Shapiro and Daiches, however, gloss over the absence of meaningful interaction between Whitman and the voiceless, faceless, undifferentiated people he for the most part observes from a protective distance.

Hugh I'Anson Fausset (127, 128) describes Whitman as "a ubiquitous observer" who "includes everything in the sweep of his observant affection"—which is truly a lovely phrase. For Tony Tanner (82) the catalogues constitute the record of the poet's "wondering eye" and at the same time satisfy a deep personal need: "Whitman wants to convey his sense that somehow the teeming differing crowd [in #15] is basically a sort of family, and if we can respond to his vision then many of his so-called catalogues come alive and knit themselves together." Zweig (123, 256) also recognizes the significance of these records of "a passionate observer, 'absorbing' visual impressions, 'devouring' colors. The drama of eyesight—the world flowing variously and smoothly into the 'space of a peachpit'—would be a cornerstone of 'Song of Myself.'" The catalogues "are the very workings of self-change. The digestive and devouring action of the poem passes through them."

Lewis Hyde (163) goes one step further in discussing the undifferentiated qualities of Whitman's kosmos as unfolded in his inventories. Each element, he declares, "seems equally fascinating" because the "poet's eye focuses with un-qualified attention on such a wide range of creation, . . . our sense of discrimina-tion soon withdraws for lack of use, and that part of us which can sense the un-derlying coherence comes forward." For the poet "puts hierarchy to sleep."

Quentin Anderson (1971, 95) makes a similar comment: "It is mere grammati-cal pedantry to think of his catalogues as having the end of inclusion: at their brilliant best, they are successful efforts to melt things together, to make the sum of things ring with one note." John Kinnaird (29) argues that "we are really never in a consciously American world, but always within the purely magical universe of Whitman's 'self' and its strange visitations. . . . we are always within a timeless and 'primeval' democracy; we never find ourselves transported to transcendental realms called 'America' or the 'New World'; we are never in a world of nationalism and ideology." Leo Spitzer (275), however, finds "the complexity of the modern world" in what he calls Whitman's "chaotic enumeration. . . . This poetic device consists of lumping together things spiritual and physical, as the raw material of our rich, but unordered modern civilization which is made to resemble an orien-tal bazaar."[5]

V. K. Chari (51) fits the catalogues into his mystical reading of the poem. For in them Whitman seeks "to capture the essence of existence in the single object, and capture experience itself in the single instant or 'fact of consciousness,' and unite these enumerated objects and instants, not in any complex texture of relationships, but in the paradoxical entity of the *One that is the Many.*" Ac-cording to Arthur Wrobel (21), in the catalogues Whitman "exults in his unity with this rich and providential Nature . . . [and] ecstatically permits the self to dissolve into the larger union of all life where all contradictions are resolved into the perfect revelation of Oneness and where this cumulative imagery fuses with the self."[6]

Michael D. Reed (153) arrives at a somewhat similar conclusion by way of Otto Fenichel's discussion in *The Psychoanalytic Theory of Neurosis* of the absence of ego in a newborn child: "It is this sense of fusion, this sense of the loss of the boundaries of self, that Whitman expresses through his catalogue rhetoric. The individual ego, Whitman's persona of 'Song of Myself,' expands its boundaries to accept all things and people, and in so doing, becomes no longer the separate ego it is in the beginning of the poem, but an ego that has no boundary or only the most fluid form of definition. . . . Whitman's catalogue rhetoric expresses a fantasy that comes from the initial stage of life, the fantasy of fusion and merger with the world outside one's ego [which] is central to 'Song of Myself' from the opening of the poem."[7]

The catalogues, Gelpi (184, 185) alleges, take on something of primitive magic, "for Whitman is operating so deeply from the primitive unconscious that the catalogues act as a kind of verbal totemism on a sweepingly democratic scale. He possesses things by naming them simultaneously; he extends himself into them and draws them into definition and relationship in himself. Thereby Whitman becomes the shaman of an increasingly urban tribe."

The way Whitman looks at the world in his catalogues, Buell (1968, 330, 331, 334) claims, "has its roots in transcendentalist idealism but was shared with Emerson and Thoreau by Whitman and, to a lesser extent, Melville. . . . The fact that the transcendental catalogue is based upon the sense of the universe's spiritual unity in diversity makes it unique in Western literature."[8]

Cavitch (1985, 51) offers a correction to what may well be an overemphasis on the intellectual sources of these catalogues, when he says that they "reflect the shower of perceptions [Whitman] received as a child from his mother, when every thought or feeling seemed to originate in her or flow to her. His childhood sensations were never simply internal events; they were confused with external sensations that came to him or fled from him as part of his double consciousness of sharing his mother's experience." The difficulty, of course, is that Cavitch's thesis rests on plausible speculations not susceptible to proof.

Whitman's catalogues, then, revive and alter a form introduced by Homer, reflect the perceptions of idealistic transcendentalism, and anticipate the perceptions of writers like Virginia Woolf. Or, to put it another way, the catalogues confirm plenitude and Freudian examination of the psyche. The endless movement of the surveys, with vantage points on land and from the air, achieves the kaleidoscopic coverage of the modern camera, conforms to modern scientific theories of a universe in flux, and at the same time unfolds American, and human, diversity. Detailed analysis of individual lines will reveal autobiographical associations as well as subtle concealed relationships of various kinds. The seeming disorder of Whitman's lists has its own kind of order and logic that may elude readers unless they undertake the enormously difficult task of seeking out through understanding and, more important perhaps, feeling the poet's complex sensibility.

Perhaps Whitman himself should have the last word. In a conversation in 1889 with Horace Traubel (4:324), he observed of his critics: "It is that catalogue business that wrecks them all—that hauls them up short, that determines their opposition: they shudder at it. . . . They call the catalogue names: but suppose they do? it *is* names: but what could be more poetic than names? . . . I have often resolved within myself that I would write a book on names—simply names: it has been one of my pet ambitions never realized."

Notes

Introduction

1 *Essays from "The Critic"* (Boston: Osgood, 1882), 177.

2 References in the text and the notes cite the author's name followed by a page number. If the author has written several works, the reference reads: Smith 1958, 17. Full descriptions appear in the Bibliography.

3 Although Berryman (388) wrote the essay in 1957, it was published posthumously in 1976.

4 Edward Fitzgerald observes in a letter: "I often think it is not the poetical imagination, but bare Science that every day more and more unrolls a greater epic than the Iliad— the history of the World, the infinitudes of Space and Time." See Robert Bernard Martin, *With Friends Possessed—A Life of Edward Fitzgerald* (New York: Atheneum, 1985), 140.

5 *Gilgamesh*, a Babylonian epic written about 2000 B.C., records the education of a youth who, to establish a name for himself, must encounter "the demonic Humbaba," and "pass through the stages of melancholia and dissolution of the self." The epic presents "the paradigm of primary social relationships: male bonding, husband and wife, brother and brother." See John Gardner and John Maier, *Gilgamesh* (New York: Knopf, 1984), 15, 42.

6 See also Fiedler (13) and Holbrook Jackson (258), who writes of "a continuum of moods with a will to live and grow."

7 See also Henseler (30).

8 Burroughs's assertion that the poet himself provides the unity of the poem is essentially repeated by Schmidt (233), Canby (113), and Daiches (1955a, 113).

9 J. E. Miller (1957, 14) acknowledges that he is "among those critics who highlight some significant aspects, leaving other and important things conveniently untouched." Although his own approach to the poem is predominantly mystical in orientation, Tuveson (212) rejects the schematization of Miller's "inverted mysticism." "We should not expect any formal, articulated structure," Tuveson maintains. "The 'forming Spirit' in unfolding itself seems to tumble together all the aesthetic forms, without rational composition." Berryman (232) also objects to Miller's terminology.

10 For additional "partitive" structures, see McElderry, F. D. Miller, Nagle, Pollak, and Robbins. Levine (471) seeks to demonstrate that Whitman reflects "contemporary political concerns in the figurative language" of his poem by means of "a three-part plot . . . , a structure of Union [#1–24], Disunion [#25–29], 'crisis sections', and Reunion [#30ff], which anticipates the painful trajectory of American destiny in the era of the Civil War." Note also Fasel (19–23).

The Mosaic of Interpretations

1 David Morse (165) describes Whitman's entrance into poetry with bounciness: "Whitman appears before a startled Parnassus as the first poetic trade unionist, presenting a series of non-negotiable demands and brusquely determined to carry the day." Roberts W. French (1981, 2) characterizes Whitman's voice as "that of a man possessed. He has had a vision that will not let him go; it has taken hold of him and changed his life. Like the Old Testament prophets, [Whitman] must proclaim what has been revealed to him."

2 Lieber (79) describes the I as "that aspect of selfhood which is individual" and "soul" as "that aspect of selfhood which is both individual and cosmic."

3 See the manuscript as reproduced by Anderson (1974, 156): "while old as creation" is Whitman's addition to Bucke's text.

4 Cox (188) observes that grass "for Whitman is as plurisignitive as the scarlet letter is for Hawthorne." J. E. Miller (1962, 115) asserts that "the leaf of grass has no limits in its symbolic meaning—it means *everything, all*, the *total.*" See also Gelpi (183).

5 See Anderson (1971, 161–62) and also Cooke (1950, 229–30).

6 See also Fausset (126).

7 As for bodily parts, the mouth and the genitals are more visible and significant in the poem than the lungs.

8 Calvin Bedient (15–16) concludes that the sounds of the two vulgarisms in this passage—"mad for it" and "belched"—"were invariably healthy; they could not offend, God himself would smile at them."

9 See also Adams, in 24:529–44 below.

10 Personal communication.

11 See *CRE*, 30–31n; also Lewis (1965, 6).

12 See Breitwieser (131) for a remarkable construction of this passage: "'Stout as a horse,' [the I] is not guilty of the gritless representativeness of the antebellum presidents." See also Fausset (129) and E. H. Miller (1979, 85).

13 Stephen Adams (7–8) offers the suggestion that Whitman's silence is the equivalent of the "sublime of silence" found in the luminist painters of the era. Adams also quotes Claes Oldenburg, an idiosyncratic twentieth-century American sculptor: Whitman "is the master of nothing happening. He is supersensitive to silences and long periods." Adams relates this quality of Whitman's poetry "to his interest in the East . . . ; it also links Whitman to the luminists, whose reflectiveness and characteristic empty spaces suggest parallels with Oriental art."

14 Shephard (1953, 73) suggests that the "divinity of the bedfellow is lost by a shift to the lower case."

15 Gelpi's commentary is in part anticipated by E. H. Miller (1968, 90).

16 Burke (88) also suggests that the baskets may "correspond food-wise" to the "polished breasts of melons" in 49:1287.

17 See also Black (1975, 102–3).

18 Renner's source for this construction is Peter L. Berger's *The Sacred Canopy: Elements of a Sociological Theory of Religion* (Garden City: Doubleday, 1967).

19 See Thoreau's *Journals*, 1852 August 8 (4:291); and *The Variorum Walden*, ed. Walter Harding (New York: Twayne, 1962), 122.

20 See also 43:1107–19 below.

21 See also Cowley (xii–xiii, xvii). John Updike (33) believes that Whitman "was no doubt

inspired by a personal experience, sexual or mystical." Others are convinced that Whitman describes a sexual experience with a male, not necessarily real but fantasized. On July 22, 1878, Whitman experienced a similar visitation or epiphany; see *PW,* 1:174–75.

22 See Allen (1946, 242–43), and Asselineau (1962, 9). Whitman comments (*PW,* 1:250) on the doctrine of Quakers pertaining to "birth in the soul."

23 Howard might have noted also that while Whitman's vision seems to unite him to his "brothers," Emerson is released from such bonds to become "the lover of uncontained and immortal beauty." See *Emerson's "Nature"—Origin, Growth, Meaning,* ed. Merton M. Sealts, Jr., and Alfred R. Ferguson (New York: Dodd, Mead, 1969), 8. In addition, Whitman's sexualization of the experience has no counterpart in Emerson, Hicks, or Hegel.

24 Allen (1955a, 158) observes that "the union of body and soul in sexual terms . . . is a problem for the psychoanalysts."

25 Michael Orth (18) disagrees: "Fellatio leading to *Samhadi,* to love and union with the ultimate, is completely in keeping with the imagery of the rest of the poem."

26 Similarly Kepner (195–96) argues that in this "sexual-mystical moment of insight" Whitman "can see the soul in every part of his body." In contrast with Nambiar's reading of the line, "How you settled your head athwart my hips," Sarracino (5–6) interprets the act as "an image of a turning back upon oneself, a circle, for his soul 'turns over' upon him, turns inward in an experience of union rendered in sexual terms."

On the basis of vaguely similar parallels, Massud Farzan (574) proposes that "it is altogether conceivable that Whitman had been influenced more by Persian Sufi poetry than any other mystical works." Farzan is no more convincing than Lord Strangford, who cited parallels in 1866; see Blodgett (198). Conway (1:218) also notes "the marvelous resemblance . . . to ancient Persian poetry."

27 Kaplan (191n, 200n) observes that Vincent van Gogh may have been referring to this passage in a letter to his sister in 1888 (*The Complete Letters of Vincent van Gogh* [Greenwich: New York Graphic Society, 1958?], 3:445). He finds a "counterpart to the ecstasy" in Rainer Maria Rilke's account of a mystical experience (*Duino Elegies* [New York: Norton, 1939], 124–27) and Tennyson's description of what he calls "a kind of waking trance" (see Walter Franklin Prince, *Noted Witnesses for Psychic Occurrences* [Boston, 1928], 144).

A change in emphasis in Whitman criticism may be indicated in the treatment of mysticism in the two versions of Allen's *Handbook,* 1946 and 1975: the discussion of the subject contracts from fifteen pages (241–54) to ten pages (192–201).

28 See also Black (1975, 104n).

29 White (356) is too clinical when he states categorically that Whitman "is afraid of the very feminine woman because she is a challenge to his masculinity and because she is a rival for his subconscious love object." Rich (17) maintains that Whitman's "homoerotic poetry does not represent a flight from woman but a recognition of woman." Erik Erikson (207–8) corrects the simplistic treatment of bisexuality that one frequently finds in literary commentary.

30 See Zweig's somewhat similar account (252–53).

31 Middlebrook (46–47) comes essentially to the same conclusion by equating Whitman's Soul with Coleridge's Imagination. See also Couser (83–84) and Gatta (176, 180).

32 Pease (144) has a strained explanation of the "hum" of the "valved voice": "In 1855, very few people were humming. The terms that could hum along with their speech had

entered into the terms of the national debate. When, in this passage, Whitman turns these terms of dispute back into a 'hum,' he means to bring the nation's arguments back into harmony with the preagreed-upon principles." Allen Grossman (195–96) considers the sexual union "as a moment of primal consciousness," from which is obtained "an unprecedented trope of inclusion. . . . The log of presence . . . attendant upon the reduction of all things to appearance [is] the reduction of all things to univocal meaning . . . continuity figured as the 'hum' of subvocal, absorbed, multitudinous, continuously regulated 'valved' voice, or 'this soul.'" Such intellectualizations would have been almost incomprehensible to Dr. John Johnston, an English admirer who found emotional as well as intellectual gratification in Whitman's poetry. In a letter to the poet in 1891 he recalled "the sound of your 'valved voice,' and I seem to live over again those two red letter—nay rather epoch-making—days of my life which I spent with *you*, my dear, old Camerado & Elder Brother"; see *Corr.* 5:184n.

33 According to French (1981, 2), the merger of body and soul "has brought the poet to a new awareness of existence; he has gone to the center and found there, as Dante did, the love that moves the sun and other stars. From this experience comes the prophetic force that generates 'Song of Myself.'"

34 Blasing (123) offers this catalogue of Whitman's catalogue: "the grass is a 'flag' of his hopeful 'disposition,' an objective sign of a subjective or psychological nature; it is a 'remembrancer' of the Lord, a token 'designedly dropt' from above, to signify divine immanence and sanction; it is a tautological answer to the questioner, 'the produced babe of the vegetation' mirroring the 'child'; it is the 'uncut hair of graves,' or death absorbing and transforming all meanings into nature; it is language both as a physiological process—nature's oral music of 'so many uttering tongues'—and as writing, a 'uniform hieroglyphic'; and like any theory of language, it implies a politics, for its universal literacy underwrites democratic equality."

35 For other discussions of slavery, see #10 below.

36 The commentary on this section is neither lengthy nor impressive, partly perhaps because Whitman here repeats themes and motifs. Reiss (85) proposes that line 124, "I pass death with the dying, and birth with the new-washed babe," is attributable to nineteenth-century interests in clairvoyance and confrontations with "extra-terrestrial beings." But overemphasis on "animal magnetism" warps Reiss's discussion and perspective.

   "To draw attention to the poem's function as a social drama that passes both poet and reader through a process of transformation," Jeffrey Steele (75, 78–79) proposes that Whitman presents himself in the "merge" passage as "the reader's 'lover,' . . . tenaciously demanding sexual engagement, ultimately inseminating us with his meaning. . . . The effect of this is to place the reader in a classically feminine position, subject to the demands of a patriarchal voice that molds 'her' consciousness."

37 According to Martin (1975, 89–90), Whitman depicts "the progress of life through sexual metaphor" concealed in the pictures of the child in the cradle, the couple on the "bushy hill," and the suicide. Then he draws this somewhat farfetched conclusion: Whitman "must accept the penis beneath the foreskin, the erect penis, and the penis after intercourse," which, we are informed, constitutes "an acceptance of life as a whole in all its multiplicity."

38 Asselineau (1962, 234) points out that "pave" is a "personal abbreviation of 'pavement' and 'sluff' [of bootsoles] a personal onomatopeia."

39 Daiches (1959, 47) finds parallels in Whitman's Brooklyn and T. S. Eliot's London: "Both poets were similarly aware of the rhythms of modern life. Both used the mosaic of ideas, the special kind of poetic dialectic achieved by patterning fragments of the civilisation you are presenting into a kind of eloquent and symbolic jigsaw. Whitman did that in his own way before Eliot did and it seems to me that no American poet, whether he accepts or rejects Whitman, can fail to have profited."

40 Jerome Loving (81) concurs: "Whitman sounds like an abolitionist [here], but he was really concerned about the white man."

41 Evidently unaware of Crawley's comment, White (354) also finds the I "Christlike" in this passage.

42 In comparison with Bradley's, Georgiana Pollak's metrical discussion (384–94) is naive.

43 Hyde (179–81) also refers to Osiris and reproduces the plate depicting the god as a mummy. See also the discussion in Irwin (281–305) and Shephard (1953, 74–75).

44 See also Rountree (554) and Schyberg (99). Renner (1978, 149–55), advances the allegorical thesis that the woman is Texas, now free from Mexican tyranny, and that the male bathers are the twenty-eight states then in the Union. Thus the poem fulfills "19th century doctrines of Manifest Destiny." Although Renner believes that Whitman's contemporaries understood this construction, one may wonder why no one discovered the poet's intentions until 1978.

45 According to Martin (1975, 91), "Not only is this one of the loveliest poems I know, it is also a clear defense of the anonymity of sexual encounter. . . . The experience could well be repeated in almost any steam bath of a modern large city." Bychowski (239) finds it "revealing" that Whitman describes sexual ecstasy "in terms of a woman." See also Marki (155) and Lewis (1955, 49). Sandra M. Gilbert (130) characterizes the situation as "an encoded fantasy of transsexualism."

46 See also E. H. Miller (1968, 131, 155).

47 There are echoes of this section in Gerard Manley Hopkins's "Epithalamion," in *Poems,* ed. Robert Bridges, 2nd ed. (London: Oxford, 1943), 89; and in Symonds's *Memoirs,* ed. Phyllis Grosskurth (New York: Random House, 1984), 167. Pamela Postma (42, 43) offers an interpretation neither new nor persuasive: "The poet *is* the woman in the house, just as he is the bathers in the sea." Then she adds: "for the artistic temperament to exist, it has first to be born, and this is precisely what happens to the twenty-eight bathers floating in their amniotic sea. They are all the woman's sons; they are also the poet's poems."

48 Whitman describes "the butcher boy" and blacksmiths in *The Aurora* in March 1842; see Rubin and Brown (21, 138) and Fishkin (32).

49 Carlisle is commenting on the 1881 version of the text in which line 227 is expanded and a new line added: "To niches aside and junior bending, not a person or object missing, / Absorbing all to myself and for this song." The new line states explicitly the process at work in the poet's incorporation of experiences, views, and people for his artistic ends.

50 The source of the neomarxist commentary is G. J. Barker-Benfield's article in *Social-Historical Perspective,* ed. Michael Gordon (New York: Saint Martin's Press, 1973), 336–72.

51 See *NUPM,* 1:390–91n, 396; Spiegelman (169), and *DBN,* 2:574–75.

52 Schyberg also cites 41:1035, 45:1170–78, and 47:1253.

53 Bingham's painting is reproduced in *Walt Whitman Review,* 15 (1969):256.

54 Aspiz (1980, 57) notes the prevalence of opium addiction among Long Islanders at mid-century. See also Rubin (231, 342–44). Lewis (1965, 5–6) believes that the "lunatic" refers to an unexplained family situation and that the prostitute in line 302 is Andrew Whitman's wife. Gilbert (136) suggests that lines in Fanny Fern's "Hour-Glass Thoughts" "may well have functioned as models to be reworked in Whitman's own catalogues."

55 Carlisle's structural analysis appears in the Introduction, xxiii.

56 In *Musical Settings of American Poetry* (New York: Greenwood, 1986), 401–2, Michael A. Hovland lists fourteen settings of "Song of Myself," four of which are based on #21.

57 James B. Ransom.

58 Myers also cites 7:124 in support of his argument.

59 Harry B. Reed (130) finds a "Wordsworthian tinge" in what he calls "Whitman's Arcadian imagination"; and Orth (20) proposes that "The Body and the Soul, the poet and the night, move from their Calamus friendship into a love affair." Don Summerhayes (218) points out that the title of James Joyce's early exercise book *Shine and Dark* is "borrowed" from "Earth of shine and dark mottling the tide of the river!" (line 443).

60 Tuveson (213–14) notes that the sea "is compared implicitly, as in other poems of Whitman's, to semen." But the sea also has clear maternal associations in "Out of the Cradle Endlessly Rocking" and "As I Ebb'd with the Ocean of Life." Faner (208) likens the repetition of "sea" in lines 457–59 to passages in Donizetti's opera *La Favorite*.

61 See Richard M. Dorson (288–300) and Kenneth G. Johnston and John O. Rees, Jr. (9–10). Whitman's familiarity with Mose is evident in one of his newspaper articles discussing the Bowery; see Charles I. Glicksberg (59).

62 This passage has also been discussed in terms of Hegel's influence by Mody C. Boatright (148–49), who in turn has been refuted by Olive W. Parsons (1093). Robert J. Scholnick (386) argues that Whitman's knowledge of contemporary science establishes "an essential context for understanding his work," and discusses the influence of Edward Livingston Youmans (1821–1887) and Robert Chambers (1802–1871).

63 See also Henseler (30). The line in 1867 became "Walt Whitman am I, of mighty Manhattan the son"; in 1876 "Walt Whitman am I, a Kosmos, of mighty Manhattan the son"; and finally in 1881 "Walt Whitman, a kosmos, of Manhattan the son" (*CRE,* 52).

64 Gohdes (1962, 18) notes an eight-page description of New York roughs in Junius H. Browne's *The Great Metropolis: A Mirror of New-York* (1869). The sixth chapter begins: "A more despicable, dangerous, and detestable character than the New-York rough does not exist." Higginson, according to Scott Giantvalley (19), believes that Whitman's interest in manliness should be called "Boweriness."

65 Thomas (1987, 72, 73) insists that "kosmos" is "his trademark" and "the very distillation of his creed," but he also believes that Whitman uses the word "to criticize important socioeconomic trends in contemporary America . . . summed up in that single, controversial word 'monopoly.'" Snyder (67) discovers a Falstaffian parallel: "the 'I' makes the world his body, which he force-feeds so that it swells to the dimensions of a veritable kosmos." Wallace (58) argues that "kosmos" is a mark which "clearly reflects the swagger and brag of the humorous backwoodsman."

66 See also Charles Eliot Norton (Asselineau, 1960, 74), Higginson (83), O'Higgins (704), and Daiches (1955a, 110–11).

67 See also Gelpi (190).

68 According to Hyde (167, 166), Whitman "takes his own body to be the font of his reli-

gion," as he becomes "what has traditionally been known as an enthusiast . . . to be possessed by a god or inspired by a divine afflatus."

69 Cowley, however, concludes that when Whitman wrote these lines, "and for some years afterwards, he was in danger, as the psychologists would say, 'of losing contact with reality'"; see *The Complete Poetry and Prose of Walt Whitman* (New York: Pellegrini & Cudahy, 1948), 19.

   Earlier interpreters, reacting with Victorian defensiveness, elevate the physical and sexual into a mystical or religious context; see Symonds (48), Smuts (126), and Beach (380). Most recent commentators do not deny the sexuality; see Thomas (1987, 66, 67), Dudding (10), Carlisle (189), Gelpi (192), and E. H. Miller (1968, 28). Blasing (120–21) emphasizes the "inherently metaphoric nature of language" which "enables the poet to speak in continuous double-entendres. . . . Whitman's originally metaphoric language is a hieroglyph, in which nature and the human body are superimposed as isomorphic transparencies. Thus it is indeed impossible to worship one more than the other. Language becomes the universal ritual in which oracle and oratory, revelation and rhetoric coincide."

70 Stephen Adams (5) proposes that Whitman paints in words a dawn scene not unlike those in the paintings of the luminist Fitz Hugh Lane: "the embodiment of renovative, generative sexuality." See also Nagle (29).

71 R. P. Adams (133–34), in the most detailed reading of this passage, notes the "harmony" of the scene "with the speaker's illuminations" in sections 3, 5, 21, 22.

72 Note also Cavitch (1978, 117).

73 *Moby-Dick,* ed. Harrison Hayford and Hershel Parker (New York: Norton, 1967), 423. M. Beck (15) compares it to Zarathustra's "Speak and Break!" in "The Night Song"; see *The Portable Nietzsche,* ed. Walter Kaufmann (New York: Viking, 1954), 217–19.

74 See also Nagle (29).

75 See also R. P. Adams (135) and Bauerlein (quoted above, 2:22–29).

76 Crawley (18–19) observes that Whitman's "characteristic freshness and vitality of expression did not appear until he rebelled against forcing his ideas into preestablished molds." Until about 1847, "the ideas and spirit were there struggling for poetic expression."

77 Blasing (139) argues that since "language is self-generating and self-authorizing," Whitman is "not master of what he says; even he cannot contest his words." Yet at the same time, in a most ingenious paradox, a challenge "is made possible by his own authorizing articulation . . . and his question ['Do you not know how the buds beneath are folded?'] amounts to an affirmation." Perhaps it is time to summon Dr. Johnson to our assistance.

78 Berkove (36) suggests a pun on "receding" as "re-seeding": "the dirt recedes (or re-seeds) before the *scream* reaches it."

79 Two of the idolaters, Dr. John Johnston and James W. Wallace (58n), observe that Whitman "was endowed with exceptionally acute senses." They report that, according to Dr. Bucke, he heard "the grass grow, and the trees coming into life."

80 Fishkin (21) suggests that Whitman is recalling a fire that years earlier he had reported in the *New York Aurora.*

81 Bettini's voice, Whitman writes, "often affected me to tears. Its clear, firm, wonderfully exalting notes, filling and expanding away; dwelling like a poised lark up in heaven; have made my very soul tremble" (*UPP,* I, 257). See also Spiegelman (169).

Sharon O'Brien suggests that the opera singer's voice becomes Willa Cather's "recurrent metonymy for the woman artist"; see *Willa Cather—The Emerging Voice* (New York: Oxford, 1987), 167. One of Cather's novels is titled *The Song of the Lark*.

82 Berryman also points to the discarded passage in a draft: "I am your voice—It was tied in you—In me it begins to talk." Coincidentally, nothing more, Picasso in one of his sketchbooks alludes to "a tenor who reaches a note higher than the one marked in the score. Me!" See John Richardson, "Picasso's Apocalyptic Whore House," *New York Review of Books,* April 23, 1987, 43.

83 Like Kramer, Joann P. Krieg (29) finds "homoeroticism" in the description of the tenor's mouth, which also echoes, she says, an early version of "A Noiseless Patient Spider." See also J. E. Miller (1962, 140): "First the poet is 'sailed' by the music, a sensation made meaningful by another, and extraordinary, metaphor—'bare feet . . . licked by the indolent waves.' Such a feeling of sensual ecstasy is transformed suddenly into a feeling of violent fear, conveyed through the image of the hostile hail, suggesting that even this signature of the universe has made the poet an outcast. But next the agitation disappears; there comes in its place a quiet which, at first peaceful, suddenly seems near the stasis of death. 'Steeped amid honeyed morphine' evokes the very essence of drugged immobility and suggests an imminent disengagement with life. Even breathing seems cut off in imitation of death. Then, 'at length,' the poet is 'let up again'—an indication that he was *possessed* by the music and made to conform emotionally to its every whim and will."

84 Law notes similar feelings of suffocation in 28:639 and 45:1170.

85 Warren (1984a, 38) argues that the "poet's passive role comes clear in the use of the passive voice and past participles," such as "licked," "exposed," and "steeped."

86 Aspiz (1984, 386) suggests that Whitman may be attempting "to differentiate himself from mere self-abusers." "Mine is no callous shell" has been attributed to Hegelian influence by Boatright (140–41), whose argument is rejected by Parsons (1085–86). Fausset (120) proposes that Whitman had truly a "callous shell": "He could feel momentarily the last gasp of the cholera patient in his throat, but he could not pass beneath that into the mind and soul of the sufferer at grips with the mystery of death, as Tolstoy did."

87 See also the reply of Conner (100) to Van Doren: "The Whitman who wrote, 'To touch my person, etc.' must have found it hard to believe that the world to which he thrilled was, as Emerson said, but 'a vast picture which God paints on the instant eternity for the contemplation of the soul.'"

88 See Carlisle (191), Marki (162–63), and Rosenthal and Gall (30). Schyberg (118) avers that the "unique" experience recorded in #27 "certainly unveils the 'I' who wrote 'Song of Myself' . . . [betraying] the strange adolescence of Whitman's whole attitude." Schyberg notes similar "autoerotic" emotions in sections 5, 22, and 26.

89 See also Allen (1955a, 161), Marki (163), Middlebrook (57), and Aspiz (1984, 387).

90 In a later work J. E. Miller (1962, 146) says, "the poet achieves intense self-awareness only through sexual awakening."

91 See also Dutton (69–70): the I "cannot turn in on itself without narrowing itself; the senses are divine, but they should radiate outwards, and human beings should be like animals, they should include and not exclude."

92 Fussell's frontier thesis determines his interpretation. Predictably the "friendly and flowing savage" in #39 is also an Indian, as Whitman presumably unfolds the American experience. Robin Magowan (75) considers it "one of the great comic moments in

literature comparable to that of Lucius when he finds himself mistakenly transformed into an ass in Apuleius' novel." What is truly comic is Magowan's contention that Whitman takes on the identity of a cow and "his cowlike nature" is horrified.

93 See also Martin (1979, 27): "The references to 'sheathed' and 'hooded' seem almost certainly to refer to the uncircumcised penis."

94 See also Aspiz (1984, 387), Hyde (180–81), and #11.

95 Rosenthal and Gall argue that "questions of Whitman's hetero- or homosexuality are irrelevant" as is the "fairly explicit description of fellatio" in the trial line, "Must you bite with your teeth with the worst spasms at parting?"

96 Hyde (177) offers a similar interpretation, "the sensual reception of the other leads toward new life."

97 For a syntactical analysis of the passage, see Walter Sutton (121).

98 See also Renner (1984, 121–22). Of this passage on the animals Willa Cather observes Whitman's limitation to "physical things" in which "an element of poetry" is present, but: "If a joyous elephant should break forth into song, his lay would probably be very much like . . . 'Song of Myself.' It would have just about as much delicacy and deftness and discrimination"; see *The Kingdom of Art: Willa Cather's First Principles and Critical Statements 1893–1896,* ed. Bernice Slote (Lincoln: University of Nebraska Press, 1966), 352.

99 In an earlier study (1957, 21), J. E. Miller observes that the horse despite its "innocence and purity" cannot "achieve" the poet's "mystical experience."

100 Martin (1975, 93) notes, gratuitously, that "Whitman makes vivid the banal sexual metaphor of 'riding' someone."

101 According to Sutton (122), the journey extends from #32 to #44.

102 See also Black (1969, 226) and Middlebrook (62–63). Snyder (82n) finds "deliberate symbolism" in Whitman's numbering of this section because of its association with the crucifixion and resurrection of Christ.

103 Reiss (85) likens the I here to "a clairvoyant whose vision is unlimited"; Wallace (63) believes that Whitman's claim "of being a sort of mystic Paul Bunyan renders him ridiculous." Or perhaps a wonderfully megalomaniacal child-man, in the American vein. Bidney (39–40) points out "the degree of compassionate empathy" and the great "strain" of Whitman's demands on his readers to encompass his "vision."

104 According to Dr. John Johnston and James W. Wallace (46), after Whitman learned from an old whaler that "it was a very exceptional thing for a whale to have more than one calf," he corrected the line.

105 The book to which Beaver refers is C. S. Rafinesque's *Celestial Wonders and Philosophy; or, The Structure of the Visible Heavens* (1838).

106 Drawing upon Lacan's interpretation of Freud, C. Carroll Hollis (1983, 195–97) maintains that "swallowing soul" is metonymic rather than metaphoric, related to our first "experiential knowledge" of nursing.

107 For positive responses, see Ingersoll (264) and Mendelson (126–27).

108 Bernard A. Goldberg (64) proves to his own satisfaction, apparently, that because #14–15 and #33 deal with two important holidays, July Fourth and Thanksgiving Day, both festivals of thanksgiving, "the poet has become for the moment the main event in the New World's feast of thanksgiving—in a word, a symbolic turkey."

109 See Goodale (203n), and the eyewitness account of Dr. J. H. Bernard in Louis J. Wortham's *A History of Texas* (Fort Worth: Wortham-Molyneau, 1924), 3:239–65.

110 See Bucke's article in *The Conservator,* 7 (August 1896). Jones's letter appears in *Old*

South Leaflets (Boston, n.d.), 7:36–39. Also see Adicks, who analyzes changes in this section from 1855 to the final edition.

111 Bedient (32) rejects what he calls "the most common error" of construing the opening lines of #37 and #38 as "a genuine, even awful crisis of doubt." Whitman, he argues, "goes out of his way . . . to explain that this is all hamming and shamming (almost reprehensibly so: 'Agonies are one of my changes of garments'!)."

112 Whicher believes that "a breath of nightmare returns [in 49:1292–98] and the poet must reconsider his victory."

113 Aspiz (1980, 58) describes the recurrent cholera epidemics in New York City in 1835–36, 1849, and 1854.

114 In support of his thesis Crawley (65–66) singles out 5:82–89 and 40:1003–5, and see 10:187 and 19:372. Black (1969, 228) asserts that the I finds his identity in "the acceptance of mortality's limitations; that, paradoxically, one cannot begin to live until he has accepted that he will die." He now shares "Christ's grave." Steele (91) compares the I's experience to Nietzsche's madness when he signed letters "Dionysus" and "The Crucified."

115 Joel Jay Belson (65) argues that the "overstaid fraction" refers to "the rite of breaking the bread in the celebration of the Eucharist." Thus Whitman "becomes a celebrant . . . of Christ as well as of himself." See also Pease (150–51) and Lieber (94–95).

116 The tale appears in Benjamin Albert Botkin (29–30).

117 "Spontaneous Me," *CRE,* 105, line 41.

118 According to Asselineau (1962, 37), Whitman fulfills his claims to surpass his predecessors in the "well-defined dogma" and "precise credo" he unfolds in "Chanting the Square Deific," which appeared in the 1867 edition of *Leaves of Grass.* Robert D. Richardson, Jr. (144), finds in Whitman's treatment of the old deities "a skeptical line of thought" that is "a standard Englightenment approach." Whitman, he alleges, domesticates rather than dismisses the old myths that have no "special claims on us." See also Harry B. Reed (125–26).

119 Boatright (134 ff) refutes this position.

120 See also E. H. Miller (1968, 109). According to Martin (1975, 94), the narrator-poet wakens his lover and says "good-by," "recognizing his transitoriness."

121 Also see Conner (113) and Beach (380–81).

122 Winnicott "modifies" the Freudian view that a child's feeling of omnipotence is actually a form of regression to an imaginary, rather than real, necessity. See also Binns (1905, 101).

123 Rumi (1207–1273), the greatest of Oriental mystics, was the author of *Mesnevi,* or *Mathnawī,* and the founder of an order of dervishes.

124 This kind of explanation, subscribed to by Bloom and Middlebrook, among others, appears to represent the desires of literary historians to find a simplistic explanation of the evolution of genius. Are we to believe that without Emerson Whitman would not have emerged as Whitman? Surely the differences between the two men are as great as the similarities, which are almost exclusively intellectual. Further, the mysteries of genius and creativity are not reducible to such easy measurements: "I was never measured," Whitman claims, "and never will be measured."

125 Nothing in the poetry appears to justify this conclusion: Whitman seeks comrades, not fellow poets; love, not art. See also McElderry (28).

126 The quotation is from the earlier version of Lawrence's essay in *The Nation and The Athenæum,* reprinted by E. H. Miller (1970, 155).

127 E. H. Miller (1968, 112) finds three levels of meaning in the use of "debouch": "literally it means to emerge from the mouth or an opening, thus referring to the birth of the 'offspring' as well as to the creative act and utterance of the artist himself; in its military sense it recalls the 'sentries' guarding the sexual passageways in #28; and again in a military sense it means to move from an enclosed place into open country—all of which meanings parallel the birth throes recorded in this poem and the journey from personal and cultural repressions to freedom and affirmation."

128 Black (1975, 117) maintains that here Whitman accepts "somewhat the impossibility of restoring infantile security and the inevitability of remaining outside the exquisite flexible doors . . . , repaying with poetry the breast he sucks."

129 Herbert J. Levine (588, 589) believes that it is no "accident that the crucial word 'union' comes together with 'life' and 'happiness' from the Declaration of Independence." And so Whitman "created a poetic blueprint of an ideal America, so that his compatriots might yet retreat from disunion and constitute themselves . . . one nation."

130 According to Summerhayes (218), James Joyce in *Ulysses* (Modern Library Edition, 18) has Buck Mulligan "jauntily" quote the famous passage on contradictions; and Stanislaus Joyce in *My Brother's Keeper* "remarks that his brother made the same retort on being reproved for irresponsible drinking after the death of their mother."

131 See E. H. Miller (1968, 113).

132 In *Schubert* (London: J. M. Dent, 1987), John Reed (40) places "Der Leiermann" (The Hurdy-Gurdy Man) among those lieder in which Franz Schubert depicts "the Romantic figure of the outcast and alienated artist [and] the homeless wanderer" in "tonal images of spiritual isolation and despair."

133 Quoted in J. E. Miller, Shapiro, and Slote (75). Orth (23) terms the hawk "a bird of powerful masculinity, but also of death." According to Wallace (64), the hawk proves that "Whitman talks big in 'Song of Myself' but actually does very little." Asselineau (1962, 208) points out that the use of the word "gab" creates the "same jarring note . . . sometimes produced by the unexpected use of a slang term." Zweig (261) declares that Whitman "sees himself as a wild hawk, sounding his non-language."

William James, Sr., made the following comment on this famous passage: "You ask me 'why I do not brandish my tomahawk and, like Walt Whitman, raise my barbaric yawp over the roofs of all the houses.' It is because I am not yet a 'cosmos,' as that gentleman avowedly is, but only a very dim nebula, doing its modest best, no doubt, to solidify into cosmical dimensions, but still requiring an 'awful sight' of time and pains and patience on the part of its friends"; quoted by F. O. Matthiessen, *The James Family* (New York: Knopf, 1947), 488.

134 Hans Reisiger (10), who hears "a cry [ring] out, lonely, sad, and yet rapturous, similar to that of the nocturnal cry of a falcon," is reminded of a poem by Gottfried Keller.

135 Beaver (62) notes that the image of "white locks" may be derived from Elijah H. Burritt's *The Geography of the Heavens* (1855).

136 Snyder (103-4) argues that Whitman at the end "kills" his poem as well as "the people and things in it" and "fills up the void with a formulaic self which can be no self at all. The 'I' is no longer really talking to the reader. He withdraws within his own tautology. Rather, he seeps out into the universe and makes the universe tautological." Quite a trick!

137 The omission of the period at the end of the last line has generated conjectures as to Whitman's intention. It would be wonderfully subtle (and modern) if Whitman set out to suggest eternal recurrence in nature and his poetry through the omission of termi-

nal punctuation, as Jon Bracker (21–22) and Cowley propose, but Arthur Golden (27–29) argues convincingly that the omission is simply a typographical error.

138 Martin (1975, 95) believes that the poem "shows how the poet translates his love for the world, his cosmic promiscuity, into a myth of the wandering lover sacking his partners in all places and at all times." What reductiveness, and with a pun too!

139 *The Variorum Walden*, ed. Walter Harding (New York: Twayne, 1962), 254–55.

Whitman's Catalogues

1 Clara Barrus, *Whitman and Burroughs, Comrades* (Boston: Houghton Mifflin, 1931), 64.

2 Thomas (1987, 49), unlike Bier, has a feeling for Whitman's wit: "critics have been in the habit of casually referring to Whitman's lists as 'inventories,' while failing to relish the ironic appropriateness of the term, when applied to the work of a poet who can pointedly ask: 'Shall I make my list of things in the house and skip the house that supports them?' [22:465]."

3 See Anderson (1974, 188–89).

4 See Asselineau (1962, 103–4).

5 Curiously, little attention has been paid to Whitman's admission in *Specimen Days* (*PW*, 13) that in his youth he was an omnivorous reader of *The Arabian Nights' Entertainment.*

6 See also George Rice Carpenter (170).

7 The syntactical examination by Tenney Nathanson (123–24) despite the novelty of the approach also arrives at a similar conclusion.

8 Also see Buell (1973, 159) and Tony Tanner (79).

Bibliography

Abrams, Robert E. "The Function of Dreams and Dream-Logic in Whitman's Poetry." *Texas Studies in Language and Literature,* 17(1975):599–616.

Adams, Richard P. "Whitman: A Brief Revaluation." *Tulane Studies in English,* 5(1955): 111–49.

Adams, Stephen. "The Luminist Walt Whitman." *American Poetry,* 2, no. 2 (Winter 1985): 2–16.

Adicks, Richard R. "The Sea-Fight Episode in 'Song of Myself.'" *Walt Whitman Review,* 13(1967):16–21.

Alcott, Bronson. *Journals.* Ed. Odell Shepard. Boston: Little, Brown, 1938.

Allen, Gay Wilson. "Biblical Echoes in Whitman's Works." *American Literature,* 6(1934): 302–15.

———. *Walt Whitman Handbook.* New York: Hendricks, 1946.

———. *The Solitary Singer.* New York: Macmillan, 1955a.

———. *Walt Whitman—Man, Poet, Philosopher.* Washington: Library of Congress, 1955b.

———. *Walt Whitman Abroad.* Syracuse: Syracuse University Press, 1955c.

———. *Walt Whitman as Man, Poet, and Legend.* Carbondale: Southern Illinois University Press, 1961.

———. *A Reader's Guide to Walt Whitman.* New York: Farrar, Straus & Giroux, 1970.

Allen, Gay Wilson, and Charles T. Davis, eds. *Walt Whitman's Poems.* New York: New York University Press, 1955.

Anderson, Quentin. *The Imperial Self—An Essay in American Literary and Cultural History.* New York: Knopf, 1971.

———, ed. *Walt Whitman—Walt Whitman's Autograph Revision of the Analysis of "Leaves of Grass."* New York: New York University Press, 1974.

Arvin, Newton. *Whitman.* New York: Macmillan, 1938.

Ashbrook, William. *Donizetti and His Operas.* Cambridge: University Press, 1982.

Aspiz, Harold. *Walt Whitman and the Body Beautiful.* Urbana: University of Illinois Press, 1980.

———. "Walt Whitman: The Spermatic Imagination." *American Literature,* 56(1984): 379–95.

———. "Sexuality and the Language of Transcendence." *Walt Whitman Quarterly Review,* 5, no. 2(Fall 1987):1–7.

Asselineau, Roger. *The Evolution of Walt Whitman—The Creation of a Personality.* Cambridge: Harvard, 1960.

———. *The Evolution of Walt Whitman—The Creation of a Book.* Cambridge: Harvard, 1962.

Bailey, John. *Walt Whitman.* New York: Macmillan, 1926.

Bauerlein, Mark. "The Written Orator of 'Song of Myself': A Recent Trend in Criticism." *Walt Whitman Quarterly Review,* 3, no. 3(Winter 1986):1–14.

Bazalgette, Léon. *Walt Whitman—The Man and His Work.* Garden City: Doubleday, Page, 1920.

Beach, Joseph Warren. *The Concept of Nature in Nineteenth-Century English Poetry.* New York: Pageant, 1956.

Beaver, Joseph. *Walt Whitman—Poet of Science.* New York: King's Crown Press, 1951.

Beck, Maximilian. "Walt Whitman's Intuition of Reality." *Ethics,* 53(1942):14–24.

Beck, Ronald. "The Structure of 'Song of Myself' and the Critics." *Walt Whitman Review,* 15(1969):32–38.

Bedient, Calvin. "Walt Whitman." In *Voices and Visions—The Poet in America,* ed. Helen Vendler. New York: Random House, 1987.

Belson, Joel Jay. "Whitman's 'Overstaid Fraction.'" *Walt Whitman Review,* 17(1971): 63–65.

Bergman, Herbert. "Ezra Pound and Walt Whitman." *American Literature,* 27(1955): 56–61.

Berkove, Lawrence I. "Biblical Influence on Whitman's Concept of Creatorhood." *Emerson Society Quarterly,* 47(2 Quarter, 1967):34–37.

Berryman, John. *The Freedom of the Poet.* New York: Farrar, Straus & Giroux, 1976.

Bidney, Martin. "Structures of Perception in Blake and Whitman: Creative Contraries, Cosmic Body, Fourfold Vision." *Emerson Society Quarterly,* 28(1982):36–47.

Bier, Jesse. *The Rise and Fall of American Humor.* New York: Holt, Rinehart and Winston, 1968.

Binns, Henry Bryan. *A Life of Walt Whitman.* London: Methuen, 1905.

———. *Walt Whitman and His Poetry.* 1920; rptd. [n.p.]: Folcroft Press, 1969.

Black, Stephen A. "Whitman and the Failure of Mysticism: Identity and Identifications in 'Song of Myself.'" *Walt Whitman Review,* 15(1969):223–30.

———. *Whitman's Journeys into Chaos—A Psychoanalytic Study of the Poetic Process.* Princeton: Princeton University Press, 1975.

Blackwell, Louise. "'Song of Myself' and the Organic Theory of Poetry." *Walt Whitman Review,* 12(1966):35–41.

Blasek, Kent. "Walt Whitman and American Art." *Walt Whitman Review,* 24(1978): 108–18.

Blasing, Mutlu Konuk. *American Poetry—The Rhetoric of Its Form.* New Haven: Yale, 1987.

Blodgett, Harold. *Walt Whitman in England.* Ithaca: Cornell, 1934.

Bloom, Harold. *A Map of Misreading.* New York: Oxford, 1975.

———. *Poetry and Repression—Revisionism from Blake to Stevens.* New Haven: Yale, 1976.

———. "Whitman's Image of Voice: To the Tally of My Soul" (1982), in *Modern Critical Views—Walt Whitman.* New York: Chelsea, 1985.

Boatright, Mody C. "Whitman and Hegel." *Studies in English (University of Texas),* 9(1929):134–50.

Botkin, Benjamin Albert. *A Treasury of American Folklore.* New York: Crown, 1944.

Bracker, Jon. "The Conclusion of 'Song of Myself.'" *Walt Whitman Review,* 10(1964): 21–22.

Bradley, Sculley. "The Fundamental Metrical Principle of Whitman's Poetry." *American Literature,* 10(1939):437–59.

———. "The Problem of a Variorum Edition of Whitman's *Leaves of Grass.*" In *English Institute Annual.* New York: Columbia University Press, 1942.

Braudy, Leo. *The Frenzy of Renown—Fame and Its History.* New York: Oxford, 1986.

Breitwieser, Mitchell Robert. "Who Speaks in Whitman's Poems?" In *The American Re-*

naissance: New Dimensions, ed. Harry R. Garvin. Lewisburg: Bucknell University Press, 1985.

Bridgman, Richard. "Whitman's Calendar Leaves." *College English,* 25(1963–64):420–25.

Brooks, Van Wyck. *America's Coming of Age.* New York: Huebsch, 1915.

———. *The Times of Melville and Whitman.* New York: Dutton, 1947.

Brown, Calvin S. *Music and Literature—A Comparison of the Arts.* Athens: University of Georgia Press, 1948.

Bucke, Richard Maurice. *Walt Whitman.* Philadelphia: McKay, 1883.

———. *Cosmic Consciousness.* New York: Dutton, 1901.

Buell, Lawrence. "Transcendentalist Catalogue Rhetoric: Vision Versus Form." *American Literature,* 40(1968):325–39.

———. *Literary Transcendentalism—Style and Vision in the American Renaissance.* Ithaca: Cornell, 1973.

Burke, Kenneth. "Policy Made Personal—Whitman's Verse and Prose—Salient Traits," in Hindus, 74–108.

Burroughs, John. *Notes on Whitman as Poet and Person.* 1867; rptd. New York: Haskell House, 1971.

———. *Whitman—A Study.* Boston: Houghton Mifflin, 1896.

Bychowski, Gustav. "Walt Whitman—A Study in Sublimation." *Psychoanalysis and the Social Sciences,* 3(1951):223–61.

Campbell, Killis. "The Evolution of Whitman as Poet." *American Literature,* 6(1934): 254–63.

Canby, Henry Seidel. *Walt Whitman—An American.* Boston: Houghton Mifflin, 1943.

Carlisle, E. Fred. *The Uncertain Self: Whitman's Drama of Identity.* Ann Arbor: Michigan State University Press, 1973.

Carlson, Eric W. "Whitman's *Song of Myself* [51–57]." *Explicator,* 18(1959):item 13.

Carpenter, Edward. *Days with Walt Whitman.* London: Allen & Unwin, 1906.

Carpenter, Frederic I. *American Literature and the Dream.* New York: Philosophical Library, 1955.

Carpenter, George Rice. *Walt Whitman.* New York: Macmillan, 1909.

Catel, Jean. "Whitman's Symbolism," in Allen 1955c, 76–89.

Cavitch, David. "Whitman's Mystery." *Studies in Romanticism,* 17(1978):105–28.

———. *My Soul and I—The Inner Life of Walt Whitman.* Boston: Beacon, 1985.

Chapman, John Jay. *The Selected Writings.* Ed. Jacques Barzun. New York: Farrar, Straus and Cudahy, 1957.

Chari, V. K. *Whitman in the Light of Vedantic Mysticism—An Interpretation.* Lincoln: University of Nebraska Press, 1964.

Chase, Richard. *Walt Whitman Reconsidered.* New York: William Sloane, 1955a.

———. "Go-Before and Embryons: A Biographical Reprise," in Hindus, 32–54.

Chukovsky, Kornei. "Many Thanks, Walt Whitman! On the 150th anniversary of Whitman's birth." *West Hills Review,* 1(Fall 1979):69–73.

Clifford, William Kingdon. *Lectures and Essays.* Eds. Leslie Stephen and Frederick Pollock. London: Macmillan, 1879. 2 vols.

Coleman, Philip Y. "Walt Whitman's Ambiguities of 'I.'" *Papers on Language and Literature,* 5, supplement 2(Summer 1969):40–59.

Colum, Mary M. *From These Roots—The Ideas That Have Made Modern Literature.* New York: Columbia University Press, 1937.

Conner, Frederick W. *Cosmic Optimism.* Gainesville: University of Florida Press, 1949.

Conway, Moncure Daniel. *Autobiography, Memories and Experiences.* 1904; rptd. New York: Negro Universities Press, 1969.

Cook, Raymond A. "Empathic Identification in 'Song of Myself': A Key to Whitman's Poetry." *Walt Whitman Review,* 10(1964):3–10.

Cooke, Alice Lovelace. "Whitman's Indebtedness to the Scientific Thought of His Day." *Studies in English (University of Texas),* 14(1935):89–122.

———. "A Note on Whitman's Symbolism in 'Song of Myself.'" *Modern Language Notes,* 65(1950):228–32.

Couser, G. Thomas. *American Autobiography—The Prophetic Mode.* Amherst: University of Massachusetts, 1979.

Cowley, Malcolm, ed. *Walt Whitman's Leaves of Grass—The First (1855) Edition.* New York: Viking, 1959.

Cox, James M. "Walt Whitman, Mark Twain, and the Civil War." *The Sewanee Review,* 69(1961):185–204.

Crawley, Thomas Edward. *The Structure of "Leaves of Grass."* Austin: University of Texas Press, 1970.

Creeley, Robert, ed. *Whitman.* Middlesex: Penguin, 1973.

Crisler, Jesse S. "Gay Walt: 'Wit' in *Song of Myself.*" *Whimsy II* (1984):20–23.

Cumming, Mark. "Carlyle, Whitman, and the Disimprisonment of the Epic." *Victorian Studies,* 29(1986):207–26.

Daiches, David. "Walt Whitman: Impressionist Prophet," in Hindus, 109–22.

———. "Walt Whitman—Philosopher," in Allen 1955b.

———. "Whitman as Innovator." In *The Young Rebel in American Literature,* ed. Carl Bode. London: Heinemann, 1959.

Davenport, Guy. "Walt Whitman an American." *Parnassus: Poetry in Review,* 5(1976): 35–48.

Davidson, James. "Whitman's 'Twenty-Eight Young Men.'" *Walt Whitman Review,* 12(1966):100–1.

Davidson, Loren K. "Whitman's 'Song of Myself'—An Analysis." *Litera,* 7(1960):49–89.

De Falco, Joseph M. "The Narrative Shift in Whitman's 'Song of Myself.'" *Walt Whitman Review,* 9(1963):82–84.

De Selincourt, Basil. *Walt Whitman—A Critical Study.* London: Secker, 1914.

Donoghue, Denis. *Connoisseurs of Chaos—Ideas of Order in Modern American Poetry.* New York: Macmillan, 1965.

Dorson, Richard M. "Mose the Far-Famed and World-Renowned." *American Literature,* 15(1943):288–300.

Dowden, Edward. "The Poetry of Democracy: Walt Whitman," in E. H. Miller 1969, 39–49.

Dubois, William Robert. "Walt Whitman's Poetry: A Record of Crises in Identity." Dissertation, 1970. Ann Arbor: University Microfilms, 1971.

Dudding, Griffith. "The Function of Whitman's Imagery in 'Song of Myself,' 1855." *Walt Whitman Review,* 13(1967):3–11.

Duncan, Robert. "Changing Perspectives in Reading Whitman," in E. H. Miller 1970, 73–102.

Dutton, Geoffrey. *Whitman.* New York: Grove Press, 1961.

Eby, Edwin Harold. *A Concordance of Walt Whitman's "Leaves of Grass" and Selected Prose Writings.* Seattle: University of Washington, 1955.

Egan, Jr., Ken. "Periodic Structure in 'Song of Myself.'" *Walt Whitman Quarterly Review,* 4, no. 4(Spring 1987):1–8.

Ellis, Havelock. *The New Spirit.* 1890; rptd. Washington: National Home Library, 1935.

Emerson, Ralph Waldo. *The Correspondence of Emerson and Carlyle.* Ed. Joseph Slater. New York: Columbia University Press, 1964.

Erikson, Erik. *Young Man Luther.* 1958; rptd. New York: Norton, 1962.

Essays from "The Critic." Boston: Osgood, 1882.

Faner, Robert D. *Walt Whitman and Opera.* Philadelphia: University of Pennsylvania, 1951.

Farzan, Massud. "Whitman and Sufism: Towards 'A Persian Lesson.'" *American Literature,* 47(1976):572–82.

Fasel, Ida. "'Song of Myself' as Prayer." *Walt Whitman Review,* 17(1971):19–22.

Fausset, Hugh l'Anson. *Walt Whitman: Poet of Democracy.* New Haven: Yale, 1942.

Feidelson, Jr., Charles. *Symbolism and American Literature.* Chicago: University of Chicago Press, 1953.

Fiedler, Leslie A., ed. *Whitman.* New York: Dell, 1959.

Fishkin, Shelley Fisher. *From Fact to Fiction—Journalism and Imaginative Writing in America.* Baltimore: Johns Hopkins, 1985.

Foster, Steven. "Bergson's 'Intuition' and Whitman's 'Song of Myself.'" *Texas Studies in Literature and Language,* 6(1964):376–87.

French, Roberts W. "The Voice of the Prophet: Collapse and Regeneration in 'Song of Myself.'" *The English Record,* 32(Winter 1981):2–5.

———. "Whitman's 'Overstaid Fraction': Section 38 of 'Song of Myself.'" *Walt Whitman Quarterly Review,* 5, no. 3(Winter 1988):17–22.

Fussell, Edwin. *Frontier: American Literature and the American West.* Princeton: Princeton University Press, 1965.

Gardner, John, and John Maier. *Gilgamesh.* New York: Knopf, 1984.

Gatta, Jr., John. "Whitman's Re-Vision of Emersonian Ecstacy in 'Song of Myself.'" In *Walt Whitman Here and Now,* ed. Joann P. Krieg. Westport, Conn.: Greenwood Press, 1985.

Gelpi, Albert. *The Tenth Muse—The Psyche of the American Poet.* Cambridge: Harvard, 1975.

Giantvalley, Scott. "'Strict, Straight Notions of Literary Propriety': Thomas Wentworth Higginson's Gradual Unbending to Walt Whitman." *Walt Whitman Quarterly Review,* 4, no. 4(Spring 1987):17–27.

Gilbert, Sandra M. "The American Sexual Poetics of Walt Whitman and Emily Dickinson." In *Reconstructing American Literary History,* ed. Sacvan Bercovitch. Cambridge: Harvard, 1986.

Gilchrist, Anne. "An Englishwoman's Estimate of Walt Whitman." In *Anne Gilchrist: Her Life and Writings,* ed. Herbert Gilchrist. New York: Scribner & Welford, 1887.

Ginsberg, Allen. "Allen Ginsberg on Walt Whitman: Composed on the Tongue," in Perlman, Folsom, and Campion, 231–54.

Glicksberg, Charles I. *Walt Whitman and the Civil War.* Philadelphia: University of Pennsylvania, 1933.

Gohdes, Clarence. "A Comment on Section 5 of Whitman's 'Song of Myself.'" *Modern Language Notes,* 69(1954):583–86.

———. "Section 50 of Whitman's 'Song of Myself.'" *Modern Language Notes,* 75(1960):654–56.

———. "Whitman as 'One of the Roughs.'" *Walt Whitman Review,* 8(1962):18.

Goldberg, Bernard A. "Patriotic Allusions in Sections 15 and 33 of 'Song of Myself.'" *Walt Whitman Review,* 21(1975):58–66.

Golden, Arthur. "The Ending of the 1855 Version of 'Song of Myself.'" *Walt Whitman Quarterly Review,* 3, no. 4(Spring 1986):27–29.

Goodale, David. "Some of Walt Whitman's Borrowings." *American Literature,* 10(1938):202–13.

Goodblatt, Chanita, and Joseph Glicksohn. "Cognitive Psychology and Whitman's 'Song of Myself.'" *Mosaic,* 19(1986):83–90.

Gosse, Edmund. *Critical Kit-Kats.* New York: Dodd, Mead & Co., 1900.

———. *Transatlantic Dialogue—Selected American Correspondence of Edmund Gosse.* Eds. Paul F. Mattheisen and Michael Milgate. Austin: University of Texas Press, 1965.

Green, Martin. "Twain and Whitman," in Murphy, 424–27.

Grossman, Allen. "The Poetics of Union in Whitman and Lincoln: An Inquiry Toward the Relationship of Art and Policy." In *The American Renaissance Reconsidered,* eds. Walter Benn Michaels and Donald E. Pease. Baltimore: Johns Hopkins, 1985.

Harris, Natalie. "Whitman's Kinetic Criticism." *American Poetry,* 2, no. 3(Spring 1985):19–33.

Hartmann, Sadakichi. *Conversations with Walt Whitman.* New York: E. P. Coby, 1895.

Hawthorne, Julian, and Leonard Lemmon. *American Literature—A Text-book for the Use of Schools and Colleges.* Boston: Heath, 1892.

Henseler, Donna L. "The Voice of the Grass-Poem 'I': Whitman's 'Song of Myself.'" *Walt Whitman Review,* 15(1969):26–32.

Higginson, Thomas Wentworth. *Contemporaries.* 1900; rptd. Upper Saddle River, N.J.: Literature House, 1970.

Hindus, Milton, ed. *Leaves of Grass One Hundred Years After.* Stanford: Stanford University Press, 1955.

Hollander, John. *The Figure of Echo—A Mode of Allusion in Milton and After.* Berkeley: University of California Press, 1981.

Hollis, C. Carroll. *Language and Style in "Leaves of Grass."* Baton Rouge: Louisiana State University Press, 1983.

———. "Is There a Text in This Grass?" *Walt Whitman Quarterly Review,* 3, no. 3 (Winter 1986):15–22.

Holloway, Emory. "A Whitman Source." *Walt Whitman Newsletter,* 2(1956):23–24.

Howard, Leon. "For a Critique of Whitman's Transcendentalism." *Modern Language Notes,* 47(1932):79–85.

———. *Literature and the American Tradition.* New York: Doubleday, 1960.

Hutchinson, George B. *The Ecstatic Whitman—Literary Shamanism and the Crisis of the Union.* Columbus: Ohio State University Press, 1986.

Hyde, Lewis. *The Gift—Imagination and the Erotic Life of Property.* New York: Random House, 1983.

Ingersoll, Robert G. "Liberty in Literature," in Traubel, Bucke, and Harned, 252–83.

Irwin, John T. *American Hieroglyphics—Symbols of the Egyptian Hieroglyphics in the American Renaissance.* New Haven: Yale, 1980.

Jackson, Holbrook. *Dreamers of Dreams.* New York: Farrar, Straus, 1948.

James, William. *The Varieties of Religious Experience.* 1902; rptd. New York: Modern Library, n.d.

Jarrell, Randall. *Poetry and the Age.* New York: Vintage, 1953.

Johnson, David J. "The Effect of Suspension Dots, Parentheses and Italics on Lyricism of 'Song of Myself.'" *Walt Whitman Review,* 21(1975):47–58.

Johnston, John, and J. W. Wallace. *Visits to Walt Whitman in 1890–1891.* London: George Allen & Unwin, 1917.

Johnston, John H. *The Poet and the City.* Athens: University of Georgia Press, 1984.

Johnston, Kenneth G., and John O. Rees, Jr. "Whitman and Foo-foos: An Experiment in Language." *Walt Whitman Review,* 17(1971):3–10.

Kallsen, T. J. "'Song of Myself': Logical Unity through Analogy." *West Virginia University Bulletin: Philological Papers,* 9(1953):33–40.

———. "The Improbabilities in Section 11 of 'Song of Myself.'" *Walt Whitman Review,* 13(1967):87–92.

Kaplan, Justin. *Walt Whitman—A Life.* New York: Simon and Schuster, 1980.

Kaul, A. N. *The American Vision—Actual and Ideal Society in Nineteenth-Century Fiction.* New Haven: Yale, 1963.

Kazin, Alfred. *An American Procession.* New York: Knopf, 1984.

Kennedy, William Sloane. *Reminiscences of Walt Whitman.* London: Gardner, [1896].

———. *The Fight of a Book for the World.* West Yarmouth, Mass.: Stonecroft Press, 1926.

Kepner, Diane. "From Spears to Leaves: Walt Whitman's Theory of Nature in 'Song of Myself.'" *American Literature,* 51(1979):179–204.

Kinkead-Weekes, Mark. "Walt Whitman Passes the Full-Stop By. . . ." In *An English Miscellany; Presented to W. S. Mackie,* ed. Brian S. Lee. London: Oxford, 1977. Pp. 163–78.

Kinnaird, John. "*Leaves of Grass* and the American Paradox," in R. H. Pearce 1962, 24–36.

Kinnell, Galway. "Whitman's Indicative Words," in Perlman, Folsom, and Campion, 215–27.

Kramer, Lawrence. *Music and Poetry: The Nineteenth Century and After.* Berkeley: University of California, 1984.

Krause, Sydney J. "Whitman, Music, and *Proud Music of the Storm.*" *PMLA,* 72(1957):705–21.

———. "Whitman's Yawping Bird as Comic Defense." *Bulletin of the New York Public Library,* 68(1964):347–60.

Krieg, Joann P. "Whitman's *Bel Canto Spider.*" *Walt Whitman Quarterly Review,* 4, no. 4 (Spring 1987):28–31.

Kummings, Donald D. "Whitman's Voice in 'Song of Myself': From Private to Public." *Walt Whitman Review,* 17(1971):10–15.

Law, Richard A. "The Respiration Motif in 'Song of Myself.'" *Walt Whitman Review,* 10(1964):92–97.

Lawrence, D. H. *Studies in Classic American Literature.* New York: Doubleday, 1953.

Lenhart, Charmenz S. *Musical Influence on American Poetry.* Athens: University of Georgia Press, 1956.

Levine, Herbert J. "Union and Disunion in 'Song of Myself.'" *American Literature,* 59(1987):570–89.

Lewis, R. W. B. *The American Adam—Innocence, Tragedy, and Tradition in the Nineteenth Century.* Chicago: University of Chicago Press, 1955.

———. *Trials of the Word—Essays in American Literature and the Humanistic Tradition.* New Haven: Yale, 1965.

Lieber, Todd M. *Endless Experiments—Essays on the Heroic Experience in American Romanticism.* Columbus: Ohio State University Press, 1973.

Loving, Jerome. *Emerson, Whitman, and the American Muse.* Chapel Hill: University of North Carolina Press, 1982.

Lowell, Amy. "Walt Whitman and the New Poetry." *The Yale Review,* n.s., 16 (1927):502–19.

Lynen, John F. *The Design of the Present—Essays on Time and Form in American Literature.* New Haven: Yale, 1969.

McElderry, Jr., Bruce R. "Personae in Whitman (1855–1860)." *American Transcendental Quarterly,* 12(1971):25–32.

McMahon, William E. "Grass and Its Mate in 'Song of Myself.'" *South Atlantic Review,* 5(1986):41–55.

Mabbott, T. O. "Whitman's *Song of Myself,* XXIV, 19." *Explicator,* 5(1947):item 43.

Magowan, Robin. "The Horse of the Gods: Possession in 'Song of Myself.'" *Walt Whitman Review,* 15(1969):67–76.

Maria, Sister Flavia. "'Song of Myself': A Presage of Modern Teilhardian Paleontology." *Walt Whitman Review,* 15(1969):43–49.

Marki, Ivan. *The Trial of the Poet: An Interpretation of the First Edition of "Leaves of Grass."* New York: Columbia University Press, 1976.

Marks, Alfred H. "Whitman's Triadic Imagery." *American Literature,* 23(1951):99–126.

Martí, José. *Selected Writings.* Translated Juan de Onís. New York: Noonday, 1953.

Martin, Robert K. "Whitman's Song of Myself: Homosexual Dream and Vision." *Partisan Review,* 42(1975):80–96.

———. *The Homosexual Tradition in American Poetry.* Austin: University of Texas Press, 1979.

Mason, John B. "Walt Whitman's Catalogues: Rhetorical Means for Two Journeys in 'Song of Myself.'" *American Literature,* 45(1973):34–49.

Mathew, V. John. "Self in 'Song of Myself': A Defence of Whitman's Egoism." *Walt Whitman Review,* 15(1969):102–7.

Matthiessen, F. O. *American Renaissance—Art and Expression in the Age of Emerson and Whitman.* New York: Oxford, 1941.

Maxwell, William. "Some Personalistic Elements in the Poetry of Whitman." *The Personalist,* 12(1931):190–99.

Melville, Herman. *The Letters.* Eds. Merrell R. Davis and William H. Gilman. New Haven: Yale, 1960.

Mendelson, Maurice. *Life and Work of Walt Whitman—A Soviet View.* Moscow: Progress Publishers, 1976.

Metzger, Charles R. "Walt Whitman's Philosophical Epic." *Walt Whitman Review,* 15(1969):91–96.

Middlebrook, Diane Wood. *Walt Whitman and Wallace Stevens.* Ithaca: Cornell, 1974.

Miller, Edwin Haviland. *Walt Whitman's Poetry: A Psychological Journey.* Boston: Houghton Mifflin, 1968.

———, ed. *A Century of Whitman Criticism.* Bloomington: Indiana University Press, 1969.

———, ed. *The Artistic Legacy of Walt Whitman.* New York: New York University Press, 1970.

———. "Notes toward a Reading of 'Song of Myself.'" *West Hills Review,* 1(Fall 1979):79–91.

Miller, F. De Wolfe. "The Partitive Studies of 'Song of Myself.'" *American Transcendental Quarterly,* 12(1971):11–17.

Miller, Jr., James E. *A Critical Guide to "Leaves of Grass."* Chicago: University of Chicago Press, 1957.

———. *Walt Whitman.* New Haven: College and University Press, 1962.

———, ed. *Whitman's "Song of Myself"—Origin, Growth, Meaning.* New York: Dodd, Mead, 1964.

Miller, Jr., James E., Karl Shapiro, and Bernice Slote. *Start with the Sun—Studies in Cosmic Poetry.* Lincoln: University of Nebraska Press, 1960.

More, Paul Elmer. *Shelburne Essays on American Literature.* Ed. Daniel Aaron. New York: Harcourt, Brace, and World, 1963.

Morris, Wright. *The Territory Ahead.* New York: Harcourt, Brace, 1958.

Morse, David. *American Romanticism, From Cooper to Hawthorne—Excessive America.* Totowa, N.J.: Barnes & Noble, 1987.

Mücke, Heinz. "Animal Share in the Universal Union" [#32] and "The Divine Principle, God" [#48]. In *Studies in Walt Whitman's "Leaves of Grass,"* ed. Harry R. Warfel. Gainesville: Scholars' Facsimiles & Reprints, 1954. Pp. 13–14, 18.

Murphy, Francis, ed. *Walt Whitman—A Critical Anthology.* Middlesex: Penguin, 1969.

Murry, J. Middleton. "Walt Whitman: The Prophet of Democracy," in Hindus, 123–44.

Myers, Henry Alonzo. "Whitman's Conception of the Spiritual Democracy, 1855–1856." *American Literature,* 6(1934):239–53.

Nagle, John M. "Toward a Theory of Structure in 'Song of Myself.'" In *Critics on Whitman,* ed. Richard H. Rupp. Coral Gables: University of Miami Press, 1972.

Nambiar, O. K. *Walt Whitman and Yoga.* Bangalore: Jeevan Publications, 1966.

Nathanson, Tenney. "Whitman's Tropes of Light and Flood: Language and Representation in the Early Editions of *Leaves of Grass.*" *Emerson Society Quarterly,* 31 (1985):116–34.

Neuman, Mary A. "'Song of Myself,' Section 11: An Explication." *Walt Whitman Review,* 13(1967):98–99.

Noel, Roden. *Essays on Poetry and Poets.* London: Kegan Paul, Trench, 1886.

Noyes, Carleton. *An Approach to Walt Whitman.* Boston: Houghton Mifflin, 1910.

O'Connor, William D. "The Good Gray Poet." In Jerome Loving, *Walt Whitman's Champion—William Douglas O'Connor.* College Station: Texas A&M University Press, 1978.

O'Higgins, Harvey. "Alias Walt Whitman." *Harper's Monthly Magazine,* 158(1929): 698–707.

Orth, Michael. "Walt Whitman, Metaphysical Teapot: The Structure of 'Song of Myself.'" *Walt Whitman Review,* 14(1968):16–24.

Parrington, Vernon Louis. *Main Currents in American Thought.* New York: Harcourt, Brace, 1930. 3 vols.

Parsons, Olive W. "Whitman the Non-Hegelian." *PMLA,* 58(1943):1073–93.

Pearce, Howard D. "'I Lean and Loafe': Whitman's Romantic Posture." *Walt Whitman Review,* 15(1969):3–12.

Pearce, Roy Harvey. *The Continuity of American Poetry.* Princeton: Princeton University Press, 1961.

———, ed. *Whitman—A Collection of Critical Essays.* Englewood, N.J.: Prentice-Hall, 1962.

———. "Whitman Justified: The Poet in 1855." *Critical Inquiry,* 8(1981):83–97.

Pease, Donald E. *Visionary Compacts—American Renaissance Writing in Cultural Context.* Madison: University of Wisconsin Press, 1987.

Perlman, Jim, Ed Folsom, and Dan Campion, eds. *Walt Whitman—The Measure of His Song.* Minneapolis: Holy Cow! Press, 1981.

Peters, Robert L. "Verbal Musculature and Concealed Kinetics in the Early Poetry of Walt Whitman: A Study in *Projective* or Open Field Composition." *Kayak,* 8 (1966):58–63.

Phillips, Elizabeth. "'Song of Myself': The Numbers of the Poem in Relation to Its Parts." *Walt Whitman Review,* 16(1970):67–81.

Pollak, Georgiana. "The Relationship of Music to 'Leaves of Grass.'" *College English,* 15(1954):384–94.

Pongs, Hermann. "Walt Whitman and Stefan George," in Allen 1955c, 17–55.

Postma, Pamela. "Self-Marriage, Dream Children, and the Poetic Imagination: A New Reading of Whitman's 'Twenty-eight Young Men.'" *American Transcendental Quarterly,* 61(1986):37–45.

Powys, John Cowper. "Walt Whitman," in E. H. Miller 1969, 146–51.

Quinlan, Kieran. "Sea and Sea-Shore in 'Song of Myself': Whitman's Liquid Theme." In *Literature and Lore of the Sea,* ed. Patricia Ann Carlson. *Costerus,* 52(Amsterdam: Rodo 1, 1986):185–92.

Rajasekharaiah, T. R. *The Roots of Whitman's Grass.* Rutherford, N.J.: Fairleigh Dickinson University Press, 1970.

Reed, Harry B. "The Heraclitan Obsession of Walt Whitman." *The Personalist,* 15(1934):125–38.

Reed, Michael D. "First Person Persona and the Catalogue in 'Song of Myself.'" *Walt Whitman Review,* 23(1977):147–55.

Reisiger, Hans. "A Child Went Forth," in Allen 1955c, 7–15.

Reiss, Edmund. "Whitman's Debt to Animal Magnetism." *PMLA,* 78(1963):80–88.

Renner, Dennis K. "The Conscious Whitman: Allegorical Manifest Destiny in 'Song of Myself.'" *Walt Whitman Review,* 24(1978):149–55.

———. "Tradition for a Time of Crisis: Whitman's Prophetic Stance." In *Poetic Prophecy in Western Literature,* eds. Jan Wojcik and Raymond-Jean Frontain. Rutherford, N.J.: Fairleigh Dickinson University Press, 1984.

Reynolds, David S. *Beneath the American Renaissance—The Subversive Imagination in the Age of Emerson and Melville.* New York: Knopf, 1988.

Rich, Adrienne. "Poetry, Personality and Wholeness: A Response to Galway Kinnell." *Field: Contemporary Poetry and Poetics,* 7(Fall 1972):11–18.

Richardson, Jr., Robert D. *Myth and Literature in the American Renaissance.* Bloomington: Indiana, 1978.

Robbins, J. Albert. "The Narrative Form of 'Song of Myself.'" *American Transcendental Quarterly,* 12(1971):17–20.

Rose, Alan H. "Destructive Vision in the First and Last Versions of 'Song of Myself.'" *Walt Whitman Review,* 15(1969):215–22.

Rosenthal, M. L., and Sally Gall. *The Modern Poetic Sequence: The Genius of Modern Poetry.* New York: Oxford, 1983.

Rountree, Thomas J. "Whitman's Indirect Expression and Its Application to 'Song of Myself.'" *PMLA,* 73(1958):549–55.

Rourke, Constance. *American Humor—A Study of the National Character.* 1931; rptd. New York: Doubleday, 1953.

Rubin, Joseph Jay. *The Historic Whitman.* University Park: Pennsylvania State University Press, 1973.

Rubin, Joseph Jay, and Charles H. Brown, eds. *Walt Whitman of the New York "Aurora."* State College, Pa.: Bald Eagle Press, 1950.

Rukeyser, Muriel. *The Life of Poetry.* New York: Current Books, 1949.

Rule, Henry B. "Walt Whitman and George Caleb Bingham." *Walt Whitman Review,* 15(1969):248–53.

Sabo, William J. "The Ship and Its Related Imagery in 'Inscriptions' and 'Song of Myself.'" *Walt Whitman Review,* 24(1978):118–23.

Sarracino, Carmine. "Figures of Transcendence in Whitman's Poetry." *Walt Whitman Quarterly Review,* 5, no. 1(Summer 1987):1–11.

Schmidt, Rudolf. "Walt Whitman, The Poet of American Democracy," in Traubel, Bucke, and Harned, 231–48.

Scholnick, Robert J. "'The Password Primeval': Whitman's Use of Science in 'Song of Myself.'" In *Studies in the American Renaissance 1986.* Charlottesville: University of Virginia Press, 1986.

Schumann, Detley W. "Enumerative Style and Its Significance in Whitman, Rilke, Werfel." *Modern Language Quarterly,* 3(1942):171–204.

Schyberg, Frederik. *Walt Whitman.* Translated by Evie Allison Allen. New York: Columbia University Press, 1951.

Shapiro, Karl. *Start with the Sun—Studies in Cosmic Poetry.* Lincoln: University of Nebraska Press, 1960.

Shephard, Esther. *Walt Whitman's Pose.* New York: Harcourt, Brace, 1938.

———. "Possible Sources of Some of Whitman's Ideas and Symbols in *Hermes Mercurius Trismegistus* and Other Works." *Modern Language Quarterly,* 14(1953):60–81.

Shipley, Maynard. "Democracy as a Religion." *The Open Court,* 33(1919):385–93.

Sixbey, George L. "'Chanting the Square Deific'—A Study in Whitman's Religion." *American Literature,* 9(1937):171–95.

Smith, Barbara Herrnstein. *Poetic Closure—A Study of How Poems End.* Chicago: University of Chicago Press, 1968.

Smith, Fred Manning. "Whitman's Poet-Prophet and Carlyle's Hero." *PMLA,* 55(1940):1146–64.

———. "Whitman's Debt to Carlyle's *Sartor Resartus.*" *Modern Language Quarterly,* 3(1942):51–65.

Smuts, Jan Christian. *Walt Whitman—A Study in the Evolution of Personality.* Ed. Alan L. McLeod. Detroit: Wayne University Press, 1973.

Snyder, John. *The Dear Love of Man: Tragic and Lyric Communion in Walt Whitman.* The Hague: Mouton, 1975.

Spiegelman, Julia. "Walt Whitman and Music." *South Atlantic Quarterly,* 41 (1942):167–76.

Spitzer, Leo. "*Explication de Texte* Applied to Walt Whitman's Poem 'Out of the Cradle Endlessly Rocking,'" in E. H. Miller 1969, 273–84.

Steele, Jeffrey. *The Representation of the Self in the American Renaissance.* Chapel Hill: North Carolina University Press, 1987.

Stevenson, Robert Louis. "The Gospel According to Walt Whitman," in E. H. Miller 1969, 64–69.

Stovall, Floyd. "Main Drifts of Whitman's Poetry." *American Literature,* 4(1932):3–21.

Strauch, Carl F. "The Structure of Walt Whitman's 'Song of Myself.'" *English Journal,* 27(1938):597–607.

Summerhayes, Don. "Joyce's *Ulysses* and Whitman's 'Self.'" *Wisconsin Studies in Contemporary Literature,* 4(1963):216–24.

Sutton, Walter. "Whitman's Poetic Ensembles," in R. H. Pearce 1962, 119–31.

Symonds, John Addington. *Walt Whitman—A Study.* London: Nimmo, 1893.

Tannenbaum, Earl. "Pattern in Whitman's 'Song of Myself'—A Summary and a Supplement." *CLA Journal,* 6(1962):44–49.

Tanner, James T. F. "The Superman in Leaves of Grass." *Walt Whitman Review,* 11(1965):85–100.

Tanner, Tony. *The Reign of Wonder: Naivety and Reality in American Literature.* Cambridge: University Press, 1965.

Tapscott, Stephen J. "Leaves of Myself: Whitman's Egypt in 'Song of Myself.'" *American Literature,* 50(1978):49–73.

Thomas, M. Wynn. "*Song of Myself* and Possessive Individualism." *Delta,* 16(May 1983):3–17.

———. *The Lunar Light of Whitman's Poetry.* Cambridge: Harvard, 1987.

Thompson, Leslie M. "Promise of America in Whitman and Thomas Wolfe: 'Song of Myself' and *You Can't Go Home Again.*" *Walt Whitman Review,* 12(1966):27–34.

Thomson, James. *Walt Whitman—The Man and the Poet.* 1910; rptd. New York: Haskell House, 1971.

Thoreau, Henry David. *The Journals.* Eds. Bradford Torrey and Francis H. Allen. 1902; rptd. New York: Dover, 1962. 2 vols.

Todd, Edgeley W. "Indian Pictures and Two Whitman Poems." *Huntington Library Quarterly,* 19(1955):1–11.

Traubel, Horace. *With Walt Whitman in Camden.* 1908–1982. 6 vols.

Traubel, Horace L., Richard Maurice Bucke, and Thomas B. Harned, eds. *In Re.* Philadelphia: David McKay, 1893.

Tuveson, Ernest Lee. *The Avatars of Thrice Great Hermes: An Approach to Romanticism.* Lewisburg: Bucknell University Press, 1982.

Updike, John. "Walt Whitman: Ego and Art." *The New York Review of Books,* February 9, 1978:33–36.

Van Doren, Mark. "Walt Whitman, Stranger." *The American Mercury,* 35(1935):277–85.

———. "Leaves of Grass: 1855–1955." In *The Merrill Studies in "Leaves of Grass,"* ed. Gay Wilson Allen. Columbus, Ohio: Merrill, 1972.

Waggoner, Hyatt H. *American Poets from the Puritans to the Present.* Baton Rouge: Louisiana State University Press, 1984.

Wallace, Ronald. *God Be with the Clown: Humor in American Poetry.* Columbia: University of Missouri Press, 1984.

Walther, Marlene. "Cycle and Spiral in 'Song of Myself.'" In *Studies in Walt Whitman's "Leaves of Grass,"* ed. Harry R. Warfel. Gainesville: Scholars' Facsimiles & Reprints, 1954.

Warren, James Perrin. "'The Free Growth of Metrical Laws': Syntactic Parallelism in 'Song of Myself.'" *Style,* 18(1984a):27–42.

———. "The 'Real Grammar': Deverbal Style in 'Song of Myself.'" *American Literature,* 56(1984b):1–16.

Waskow, Howard J. *Whitman: Explorations in Form.* Chicago: University of Chicago Press, 1966.

Wellek, René, and Austin Warren. *Theory of Literature.* New York: Harcourt, Brace & World, 1956.

Wells, Henry W. *The American Way of Poetry.* New York: Columbia University Press, 1943.

Whicher, Stephen E. "Whitman's Awakening to Death—Toward a Biographical Reading of 'Out of the Cradle Endlessly Rocking.'" In *The Presence of Walt Whitman,* ed. R. W. B. Lewis. New York: Columbia University Press, 1962.

White, William M. "The Dynamics of Whitman's Poetry." *The Sewanee Review,* 80 (1972):347–60.

Whitman, Walt. *The Correspondence.* Ed. Edwin Haviland Miller. New York: New York University Press, 1961–1977. 6 vols.

———. *Daybooks and Notebooks.* Ed. William White. New York: New York University Press, 1978. 3 vols.

———. *I Sit and Look Out—Editorials from the Brooklyn* Daily Times. Eds. Emory Holloway and Vernolion Schwarz. New York: Columbia University Press, 1932.

———. *Leaves of Grass: Comprehensive Reader's Edition.* Eds. Harold W. Blodgett and Sculley Bradley. New York: New York University Press, 1965.

———. *Leaves of Grass—A Textual Variorum of Printed Poems.* Eds. Sculley Bradley, Harold W. Blodgett, Arthur Golden, and William White. New York: New York University Press, 1980. 3 vols.

———. *Notebooks and Unpublished Prose Manuscripts.* Ed. Edward F. Grier. New York: New York University Press, 1984. 6 vols.

———. *Prose Works 1892.* Ed. Floyd Stovall. New York: New York University Press, 1964. 2 vols.

———. *The Uncollected Prose and Poetry.* Ed. Emory Holloway. Garden City: Doubleday, Page & Co., 1921. 2 vols.

Wiley, Autrey Nell. "Reiterative Devices in *Leaves of Grass.*" *American Literature,* 1(1929):161–70.

Willard, Charles B. *Whitman's American Fame—The Growth of His Reputation in America.* Providence: Brown University Press, 1950.

Woodward, Robert H. "Davy Crockett: Whitman's 'Friendly and Flowing Savage.'" *Walt Whitman Review,* 6(1960):48–49.

Wright, James. "The Delicacy of Walt Whitman," in Perlman, Folsom, and Campion, 161–76.

Wrobel, Arthur. "Whitman and the Phrenologists: The Divine Body and the Sensuous Soul." *PMLA,* 89(1974):17–23.

Zweig, Paul. *Walt Whitman—The Making of the Poet.* New York: Basic Books, 1984.

Zitter, Emmy Stark. "Songs of the Cannon: *Song of Solomon* and 'Song of Myself.'" *Walt Whitman Quarterly Review,* 5, no. 2(Fall 1987):8–15.

Index

Index to "Song of Myself"